W9-ADP-901

WITHDRAWN

Gramley Library
Salem College
Winston-Salem, NC 27108

ELIZABETH LAURA ADAMS

DARK SYMPHONY AND OTHER WORKS

AFRICAN-AMERICAN WOMEN WRITERS, 1910–1940

HENRY LOUIS GATES, JR. *GENERAL EDITOR*
Jennifer Burton *Associate Editor*

ELIZABETH LAURA ADAMS

DARK SYMPHONY AND OTHER WORKS

Edited and with an Introduction by
CARLA KAPLAN

G. K. HALL & CO.
An Imprint of Simon & Schuster Macmillan
New York

Prentice Hall International
London   Mexico City   New Delhi   Singapore   Sydney   Toronto

Gramley Library
Salem College
Winston-Salem, NC 27108

Introduction copyright © 1997 by Carla Kaplan

All rights reserved. No part of this book may be reproduced or transmitted in any form or by any means, electronic or mechanical, including photocopying, recording, or any information and retrieval system, without permission in writing from the Publisher.

G. K. Hall & Co.
An Imprint of Simon & Schuster Macmillan
1633 Broadway
New York, New York 10019

Library of Congress Catalog Card Number: 96-43471

Printed in the United States of America

Printing Number
1   2   3   4   5   6   7   8   9   10

Library of Congress Cataloging-in-Publication Data

Adams, Elizabeth Laura.
    Dark symphony and other works / Elizabeth Laura Adams.
        p.   cm. — (African-American women writers, 1910–1940)
    ISBN 0-7838-1429-1 (alk. paper)
    1. Afro-American women—Literary collections. 2. Afro-Americans—Literary collections. 3. Afro-American women—Biography. 4. Converts, Catholic—Biography. 5. Adams, Elizabeth Laura. I. Title. II. Series.
PS3501.D2182A6   1996
248.2'42'092—dc20
[B]   96-43471
                                                                                                   CIP

This paper meets the requirements of ANSI/NISO Z39.48-1992 (Permanence of Paper).

CONTENTS

Contents

GENERAL EDITORS' PREFACE

The past decade of our literary history might be thought of as the era of African-American women writers. Culminating in the awarding of the Pulitzer Prize to Toni Morrison and Rita Dove and the Nobel Prize for Literature to Toni Morrison in 1993 and characterized by the presence of several writers—Toni Morrison, Alice Walker, Maya Angelou, and the Delaney Sisters, among others—on the *New York Times* Best Seller List, the shape of the most recent period in our literary history has been determined in large part by the writings of black women.

This, of course, has not always been the case. African-American women authors have been publishing their thoughts and feelings at least since 1773, when Phillis Wheatley published her book of poems in London, thereby bringing poetry directly to bear upon the philosophical discourse over the African's "place in nature" and his or her place in the great chain of being. The scores of words published by black women in America in the nineteenth century—most of which were published in extremely limited editions and never reprinted—have been republished in new critical editions in the forty-volume *Schomburg Library of Nineteenth-Century Black Women Writers*. The critical response to that series has led to requests from scholars and students alike for a similar series, one geared to the work by black women published between 1910 and the beginning of World War II.

African-American Women Writers, 1910–1940 is designed to bring back into print many writers who otherwise would be unknown to contemporary readers, and to increase the availability of lesser-known texts by established writers who originally published during this critical period in African-American letters. This series implicitly acts as a chronological sequel to the Schomburg series, which focused on the origins of the black female literary tradition in America.

In less than a decade, the study of African-American women's writings has grown from its promising beginnings into a firmly established field in departments of English, American Studies, and African-American Studies. A comparison of the form and function of the original series and this sequel illustrates this dramatic shift. The *Schomburg Library* was published at the cusp of focused academic investigation into the interplay between race and gender. It covered the extensive period from the publication of Phillis Wheatley's *Poems on Various Subjects, Religious and Moral* in 1773 through the "Black Women's Era" of 1890–1910, and was designed to be an inclusive series of the major early texts by black women writers. The Schomburg Library provided a historical backdrop for black women's writings of the 1970s and 1980s, including the works of writers such as Toni Morrison, Alice Walker, Maya Angelou, and Rita Dove.

African-American Women Writers, 1910–1940 continues our effort to provide a new generation of readers access to texts—historical, sociological, and literary—that have been largely "unread" for most of this century. The series bypasses works that are important both to the period and the tradition, but that are readily available, such as Zora Neale Hurston's *Their Eyes Were Watching God*, Jessie Fauset's *Plum Bun* and *There Is Confusion*, and Nella Larsen's *Quicksand* and *Passing*. Our goal is to provide access to a wide variety of rare texts. The series includes Fauset's two other novels, *The Chinaberry Tree: A Novel of American Life* and *Comedy: American Style*, and Hurston's short play *Color Struck*, since these are not yet widely available. It also features works by virtually unknown writers, such as *A Tiny Spark*, Christina Moody's slim volume of poetry self-published in 1910, and *Reminiscences of School Life, and Hints on Teaching*, written by Fanny Jackson Coppin in the last year of her life (1913), a multi-genre work combining an autobiographical sketch and reflections on trips to England and South Africa, complete with pedagogical advice.

Cultural Studies' investment in diverse resources allows the historic scope of the *African-American Women Writers* series to be more focused than the *Schomburg Library* series, which covered works written over a 137-year period. With few exceptions, the authors included in the *African-American Women Writers* series wrote their major works between 1910 and 1940. The texts reprinted include all the works by each particular author that are not otherwise readily obtainable. As a result, two volumes contain works originally published after 1940. The Charlotte Hawkins Brown volume includes her book of etiquette published in 1941, *The Correct Thing To Do—To Say—To Wear*. One of the poetry volumes contains Maggie Pogue Johnson's *Fallen Blossoms*, published in 1951, a compilation of all her previously published and unpublished poems.

Excavational work by scholars during the past decade has been crucial to the development of *African-American Women Writers, 1910–1940*. Germinal bibliographical sources such as Ann Allen Shockley's *Afro-American Women Writers 1746–1933* and Maryemma Graham's *Database of African-American Women Writers* made the initial identification of texts possible. Other works were brought to our attention by scholars who wrote letters sharing their research. Additional texts by selected authors were then added, so that many volumes contain the complete oeuvres of particular writers. Pieces by authors without enough published work to fill an entire volume were grouped with other pieces by genre.

The two types of collections, those organized by author and those organized by genre, bring out different characteristics of black women's writings of the period. The collected works of the literary writers illustrate that many of them were experimenting with a variety of forms. Mercedes Gilbert's volume, for example, contains her 1931 collection *Selected Gems of Poetry, Comedy, and Drama, Etc.*, as well as her 1938 novel *Aunt Sarah's Wooden God*. Georgia Douglas Johnson's volume contains her plays and short stories in addition to her poetry. Sarah Lee Brown Fleming's volume combines her 1918 novel *Hope's Highway* with her 1920 collection of poetry, *Clouds and Sunshine*.

The generic volumes both bring out the formal and thematic similarities among many of the writings and highlight the striking individuality of particular writers. Most of the plays in the volume of one-acts are social dramas whose tragic endings can be clearly attributed to miscegenation and racism. Within the context of

ix

these other plays, Marita Bonner's expressionistic theatrical vision becomes all the more striking.

The volumes of *African-American Women Writers, 1910–1940* contain reproductions of more than one hundred previously published texts, including twenty-nine plays, seventeen poetry collections, twelve novels, six autobiographies, five collections of short biographical sketches, three biographies, three histories of organizations, three black histories, two anthologies, two sociological studies, a diary, and a book of etiquette. Each volume features an introduction by a contemporary scholar that provides crucial biographical data on each author and the historical and critical context of her work. In some cases, little information on the authors was available outside of the fragments of biographical data contained in the original introduction or in the text itself. In these instances, editors have documented the libraries and research centers where they tried to find information, in the hope that subsequent scholars will continue the necessary search to find the "lost" clues to the women's stories in the rich stores of papers, letters, photographs, and other primary materials scattered throughout the country that have yet to be fully catalogued.

Many of the thrilling moments that occurred during the development of this series were the result of previously fragmented pieces of these women's histories suddenly coming together, such as Adele Alexander's uncovering of an old family photograph picturing her own aunt with Addie Hunton, the author Alexander was researching. Claudia Tate's examination of Georgia Douglas Johnson's papers in the Moorland-Spingarn Research Center of Howard University resulted in the discovery of a wealth of previously unpublished work.

The slippery quality of race itself emerged during the construction of the series. One of the short novels originally intended for inclusion in the series had to be cut when the family of the author protested that the writer was not of African descent. Another case involved Louise Kennedy's sociological study *The Negro Peasant Turns Inward*. The fact that none of the available biographical material on Kennedy specifically mentioned race, combined with some coded criticism in a review in the *Crisis*, convinced editor Sheila Smith McKoy that Kennedy was probably white.

These women, taken together, began to chart the true vitality, and complexity, of the literary tradition that African-American women have generated, using a wide variety of forms. They testify to the fact that the monumental works of Hurston, Larsen, and Fauset, for example, emerged out of a larger cultural context; they were not exceptions or aberrations. Indeed, their contributions to American literature and culture, as this series makes clear, were fundamental not only to the shaping of the African-American tradition but to the American tradition as well.

Henry Louis Gates, Jr.
Jennifer Burton

PUBLISHER'S NOTE

In the *African-American Women Writers, 1910–1940* series, G. K. Hall not only is making available previously neglected works that in many cases have been long out of print, we are also, whenever possible, publishing these works in facsimiles reprinted from their original editions including, when available, reproductions of original title pages, copyright pages, and photographs.

When it was not possible for us to reproduce a complete facsimile edition of a particular work (for example, if the original exists only as a handwritten draft or is too fragile to be reproduced), we have attempted to preserve the essence of the original by resetting the work exactly as it originally appeared. Therefore, any typographical errors, strikeouts, or other anomalies reflect our efforts to give the reader a true sense of the original work.

We trust that these facsimile and reprint editions, together with the new introductory essays, will be both useful and historically enlightening to scholars and students alike.

ACKNOWLEDGMENTS

I would like to express my gratitude to Marlayna K. Gates, head of Yale's Interlibrary Loan Office, for instrumental help in locating copies of Adams's early publications; to Sheed & Ward for supplying me with copies of Adams's correspondence and for kindly taking the trouble to estimate the sales figures for *Dark Symphony*; and to my research assistant at the Schomburg Center for Research in Black Culture, Jonathan Mason, for helping to locate some of Adams's early poetry. Most especially, I want to express my profound appreciation to Tara Hoover, of the Dominican College Library in Washington, D.C., who supplied me with a wealth of background material, book reviews, biographical information, and early essays by Adams; who graciously answered endless urgent requests by phone and fax; and who made this project so much her own as to become virtually a collaborator on it. It is impossible to imagine completing this project without Tara's enthusiasm, professionalism, know-how, and insights. I am also grateful to the National Endowment for the Humanities and the Aaron Diamond Fund for a fellowship at the Schomburg Center for Research in Black Culture, where most of the work for this volume was completed, and to the staff of the Schomburg Center for their help.

INTRODUCTION:
"I WANNA MARCH"

By Carla Kaplan

AN EXTRAORDINARY ORDINARY LIFE

In 1942 Elizabeth Laura Adams, then in her early thirties, published *Dark Symphony*, her extraordinary story of an independent and willful conversion to Catholicism. At the time, there were relatively few African-American Catholics—just over 300,000 as compared with nearly 6 million African-American Protestants.[1] There were fewer still who wrote about Catholicism at any length. Indeed, Adams appears to be the first African-American to have done so.[2] *Dark Symphony* became a Catholic best-seller, selling over 10,000 copies between 1942 and 1946, a total of nearly 15,000 copies in all. *Dark Symphony* earned Adams, who depended heavily on its royalties, well over $5,000. It was translated into Dutch and Italian editions and was also published in Great Britain.[3] For a few brief years Adams was a Catholic sensation. Her fan mail was published in the Catholic press.[4] Her life was profiled in Catholic magazines.[5] She was described as "your favorite" writer[6] and *Dark Symphony*, in full-page advertisements, as "the book that has the Catholic World TALKING and THINKING."[7] *Dark Symphony* was listed as one of the three most important books on blacks and the Catholic Church, alongside John LaFarge, S.J.'s *The Race Question and the Negro* and John T. Gillard, S.S.J.'s *Colored Catholics in the United States*.[8]

But in the late 1940s, Adams dropped from sight, leaving mostly unanswered questions. Why did she cease to publish? Why did the Catholic press lose interest in her? How did Catholicism fit into the life of this young, isolated, black, female writer? What does her life story reveal and, equally important, what does it conceal?

Adams's Catholicism clearly answered deep spiritual needs for peace ("a quiet place in which to pray"), guidance (a "simple wish that the Son of God would 'walk and talk'" with her), and community.[9] Her conversion occurred during a visit to the historic Santa Barbara Mission, which she describes as giving her a great sense of contentment, a "desire to attend service at the Santa Barbara Mission forever." From this visit, she relates, "conversion came to me quickly and quietly" (105–6).

The Santa Barbara Mission may have provided a sense of belonging, even of homecoming. But the Church Adams embraced turned out to be less than completely welcoming to a young black woman. Adams devotes much of her narrative to describing the obstacles Church and family posed to realizing her spiritual ambitions. Her conversion story takes shape as a struggle—deeply inflected by both gender and race—to carve out a place for herself, rebel against rigid rules and prohibitions, and assert her own agency.

Although Adams presents herself as submissive and frail, *Dark Symphony* participates in the African-American heritage of narrative double-voicedness. Her story of acquiescent, obedient girlhood is laced with private, sometimes coded rebellion. Her frailty and passivity mask resolve and determination. Even her use of the conversion narrative, an often formulaic genre which, as Virginia Brereton describes it, tends to "discourage originality of plot or expression,"[10] functions in coded, or double-voiced, ways. Adams uses her narrative to criticize the Church as much as to praise it, carefully carving out a space for "an original voice, a unique viewpoint."[11] Often presenting her story as typical, even ordinary, Adams also provides for keen awareness of the anomalousness of her situation and the singularity of her response.

The story of Adams's life is a study in the interplay between (perhaps even the ultimate indistinguishability of) the ordinary and the extraordinary. Born on February 9, 1909, as the only child of middle-class black parents in Santa Barbara, California, Adams led a quiet life, circumscribed by her parents' ideals of genteel black girlhood, by daughterly obligations, and by the responsibilities of a religious upbringing. "I was just an ordinary child," she declares (56). As she presents it, her childhood was not particularly remarkable. She studied acting and the violin. She did well in school and played with friends. She helped out around the home and wished for more excitement. Her adulthood, on the other hand, was much less ordinary. Adams had ambitions, which she realized to varying degrees, to be an actress, a musician, a writer, and a nun. Some years after her conversion, when her hopes of joining an order were blocked, she became a Franciscan Tertiary, a member of what is called the Third Order: one who, while secular, takes vows to live by moderation, temperance, and daily prayer and to remain in his or her current state—whether married or unmarried.[12]

Failed dreams, unfortunately, came to play a big part in Adams's life, a not unusual story for women and for African-American women in particular.[13] Adams's own mother, Lula Josephine Holden Adams, had been an accomplished painter whose talent, it seems, was sacrificed to the routine concerns of housekeeping. Like her mother's painting, Adams's acting and music developed into hobbies, rather than careers. As Adams puts it in "She Talks Like We Do!" (a discussion of what it is like to be an African-American woman), "You get all set and believe that a dream is going to come true—then it vanishes."[14]

Adams gave up her desire to join an order so that she could care for her mother, who was chronically ill and whose second marriage, after Adams's father's death, proved abusive. The basic outlines of this story of thwarted ambition may seem familiar. But by becoming an accomplished author and a star of the Catholic publishing circuit, Adams converted disappointment into a certain measure of accomplishment and success.

Prior to the publication of *Dark Symphony*, Adams published poems, essays, and reviews in some of the leading Catholic journals of her day, as well as in some mainstream literary venues. Portions of *Dark Symphony* were serialized in the *Torch*, which began as the monthly bulletin of the Dominican Tertiaries—an order with close historic ties to the Franciscans—and gained national prominence among Catholics when it became the official publication of the Blessed Martin Guild, one of the most powerful national organizations working on behalf of African-American Catholics. By the time Sheed & Ward, an important religious publisher, brought *Dark Symphony* out in 1942, Adams was already popular. But the terms of her popularity raise some difficult questions. Was her success in the mostly white Catholic establishment an instance of what Zora Neale Hurston derisively dubbed the "pet Negro system?"[15] Were there compromises, trade-offs, and negotiations into which she may have been forced?

Reviews of *Dark Symphony* were almost universally laudatory. But almost all of them were written by white Catholics who celebrated particular aspects of Adams's character. She was praised for consoling blacks and educating whites; for being "poised and revealing," "warm" and "spirited"; for representing "the entire colored race" and "all colored womanhood" in particular; and for telling her story "lucidly and beautifully," with "shrewd observation" and an "interesting," "beautiful," "electric" style that offers the "stirring" story of "the unsensational, frugal, clean living Negro middle class." She was praised again and again for writing without "self pity," for being "never bitter," for displaying never "a single line of rancor," and for observing "incidents of human cruelty . . . without malice." This lack of bitterness or anger was clearly particularly important to her white Catholic reviewers.[16]

Two reviews written by Ellen Tarry and Theophilus Lewis, both African-Americans, however, take a notably different approach. They are skeptical about Adams's lack of rancor. They are also—and probably not coincidentally—much more moderate in their praise. Ellen Tarry was a Catholic social worker, critic, and author who, long after she reviewed Adams's work, would go on to write *The Third Door: The Autobiography of an American Negro Woman* (1955) and *The Other Toussaint: A Post-Revolutionary Black* (1981). She also befriended Harlem Renaissance writer and radical Claude McKay and converted him to Catholicism in the forties. In a 1942 review in the *Catholic World*, Tarry suggested that what really made *Dark Symphony* "worth reading" was neither its style nor Adams's conversion, but rather the way *Dark Symphony* "breaks away from the tradition of fictional pickaninnies and Lindy-Hoppers" to counter the stereotypical picture of "the cabin in the corn patch or the rat-infested apartment in some slum area" with a picture of unsensationalized black middle-class life. Where white Catholic reviewers praise Adams for representing "the entire colored race," Tarry applauds her for demonstrating that such sweeping representations were pernicious. But, in Tarry's view, Adams's narrative strains credulity nonetheless. She implies that in spite of defying certain conventions, Adams was trying too hard to please, to make herself seem ordinary and familiar. She notes that Adams's portrayal of her parents is so positive that "one wonders if they are also human." Her story of their "stern methods" of child rearing, she writes, "does not always make interesting reading. Adams left out too much interesting, but difficult, material, Tarry suggests. "Miss Adams might have gotten even more material from her experiences during the depression years." The book, she adds, contains too many "gaps" and "too often the writer depends upon quotation."[17]

Theophilus Lewis, who wrote regularly for the radical black journal the *Messenger*, and has sometimes been considered the Harlem Renaissance's voice for the theater, was known especially for his commitment to race plays.[18] Lewis was also the only black member of the editorial board of the *Interracial Review* (which included no women on its editorial board or its governing body, the Catholic Interracial Council). Along with the *Torch*, *Interracial Review* was the most important Catholic periodical to deal with issues of race, the Catholic Church, and American society in the thirties. And unlike the *Torch*, *Interracial Review*, as its name suggests, aimed for an interracial voice. This makes it all the more notable that Lewis's review, like Tarry's, is not particularly favorable. He notes that Adams "affects a number of conceits," which may prove "annoying to the reader" and which "do not enhance the interest in her book." He goes on to assert, even more strongly, that her book "has little distinction as the story of a life" and that "one plods through the first half of *Dark Symphony* [her childhood] as a laborious chore." Lewis apparently finds *Dark Symphony* dull because it tells a story of what is for him a very ordinary life, one with which he is already too familiar: "Miss Adams has had her share of hard knocks and encounters the numerous petty discriminations which are the common experience of all Negroes," he notes. "These experiences are not the stuff of which interesting autobiography is made."[19]

Not for Tarry or Lewis perhaps. But judging from the other reviews I've quoted, the many white readers who embraced Adams's story found this tale of "petty discriminations" and "common experiences" both uncommon and inspiring. For whites, the experience of reading about the everyday life of an ordinary African-American Catholic woman may well have been extraordinary, a fact which may have been clear to Adams. As she put it in the serialized version of *Dark Symphony* (but omitted from the later, book version): "many White people have strange ideas about Negro home life. They imagine we live in shacks without rules or regulations."[20] Her disclosure that blacks lived in well-ordered homes with rigorous rules and standards may have been, as she knew, quite a revelation.

After the publication of *Dark Symphony*, Adams appears never to have published again, except for two brief and not particularly noteworthy book reviews.[21] While she is briefly mentioned in *The National Catholic Almanac*'s listing of contemporary American Catholic authors in 1942, under "Recommended Books" in *The National Catholic Almanac* for 1943,[22] and in its "Gallery of Living Catholic Authors" through 1959, her further activities seem unrecorded by the Catholic press. Indeed, although it is clear from various records that Adams was living in Santa Barbara, California, as late as 1970 and perhaps even as late as 1980, I have been unable to determine where or when she died or, more intriguingly, whether she is still alive. If so, she would have celebrated her eighty-sixth birthday early in 1996—unlikely, perhaps, given a life-long history of very delicate health, but certainly not impossible.

Such a slide from celebrity to obscurity is not, for African-Americans, a very unusual story. Zora Neale Hurston, after all, whose novel *Their Eyes Were Watching God* has been through fifty printings in the last six years alone,[23] died in a county welfare home, unknown and barely noticed by the press, in spite of her accomplishments and notoriety from the twenties through the forties. We often hear of African-American artists taken up for a brief time by the mainstream only to find themselves—if too many years pass, if they switch to different subjects, or if they are replaced by the next "exceptional" celebrity—suddenly without audience, publisher, stage, or exhibition space. Often we read of an African-American author who, fighting terrific odds, managed to squeeze one book out of a difficult, overcommitted life, but could never again beat the odds to bring out another.

The odds against Adams were extremely high. Although *Dark Symphony* describes her desire to write "plays of Negro life—adventures of the New Negro" (190), it is clear, especially from her letters to Sheed & Ward, that without substantial material and spiritual support, she could not keep working. Her many letters to various directors, managers, and bookkeepers at Sheed & Ward reveal how deeply Adams depended on her writing career to supplement other income (she also did office, secretarial, and domestic work). They also reveal that at least as late as the fifties—perhaps even beyond—Adams was determined to keep writing.

Adams's letters to Sheed & Ward display a pattern of what she called "S.O.S.'s": appeals for advances that Adams needed to pay for "very, very pressing obligations," mostly for medical care for her mother and herself. Adams had emergency surgery and a long recovery in 1947. She may have had another surgery in 1949. Throughout the forties and fifties she underwent a number of periods of hospitalization. Between 1944 and 1955 Adams contacted Sheed & Ward with over a dozen urgent requests for advances on her royalties. Sometimes she sent a telegram. Sometimes she enclosed stamps. Sometimes she asked that the money be sent to her by special delivery. Early in 1946, for example, she wrote to ask if she might "obtain fifty ($50.00) dollars advance royalty" to help with "urgent medical aid for my mother." In June of 1947 she wrote to ask if Sheed & Ward couldn't forward her the $200 advance owed by publishers in Belgium on the Dutch edition of her book. "I need the money very badly," she wrote. "I really need it." On June 22, 1948, she wrote to ask if she could have a $25 advance on her royalties to help pay for treatments for her mother's worsening neuritis. "This would mean a *great deal to me*," she added. Sometime in October of the same year, she wrote to ask if her royalties could be sent early. "This is the reason I ask," she explained:

> I have been getting along very well since the serious operation I had, but last Thursday I collapsed in the office where I am employed and had to be taken by ambulance to an emergency hospital. My physician tells me that I will have to take some treatments which are quite expensive even though a specialist is giving them to me at a reduced rate.
>
> I sincerely ask for consideration in this case. If I could have the November royalty now it would mean so much to me. . . . I have had so much sickness that it takes a lot of courage to keep up the fight . . . for it seems endless [ellipses in original].

Only a few months later, in January of 1949, she wrote again to say that "urgent financial needs" were pressing her to request a $30 advance on her next royalties. Similarly, she requested $40 in July of 1949 and, by telegram, $50 on August 18, 1950, writing: "Would you please grant special favor of advance royalty illness causes urgent need for fifty dollars. If so, please would you kindly mail it air mail special delivery." Only a few months later, on October 10, 1950, she telegrammed again: "Desperate. $85.00 need to add to hospitalization fee. Can I obtain this much advance royalty if so please wire deduct costs from royalty."

These letters reveal that Adams spent the ten years after the publication of *Dark Symphony* working at a variety of jobs and trying to write, all the while caring for her ailing mother and her own failing health. It is clear that during all these years Adams lived close to the economic edge and was constantly forced to scramble for survival. The Depression years were particularly hard on African-American women, offering what Jacqueline Jones describes as "only a precarious hold on gainful employment" for many. Often the only forms of work available, especially in agriculture or domestic service, were exempt from the protective provisions of the Industrial Recovery Act, the Social Security Act, and the Fair Labor Standards Act.[24] Although Adams seems to have secured office work ("I worked in offices for a long, long time," she wrote in a letter of October 30, 1946), her dependence on ever-diminishing royalties to pay for medical expenses suggests that she suffered considerably from such conditions in the thirties and from their aftermath in the forties. "The cost of living is very high and even though I have used a budget system it means a great deal of effort to keep all expenses at a low level while writing," she wrote in March of 1944.

She continued to long for a quiet and ordered life in which writing could be the center of her activities. A few months after her mother died, on June 21, 1952, Adams offered to relinquish all future rights to *Dark Symphony* if the publishers would grant her a one-time royalty of $375, which, she explained, would allow her to "settle up the most important bills and move with a very nice family where I could live and be happy, pay for my room and board and write after my day's work would be over." Sheed & Ward negotiated this deal with Adams, estimating that $375 was close to the amount of money she would receive if all remaining copies of *Dark Symphony* were sold. They left open the possibility of paying Adams more money if the book were ever reprinted, which it was not. Adams did apparently move in with a family named Brown in Los Angeles, in 1952,[25] but it appears that she stayed with them for only six months. The quiet, secure life she sought was still eluding her. Her reliance on her publishing income and her desperate need for financial support continued into 1953, when she again telegrammed Sheed & Ward asking for another $85 to pay for urgent hospital expenses. "Been ill in hospital now friends home could you advance $85 royalties by Sunday August 14th please deduct airmail special from royalties Dark Symphony," she wrote. This request was answered by a letter reminding her of the $375 deal and explaining that no further money "whatsoever," was owed her. "I would very much like to help you out," Sheed & Ward responded, "but it is utterly impossible. We do not owe you any money whatsoever at the moment and we are not quite sure whether DARK SYMPHONY will be reprinted again." From this point on, all substantive contact between Adams and Sheed & Ward seems to cease.

Obviously, there are many unanswered questions here. What happened, for example, to the manuscripts of "New Negro" plays that Adams apparently worked on for years? Did she send them to publishers? Did her Catholic sponsors find her stories of New Negro life less interesting than her story of her humble conversion and her life as a Catholic? Why was she taken up so enthusiastically only to disappear almost immediately? The market for African-American literature in the forties was particularly grim. The forties was one of the decades of public indifference which followed the twenties' fascination with black America. Was Adams a victim of this backlash? What did it mean to be an African-American Catholic woman in the forties? And why, after her mother's death, did Adams, who for so many years had wanted to join a convent and who so evidently needed and wanted a community of support, not join one? Was she more welcome as a Tertiary than as a sister? Was convent life, in Adams's eyes, not the right environment for an author of New Negro plays?

Just as there are many unanswered—perhaps unanswerable—questions about Adams's life, so her writing may raise more questions than it answers. In fact, I would suggest that *Dark Symphony* is at least as interesting for what it does not say, what it leaves out, what it only suggests and hints at, as for what it declares. What, for example, are the postures and self-presentations available to a young Catholic woman, needing to appear "good" to her audience and her promoters? In what ways, if any, was Adams, who came into adulthood during the twenties and converted to Catholicism in either 1928 or 1929 (depending on the sources consulted), linked to her historical moment? Why does her narrative seem so divorced from history, offering almost no mention of the Depression, the war, or the struggles of African-Americans for justice? What are Adams's terms for personal fulfillment, and how do those terms operate in their historical and social context? How ordinary, in fact, *was* Adams's life, and how does her story help us to challenge categories like "ordinary" and "extraordinary" by which Adams herself had been judged?

"I COULD SNIFF"

Toward the end of *Dark Symphony*, Adams discusses her travails as a domestic employed by immoral, insensitive, racist white families during the Depression. "I was misunderstood because I represented the New Negro—the thinking Negro" (171), she states. It is a startling comment. At first glance, *Dark Symphony* cannot help but strike the contemporary reader as a deeply conservative book, about as divorced from New Negro sensibilities and writing as one could imagine. *Dark Symphony* does not contain the righteous anger, fierce race pride, engagement with social issues, or loosening of restraints on racial and sexual representation that are generally associated with New Negro writing. It makes no mention of racial violence, although it was published just one year before mounting racial tensions erupted in over twenty-five massive urban riots. There is no mention of World War II, economics, struggles for black justice (such as the Scottsboro case of 1934), institutional racism, or the questions of racial aesthetics so central to other self-described New Negro writers. Adams's personal creed seems to be not race pride but rather being "not sensitive as to my color" (156). The Christian doctrine of forbearance and forgiveness she adopts seems at odds with many of the usual features of New Negro literature. Her mother's advice after Adams is called a "nigger" for the first time, for example, is to "love her enemies" (20). "A lady never strikes back" (18). In the spirit of Booker T. Washington, Adams was trained "to work purposefully" so as to "face undismayed the perplexities and disappointments of life" (59). In a manner reminiscent of Zora Neale Hurston's autobiography *Dust Tracks on a Road* (published the same year as *Dark Symphony* and also heavily influenced by the presence and help of white patrons)[26] there are persistent, sometimes even seemingly irrelevant, mentions of the "ever faithful" goodness of friendly whites "who tried to amend the wrongs of the easily-persuaded-to-become-prejudiced of their own group" (23).

As black Catholic historian Cyprian Davis notes in his history of black Catholics, "in this haven for writers, artists, philosophers, and politicians [the Harlem Renaissance], black Catholics were not generally conspicuous."[27] But part of *Dark Symphony*'s double-voicedness inheres in Adams's attempt to forge links to the work of the leading black artists and intellectuals of her day. She quotes from Langston Hughes ("the misunderstood" she calls him [184]), Edwin R. Embree's *Brown America*, Robert Russa Moton's *What the Negro Thinks*, Paul Laurence Dunbar, Arna Bontemps, Joseph S. Cotter, Georgia (misprinted as George) Douglas Johnson, and others. In writing about being called a "nigger," Adams quotes Countee Cullen's well-known poem, "Incident" (17). The poem's message is not forgiveness, but instead, how searing, unforgettable, and devastating such childhood experiences of racism are:

Incident

"Once riding in old Baltimore
　　Heart-filled, head-filled with glee,
I saw a Baltimorean
　　Keep looking straight at me.

Now I was eight and very small,
　　And he was no whit bigger,
And so I smiled, but he poked out
　　His tongue and called me, 'Nigger.'

I saw the whole of Baltimore
　　From May until December;
Of all the things that happened there
　　That's all that I remember."[28]

Later in *Dark Symphony*, Adams uses the words of Elise Johnson McDougald's "The Task of Negro Womanhood" (published in Alain Locke's profoundly influential anthology, *The New Negro* [1925]) to give voice to a certain feminist anger that is not otherwise very evident in her book. "It is not surprising," Adams quotes (168), "that only the most determined [Negro] women forge ahead to results other than mere survival. . . . We find the Negro woman, figuratively struck in the face daily by contempt from the world about her. *Within her soul she knows little of peace and happiness."*[29]

This strategy of using other voices, or multivocality as Mikhail Bakhtin would call it,[30] allows Adams certain narrative freedoms. Through the voices of others she can offer messages she may not want to put, explicitly, in her own voice. That is one sense in which her narrative is double-voiced and forges its links to New Negro writing. *Dark Symphony* is double-voiced, as well, in two other senses. First, throughout *Dark Symphony*, there are resonances of Adams's earlier writings, writings which are more recognizably New Negro than *Dark Symphony*. And second, throughout *Dark Symphony*, Adams is at pains to describe her desire for rebellion and the ways in which her parents try to thwart and repress that desire.

Some of Adams's other writings, such as "Our Colored Servants" (1941), which treats the willful blindness of white society, and "The Last Supper" (1943), which treats the wrongful execution of an innocent black man, do display the anger over racial injustice and the richly detailed indictment of racial stereotyping that we associate with New Negro writing. "I didn't send a floral wreath—they're far too high this year," says Adam's parodic white mistress on the death of her "beloved" servant in the poem "Our Colored Servants." "But Amanda knew I loved her—She was such a precious dear!"[31] In "The Last Supper," a year after the execution *"a man of another race* / Pleaded guilty to the murder charge." In consequence, the white narrator asks "for a parish in which to work among the colored."[32] A fascinating and profoundly sensual eroticism in the search for God or a spiritual companion is revealed in pieces such as "The Finding of a Soul" (1930), which treats an attachment between a man of science and a monk in ways that today we could only call homoerotic, and in the love poem "Until I Find You" (1936), which expresses intense physical longing for another person. "My heart yearned for the hours we spent together. And often in my dreams I beheld him . . . the holy monk . . . his Rosary and Crucifix suspended at his left side. My ears were alert as though to note the steady tread of his measured step . . . the soft tap of the sandaled feet. The memory of his voice was as a musical reverie."[33] There is an interesting formal and imaginative playfulness in many of her earlier pieces. There, Adams experiments with the voice, persona, and sensibility of someone very different from herself: a scientist in "The Finding of a Soul"; a lover in "Until I Find You"; a desperate mother in "Consecrated" (1936); insensitive white employers in "Our Colored Servants." There is a kind of hard-edged grimness in some of these pieces as well, which accords with much of the realism of New Negro writing. The mother in "Consecrated" learns that God may give but he also takes back. Her terrible loneliness is answered, finally, only by the wind, and she is left embittered. There is an overwhelming gloominess in "The Summons" (1941), which suggests that there is a power and spirit in African-American culture that can never be understood from the outside.

Most of these elements are missing from the book-length version of *Dark Symphony*. But the serialized version of *Dark Symphony* ("'There Must Be a God . . . Somewhere'") does present the kind of strong and engaging voice we might recognize as New Negro. It begins with anger over stereotypes and the silencing of black women. It protests the practice of judging blacks by categories such as extraordinary, exceptional, ordinary, and typical. In her first installment, Adams movingly writes:

> The majority of newspaper and magazine articles about my people are written by authors of other races. Now and then a broadminded Caucasian editor permits a Negro to sketch the lives of our people, but most of these writers are men. The Colored woman's attitude toward her life, her reactions to its problems, her struggles, ambitions and hopes seldom reach print in magazines published by White editors. True—the Colored woman has a voice, but it may be likened to a singer's whose vocal chords cease to function properly—the melodious tones cannot be heard because the delicate strings of the human-lyre, the throat, are mute. . . . Many people cling to pre-conceived false ideas about the Colored race. There is a popular consensus of opinion that immorality and indolence are supposedly "Negro character traits." Therefore, any commendable goal seems apart from the public's idea of being "typically Negro"

and is usually described as "different." On the other hand, many people believe we possess innate spirituality.[34]

In titling her autobiography *Dark Symphony*, Adams suggests that she is creating a space for the "melodious tones" of a muted "colored woman's" voice. But in contrast to the mature and angry tone of this passage, *Dark Symphony* often strikes a false note. In place of hard-edged, incisive passages such as the above, we find an overabundance of sentimentality and self-deprecation, especially in Adams's discussions of her childhood. Here, she strikes just the saccharine singsong rhythm she claims, in the serialized version, to detest in "religious teachers."[35] She writes about the "happy, care-free kingdom" of a first day at school (12) and describes her mother as "the oracle of oracles" (26). None of the other General Science students, she writes, "could excel the record I held for stupidity" (114).

The book version of *Dark Symphony* is not only more focused on childhood than the serialized version, it is also more childlike. Adams's story about first hearing the word "nigger," for example, which includes the Cullen poem quoted above, is narrated straight-forwardly in the serialized version. In the book version, however, it becomes a lengthy and insipid story of "Little Mary Carty . . . Mary, with the stringy, taffy-yellow hair and the winning front-tooth-missing-smile" (16), Mary, the good little white girl who loves Elizabeth "anyway" and helps restore her to "the happy, care-free kingdom" of school (12). Similarly, where the serialized version of *Dark Symphony* begins with the straightforward discussion of racial stereotyping quoted above, the opening of the book version is a strangely childlike description of childhood: "My life, as a very small child, was filled with happiness. I saw only the beauty of rose coloured dawns. No clouds were visible to darken my path" (7). Whereas in the serialized version, Adams thanks the editors of the *Torch* "for the opportunity granted me to present a Colored woman's viewpoint pertaining to religious *and racial conflicts* in a series of articles,"[36] in the book version, Adams notes that *"Dark Symphony* is *supposed* to deal primarily with my quest for Christ Our Lord" (191, my italics). Where does this "supposed to" come from?

It is unclear why Adams muted *Dark Symphony*, replacing racial messages with childhood idylls. She may have done so in compliance with an explicit editorial request, or in anticipation of what she believed her editors and intended readers wanted to hear. Her letters to her publisher show that the approval of the Catholic Church, both formal and informal, was gravely important to her. Although an official imprimatur (the Church stamp *Nihil obstat* and *Imprimatur* that translate roughly as "Nothing is objectionable"; "I approve" or "Let it be printed")[37] would probably not have been required for *Dark Symphony*, the U.S. edition does carry one,[38] and Adams was very disturbed to learn that it had been omitted in the Dutch edition.[39] We do not know what kind of editing process was necessary for Adams to obtain this approval nor what kind of input others might have had, but the marks of substantial rethinking are evident throughout the book version of *Dark Symphony*.

Dark Symphony is dedicated to three of Adams's patrons, Mother Mary Aloysius, Father Norbert Georges, and Father Francis Wendell, white Catholic friends who clearly encouraged her to write her story and perhaps even promoted its publication to encourage African-American Catholicism, a project with which they were all intimately associated. Mother Mary Aloysius is named in "She Talks Like We Do!" as the nun who sent Adams a statue of Blessed Martin de Porres.[40] Porres was a black Brazilian lay monk who was beatified in 1837. This revered monk was born in Lima in 1579, and his acts of charity and humility inspired an international movement for canonization (which was begun as early as 1659 but did not become successful until May 6, 1962). This galvanized a larger—but also controversial and contested—movement for the evangelization and training of African-American Catholics in the United States: the Blessed Martin Guild, which numbered nearly a hundred thousand members in the mid-1940s.[41] Mother Mary Aloysius's church, the Blue Chapel of the Dominican Nuns in Union City, New Jersey, was the site of the first public novena to Blessed Martin in October 1935 and remained, for many years, a national center of devotion to his cause.[42] Father Norbert Georges, a member of the Dominican Order, directed the Blessed Martin Guild, which promoted both the canonization of Martin de Porres and the cause of African-American Catholics. He also published a number of influential publications about Blessed Martin and the Guild.[43] Father Georges took over the editorship of the *Torch*, the official journal of the Blessed Martin Guild, from Father Francis Wendel, also a member of the Dominican Order, who helped Adams get published.[44] Father Georges recommended *Dark Symphony* as a guidebook to black life months before its actual appearance, indicating that he was intimately aware of, if not directly involved in, Adams's effort to turn her series of articles into a full-scale book.[45]

The influence of such patrons may have contributed its share to *Dark Symphony*'s cautious, careful voice. But for all its self-policing and cautious self-posturing, *Dark Symphony* is not simply an exercise in submission and humility. Adams managed to lace her ladylike tale with significant threads of rebellion and discontent. It is this double voicedness, I want to suggest, that makes *Dark Symphony* especially interesting to contemporary readers.

Dark Symphony may be, as Rebecca Chalmers Barton has noted, the chronicle of a "process of repression" instigated by Adams's parents.[46] But it is also the chronicle of an internal struggle, often waged covertly, against such repression: against domesticity, against the tyranny of compulsory heterosexuality, against racism, and against the rigidity of her parent's training.

Early in her autobiography, Adams relates a moment which is in many ways emblematic. In second grade she and a friend exchange "oral expressions" of what is for each "hearts' delight" (14). Her friend, Mary, "asked nothing more of life than to sit for hours slipping painted wooden beads on a piece of string" (14). But young Elizabeth does not want to sit and string. Her "heart's delight" is to "march": to step to music, to charge about in a "procession." "I kept thinking about marching and music until my feet automatically lifted themselves from the floor: and before I realized what was happening I found myself standing beside Second-Grade-Teacher's desk" (15). "I wanna march," Elizabeth boldly announces. Not surprisingly, her teacher tells her to "march right back" to her desk and stop making trouble (16). The class erupts in laughter, and Elizabeth is deeply humiliated.

If simply getting up and marching is not an option, Elizabeth must discover other ways to express her restlessness, her desire to step to music, her resistance to being passive and told what to do.

The model for such covert resistance begins to take shape during the fateful incident of being called a "nigger"—an incident that Adams puts at the center of her narrative and to which she alludes many times, substituting "the word" as revelation of God for this story of "the word" as revelation of racism—and her consequent "awakening of race consciousness" (23). The key moment occurs when Adams's bead-stringing friend, "Little Mary Carty," shows her how to snub racists like Lillian, a schoolyard name caller, by sniffing and turning up her nose. "I could not strike Lillian without having upon my conscience the guilt of disobedience to my parents [who expressly forbade any form of fighting whatsoever]. But I could sniff" (24), Adams writes. Sniffing in itself is an incomplete gesture, meant to be accompanied by a disdainful turned-up nose, which Adams, whose nose was "not of the streamline design," couldn't quite provide. "You'll just hafta be happy sniffin' at everybody what makes you mad," her friend Little Mary Carty offers. And this is precisely what Adams proceeds to do. Throughout *Dark Symphony*, Elizabeth Laura Adams sniffs at things that make her mad. Her awakening, it seems, is not only to the cruelty of racism, but also to the fact that even though she was forbidden to fight back or contest her tormentors—"a lady never strikes back"— there *was* a form of rebellion she could engage in.

One of the things she sniffs at is the domestic life she also celebrates. One of Adams's purposes in *Dark Symphony* is clearly to render a positive portrait of African-American domestic life. Hence, she describes her home in glowing, exemplary terms: "a large, roomy place" with "an old grandfather clock," upholstered furniture, "a brightly polished mahogany piano," "artistically arranged" tables and lamps, "soft carpet" (31), and loving, but strict, parents. Adams knows that this is not the picture of black life to which her readers may be accustomed, and she insists on its veracity: "The prose-paintings of my home life are not fake replicas of life scenes portraying a back-ground of cultural pretense. They are genuine" (44). Her problem, however, was that not everything was truly perfect, as it never is in real families. In Adams's case, her parents' zeal to prove themselves to be orderly and disciplined, contrary to the derisive stereotypes of disordered and chaotic black families, translated into rigor that really was, as reviewer Ellen Tarry suggested, somewhat inhuman. Adams negotiates this dilemma between what she may have wanted to say and what may have been the truth of her home life by making explicit statements about the perfection of her parents on the one hand— "my mother was very tactful" (18); "Mamma was very religious" (21); "the oracle of oracles—Mother" (26); "no child ever received more love from parents than I" (55)—while describing, on the other hand, a number of chilling scenes and practices, like the "over-abundance of energy" her mother managed, miraculously, to summon up "at whipping time" (57). She provides these descriptions always in a matter of fact, even-handed, voice: "the purpose of my parents' strict training was to prepare me to work purposefully that I might face undismayed the perplexities and disappointments of life" (59). The double-voicedness of these descriptions means that she need never *say* what was wrong with her parents' methods; we see it all too clearly. Whenever she does say something negative, she moves quickly to qualify. "By the time I was nine years of age," Adams relates, for example, "my parents had trained me to respond to their commands by a gesture. If they had placed me in a circus I would have won out in competition with a well-trained seal without the slightest effort" (60). "When friends came to our house I waited upon them as though I were a servant" (61). Adams follows with an exoneration that may only serve to indict her parents further. "Though it may appear to a reader that my parents' method of child training was too severe," she writes, "future chapters will bear testimony to the profound influence it had upon my life" (63). Since Adams reveals herself to be in myriad subtle forms of lifelong rebellion, that influence, we are able to infer, may not have been altogether pretty.[47]

Adams sniffs, even more loudly, at marriage. "Mother," described by Adams as "an adherent to the old-fashioned teaching that the most essential requisite of a loyal wife is willingness to make any sacrifice that benefits her family" (46), is not made out to be particularly happy. Her father, while loving and often more lenient than her mother, is also a patriarch who, in Adams's view, expects service and objectifies and infantilizes his wife:

> My father's love for Mother was like that which a curator of a museum has for the possessions entrusted to his guardianship. He values them and exercises extreme caution to insure the protection of each treasure. He cherishes the treasures and is pleased when others can appreciate their worth, but he rarely takes them away from the security of the museum to be placed on display in the homes of friends. And so likewise was Father's love for Mother. He surrounded her with every luxury his income afforded, but he preferred his wife to have no interest in civic affairs. A wife's place, he believed, was in the home—to be adored by her husband, worshiped [sic] by their child. (46–47)

Adams's response to what she observes in her parents' "ideal" marriage is outright rejection of marriage and an early or proto feminism. Even as a young child, she reveals, she was "not inclined to care for my dolls (disliking to wash, iron, or sew for them)" (53). Taught by her mother that "wedded life will not be a path of orange-blossoms" and that as a future wife she "must learn how to be self-sacrificing, patient, tolerant and industrious" (100), Adams managed to vent her feelings on the smoking jacket and slippers she had to fetch for her father nightly:

> Who would want to get married, anyway, I asked myself, if it meant waiting on someone else the rest of one's life!
> If Mother was occupied elsewhere I took my spite out on the slippers—sometimes banging them against the chair or beating them with my fists, muttering:
> "Crazy husban'."
> "Silly husban'."
> "Hateful husban'."
> "When I marry I won't wait on my husban'! I won't! I won't! I won't!"
> Once in a while Mother, hearing me mutter[,] would call out, "Did you just say something?"

"Just talkin' to myself, Mamma dear," I would reply, with a sigh. (100)

Adams goes one better than refusing to wait on her future husband; she avoids marriage and motherhood altogether. As a Catholic Tertiary, she certainly submitted to the idea of higher authority, but this was not the same authority as the one she had witnessed at home. Indeed, it even ran contrary to her parents' authoritarian plans for her life. There is a long tradition of black women being able to "maintain an organized resistance to patriarchy within the black religious experience," Cheryl Gilkes argues.[48] Adams may be part of a less-commented-upon tradition, one of unorganized or personal resistance that also uses the Church, a way of keeping alive what Gilkes calls the "dynamics of conflict" without ever seeming to endorse or practice them.

Adams describes her childhood home as comfortable, ordered, even lush at times. But like other African-American women writers, such as Zora Neale Hurston or Nella Larsen (whose descriptions of domestic interiors Adams's often resemble), what seems a desirable domestic space is not necessarily as safe or as pleasant as it appears.[49] An added benefit of her conversion and her decision to become a Tertiary, even if it had little or nothing to do with her motives for becoming a Catholic, could have been its use as a rationale for eschewing an ordinary, domestic, married life. There may also have been secret satisfaction in breaking her father's repeated edict: "'You cannot become a Catholic!' and 'I will not permit you to become one'" (106).[50]

The one thing Adams "sniffs" at most consistently in *Dark Symphony* is racial injustice and racial inequality. Adams's parents were unequivocally opposed to her taking part "in racial arguments anywhere at anytime" (113). In their view, a willingness—let alone a propensity—to engage in "controversy" was an affront to both breeding and decency. In the face of the gravest and most painful expressions of racism, they schooled her in forgiveness, forbearance, and faith in God.

As a child, however, Adams's own instincts were much more confrontational: "Fight! Fight! Fight! I wanted to fight!" she admits (83). This New Negro attitude had no place in a home that was strictly old-school. Her mother's teaching on race was that people are divided up into categories and that a white preference for whites was no different from Elizabeth's own preference for candy, that an avoidance of blacks by whites was no different from Elizabeth's avoidance of spinach. Her father's teaching, similarly, was that "every person in the world had 'a place'" (113) and that the key thing was neither to covet nor to deride anyone else's place.

Part of trying to find her own place involved challenging racial categorization. But when Adams so much as questions her parents about stories she had heard of racial prejudice in classrooms, they erupt in a fury of startling anger and invective: "Has any white teacher ever refused to teach you? Answer me!" her mother insists (95). "No, Ma'am," Adams meekly replies (95).

> Mother raised her voice higher: "Then what have you to complain about? Answer me!"
>
> I answered, admitting that no white teacher had ever refused to teach me.
>
> Then Father said: "Young lady—I may as well tell you now that I don't propose to stand by and see your mother work herself to death while you waste time and energy fighting the Civil War all over again. Now stop wagging your tongue over adult problems. Do you hear me?"
>
> Politely, meekly, reverently, and resignedly, I breathed: "Yes, Papa dear."
>
> I was ready to leave the room, but Mother called me to attention.
>
> "Stand still, *you fidgety little maggot!*" she said, "and listen to what I have to say. I don't propose to stand by and see your father work himself to death while you waste time and energy taking part in controversies. Do you hear me?" (96, my italics)

This outburst follows a lecture by her mother on slavery which concludes in a manner that is hard not to read as parodic—particularly of Booker T. Washington—but that I think we are meant to take as sincerely felt and as representative of an "Old Negro" view: "if poor, despised slaves were honest, industrious and trusty," her mother declares, "their descendants for generations to come will be endowed with good heritage" (92). Adams responds by finally promising "to stay away from those terrible things called controversies" (93).

As soon as Adams feels herself drawn to religion, to its rituals and its quiet and the physical beauty of the church, she becomes involved in racial controversies. While still attending services with her mother, Adams notes that during Holy Communion "the clergyman was wiping the Chalice where my lips had touched it, briskly polishing it as though it were tarnished. Then turning the Chalice round he served the White communicant kneeling beside me. . . . The thought came to my mind like a newspaper headline: 'RACE PREJUDICE AT THE ALTAR!'" (125). Before she or her mother can decide how to respond, they are asked by the clergyman, with "tears filling his eyes and streaming down his cheeks" to stop coming to that church because "White communicants did not want to kneel at the altar with Negroes" (125).

Adams continues to search for a spiritual home, but not by ignoring such racism. She resolves to "find out everything I wanted to know about God if it took me the rest of my life" (128). But she also determines to settle the question—for herself—of where such race prejudice came from. "Unless I could be convinced," she writes, "that His Son's death for the redemption of all people included the Colored, I could put my time to better use than praying to One Who heard only the fair of skin" (128).

One of the things that draws her to the Catholic Church is the confessional. Rather than see confession primarily as a place to talk about herself, Adams sees it as "an ideal place . . . to ask questions about God" (128), presumably to pursue her inquiry into God's racial views without anyone knowing, since "the confessional was dark," that the investigator herself was black (129).

In devoting so much of *Dark Symphony* to racial controversy, Adams clearly challenges her parents' anti-confrontational ideology. Even before publishing *Dark Symphony*, Mary Scally reports, Adams kept what she called "'Scrap-Book Letters,' so called because of the newspaper clippings and magazine articles pasted between the messages, telling of the sufferings and achievements of the Negro, *which she sent to interested people in all parts of the world.*[51] In *Dark Symphony*, not only does Adams emphasize and criticize instances of white racism, but she also celebrates African-American women, such as Juliette Derricotte. Derricotte was Dean of Women at Fisk University and an international campaigner for African-American rights. She died of injuries from a car accident because no white hospital would treat her. Because she spoke out on behalf of African-Americans and fought racial prejudice, even when it did not seem strictly ladylike to do so, Derricotte became a heroine and role model to many young black women.[52]

It is not surprising that Adams would be one of the young women to look to someone like Derricotte. Adams was sorely in need of role models. All of the role models in her life who encouraged her to rebel and fight back—a devoted grandfather who encouraged her to rough-house and play outdoors, a music-loving father who sometimes winked at her mother's strictness, who had "socked that white kid in both eyes and tried to tear the pants off him" (21), when he, like Elizabeth, was first called "nigger," and who encouraged a light irreverence if not outright rebellion—died suddenly and in ways that left Adams filled with fear and a sense of isolation. Her grandfather, in particular, had seemed a bulwark against all evil. He promised the young Elizabeth that he would protect her from death itself. "'I'll be watching when you're asleep,' he promised, 'and if Ol' Death comes I'll shoot him down'" (40). The loss of her grandfather, shortly after this promise, Adams reports, "was hard to bear. The truth was bitter—bitter—bitter" (42). When her father dies, some years later, Adams is schooled by her mother simply to repress all her feelings. "'Learn the value of silence,'" her mother advises (121).

As a non-Catholic it is difficult for me to speculate about the ways in which the Catholic Church answered, or failed to answer, Adams's spiritual needs, her desire for "tranquility" (129), and her search for God. But joining the Catholic Church must have provided Adams with three things she desperately sought: a way of dealing with death, peace from her parents' edicts, and a community in which (as well as *with* which) she could "fight." Adams speaks a number of times of how she sought the Catholic Church, at first, as a place of refuge: "I only wanted a quiet place in which to pray" (142); "I came there simply because it was quiet."[53] Affiliations with the Catholic Church, the *Torch*, and organizations like the Blessed Martin Guild may have provided Adams with not only "tranquillity," but also a way to fight for racial justice without seeming "controversial" or ill-mannered. Such affiliations may have seemed to offer a respectable community of more or less like-minded individuals who shared her concerns and a commitment to speaking out.

"HARVESTING" 13 MILLION

To place *Dark Symphony* in context, we would need to inquire not only into how the Church answered Adams's needs, but how she answered the Church's as well. In particular, Adams would have supplied an important, even crucial, voice to two of the Catholic Church's most important initiatives of the thirties and forties: the effort to create a lay apostolate and the program for evangelizing African-Americans and "harvesting" 13 million non-Catholics, as James Mack put it.[54] To suggest that Adams may have been of use to the Church does not make its interest in her only opportunistic, or imply that her promoters were simply taking advantage of her, or suggest that she was merely a pawn. The relationship can have been a mutually beneficial one, of course. But at the same time, we need to recognize that many African-Americans during this time were questioning the depth of the Church's commitment to black America. W. E. B. Du Bois, in 1925, spoke for many African-Americans when he declared that "the Catholic Church in America stands for color separation and discrimination to a degree equalled by no other church in America, and that is saying a very great deal.[55] In 1936, George Hunton, editor of the *Interracial Review*, described an attitude of "indifference and apathy" on the part of white Catholics, an attitude, he warned, which created the "impression in the minds of many Negroes that the Catholic Church does not particularly welcome the Negro."[56]

But if there was "indifference and apathy," there was also a concern, shared by many white Catholics, that African-Americans could be the answer to declining numbers of American Catholics, a problem some sought to solve through a lay apostolate aimed at blacks. As Francis Wendell, one of Adams's patrons and associate editor of the *Torch*, put it in a 1942 essay entitled "The Formation of a Lay Apostle," the laity had historically proved one of the most valuable resources of the Catholic Church. Given that "recent Popes have insisted on 'an apostolate of like by like,'" the Church was highly motivated to encourage such commitment. To restore the Church to its former position of strength, Wendell argues, "Lay apostles *must* be formed. The questions to be answered are: When? In what way? And by whom?"[57] Debates swirled in the Catholic press over whether African-Americans could be best converted by a black lay apostolate—"like by like"—or by a white lay apostolate—to whom they would be presumed to "look up." For proponents of both positions, the creation of a lay apostolate was widely perceived as the answer to bringing African-Americans into the Catholic Church.

Bringing African-Americans into the Church was not going to be easy, given that, historically, the racial record of the Catholic Church and of the American Catholic Church in particular had not been especially good. Beginning with slavery, there is a record of complacency about racial injustice and avoidance of controversy, ironic enough given Adams's childhood. As the *Catholic Almanac* reports, "Pope Gregory XVI had condemned the slave trade in 1839, but no contemporary pope or American bishop published an official document on slavery itself." Even unofficially, there was no clear Catholic position on slavery, and Catholics fought on both sides in the Civil War. Overall, as the *Catholic Almanac* points out, American Catholics had never been "prominent in the Abolition movement."[58]

Reconstruction did little to spark American Catholic interest in the situation of American blacks. In 1904, as Cyprian Davis reports, Rome issued a virtual mandate to the Catholic Church in the United States to loosen and ultimately erase discrimination and segregation. When this call went unanswered through the first two decades of the century, Rome continued to push for changes in policy and practice. As American Catholic clergy continued to turn a deaf ear to advocates of racial justice, the Church saw a "massive withdrawal from Catholicism" by African-Americans. In 1919 Rome asked American Catholics to specifically address the crisis of racial violence which had produced the "Red Summer" of rioting in Washington, D.C.; in Chicago; in Elaine, Arkansas; and in Knoxville, Tennessee. Once again, the response was underwhelming. "By and large," Davis writes, "Catholics, either black or white, were not in the forefront of the civil rights movement or among the leadership of the protest organizations." Indeed, he concludes, it would not be until 1958 that the U.S. bishops would finally bring themselves to take an "unequivocal stand" on racial discrimination.[59] While Rome seemed to many to represent an ideal of genuine equality and brotherhood, Catholicism as practiced in the United States had its own racial views.

This does not mean that African-Americans were ignored by the American Church. On the contrary, a number of factors converged in the thirties and forties to make African-Americans a kind of focal point of American Catholic discussion and activity. First, there were the papal encyclicals of 1939, especially the controversial *Summa Pontificatus*, "On the Unity of Human Society," of October 20, 1939, in which Pope Pius XII directly addressed the position of blacks in the Catholic Church. Reiterating the principle of "equality," the pope asserted that

> We confess that We feel a special *paternal affection*, which is certainly inspired of Heaven, for the Negro people dwelling among you; for in the field of religion and education We know that they need special care and comfort and are very deserving of it. We therefore invoke an abundance of heavenly blessing and We pray fruitful success for those whose generous zeal is devoted to their welfare.[60]

Whether American Catholics suddenly began to feel this "paternal affection" or were instead struck by the possibilities of a large "harvest" of new converts, the thirties and forties saw a large movement for the evangelization of African-Americans. One view had it that this was a convenient population ripe for national, as opposed to international, missionary work. As Father John

LaFarge, founder of the *Interracial Review* and the Catholic Interracial Council, put it in "The Conversion of the American Negro":

> to convert the Negroes we do not have to travel to distant places, live in great physical hardship under unusual circumstances; we do not learn intricate tribal customs or acquire complicated languages, or deal with foreign and suspicious governments. They are here at home, on our streets, in our towns, in our familiar American surroundings, wearing the same clothes, speaking the same tongue.[61]

Throughout Catholic periodicals of the late thirties and forties, there are constant references to the untapped population of 13 million souls just waiting, it seemed, for Catholic enlightenment. *The National Catholic Almanac* of 1942, for example, asserts that "prayer and worship come naturally" to blacks and that Catholicism, with its rituals, "has a definite appeal to the Negro." But it also expresses concern that an "indifferent, unconcerned, and uninformed" attitude on the part of white Catholics might well hinder the approach of "the vast number of Negroes who are looking toward the Church."[62] Racial stereotyping crops up again and again in numerous essays on the "harvest" of blacks to be converted. In "12,500,000 Potential Catholics" for example, writer James Mack maintains that "when a Negro embraces the true faith he does so with a zeal and fervor characteristic of his race."[63]

In the eyes of many Catholics, the Blessed Martin movement was one of Catholicism's greatest resources in wooing and also working with blacks. As Father Norbert Georges, director of The Blessed Martin Guild and one of Adams's patrons, put it in 1945, "Blessed Martin is taking away some of the obstacles to the conversion of the Colored."[64] The Blessed Martin Guild was established in 1936 and had over 100,000 members. Its success led to the formation of numerous other organizations, such as the De Porres Interracial Center in New York City. As John T. Gillard put it, eliding the Church's resistance to canonizing Blessed Martin, "Martin de Porres stands as the radical answer of Catholicism to the pagan assumptions of racism."[65]

As a symbol, Martin de Porres could be construed in multiple ways. For many African-American Catholics, his message was one of racial pride and commitment. For many white Catholics, on the other hand, his humility and subservience provided a reassuring message that resonates strongly with Adams's favorable reception in the white Catholic press, its approval of her for representing "the entire colored race" and doing so without "rancor."

This was a very complicated period in the history of the Catholic Church, a period when it was quite feasible for different groups to share symbols and agendas they interpreted altogether differently. As Cyprian Davis explains it, the period between, during, and after World War II was one of growth for both blacks and the Catholic Church. This meant that black Catholics were experiencing not only increasing numbers, but also fundamental changes that took them from "a mission status as recipients and dependents" to a community "that began to make itself heard and heeded in the social and cultural revolution following the Second World War."[66] According to Davis, on a national level "the Catholic Church in mid-twentieth-century America acquired a reputation for racial fairness among African-Americans." It was able to do so, he writes, through calls to integrate the Church and to open all levels of Catholic life, including the priesthood, to blacks. During this period many white Catholics issued strong anti-racist statements, messages that must have proved inspiring to a writer like Adams.[67] Unfortunately, Davis adds, this imperative was "often compromised at the local level."[68]

A number of organizations helped open up the Church and encourage African-American activity. Many of them included differences of view such as those which characterized the proponents of Martin de Porres. Two of the most prominent organizations for African-American Catholics were the Federated Colored Catholics (FCC), primarily run by blacks, and the Catholic Interracial Council, primarily run by whites. The Federated Colored Catholics, Davis reports, was founded in 1924 under the directorship of black president Thomas Wyatt Turner. It split in 1932 due to irreconcilable conflicts between its leadership and that of white Jesuits John LaFarge and William Markoe, who proved unable to recognize or accept the legitimacy of black leadership. Markoe successfully gained control of the group's publication, *Chronicle*, which became the *Interracial Review*, and LaFarge worked on "infiltrating the organization" and angling for leadership. When Turner was finally ousted as president, over considerable but ultimately insufficient black protest, the FCC was drastically weakened. LaFarge took over the *Interracial Review* and folded it into his own Catholic Interracial Council in 1934.[69]

Such paternalism, resonating with echoes of Pope Pius XII's avowal of "paternal affection," was not uncommon. For example, according to Davis, Archbishop Bonzano, one of the first archbishops to recommend an aggressive program of evangelization of African-Americans, worked from the premise that blacks had "low moral standing" and "limited intelligence." At the 1918 founding of the National Catholic Association for the Advancement of Colored People, Davis notes, not a single black person was present.[70] Some saw Catholicism as an antidote to the threat of communism, believing that blacks, because of their supposedly inferior intelligence, were particularly vulnerable to indoctrination and brainwashing. Father John T. Gillard, another influential white Catholic writer on African-Americans, warned that "Twelve million Negroes in the United States are growing restless under the burden of their present disabilities. They are looking for a Moses to lead them into the Promised Land. Radicals from across the sea are capitalizing on that discontent."[71] James Mack, in his call to "harvest" 12,500,000 potential Catholics, unabashedly represents Catholicism as an antidote to radicalism,[72] as do both Norbert Georges[73] and Father William McCann, the pastor of St. Charles Borromeo Church in Harlem, who declared that "we must start a movement from within to keep the white Communists out of Harlem."[74] Adams herself was concerned that "Negroes today are turning to Communism" but she saw no easy solutions. "Both the Protestant churches and the Catholic have failed in many respects to show a true attitude toward the Negro," she argued in the serialization of *Dark Symphony*, suggesting that, without a genuine change of attitude, the Catholic Church could not hope to provide for the spiritual, political, and social needs of most African-Americans.[75]

The African-American community, not surprisingly, responded angrily to being patronized. While Protestant publications found the Catholic interest in evangelizing blacks to "bode not good to the colored people,"[76] African-American periodicals were often vociferous in their warnings of potential exploitation and appropriation, and their denunciations of Jim Crow practices such as the segregated Communion and others described by Adams.[77] On April 27, 1935, the *Afro-American* ran a story entitled "Catholics Put Father LaFarge on a Hot Spot," about community reaction to LaFarge's leadership strategies and patronizing attitudes. Noting that the Church had remained "mum" on important issues such as the Costigan-Warner anti-lynching bill, the article reported that the audience called LaFarge to account for practices such as serving mass to blacks from behind a screen, practicing racism at Communion, and opposing black social justice initiatives such as sharecroppers' unions. The Catholic Church, one angry audience member noted, has never been "accused of stirring up the colored man in defense of his rights as an American citizen." As reported in the article, numerous "leading Catholics," presumably black, questioned LaFarge's integrity and the appropriateness of his leadership of the African-American Catholic community. "He stands for domination and not cooperation," one member commented. "Father LaFarge's stand in public is quite the opposite of what we have found it to be in trying to work with him," warned another.[78]

Evidently, joining the Catholic Church as an African-American woman was hardly the way to "stay away from . . . controversies"! But if becoming part of this complex and contentious debate had the benefit of letting Adams "sniff" at her parents and "march" along with others, it is hard to believe that this is what she sought, first and foremost, from the Catholic Church. Throughout Adams's writings there is an extraordinary longing to be heard, to be recognized, and to be in meaningful dialogue with others. Many of her earlier writings, such as "The Finding of a Soul," "Until I Find You," and "Consecrated," rhapsodize about the ideal listener Adams seems to have sought. In "Until I Find You" the supplicant is a "solitary figure" remembering and longing for the miracle of communion—of connection. In "Consecrated," the mother recognizes and respects her son's desire as Adams may have hoped someone, someday, would recognize her own: "you told me of your desires, and I listened." In "She Talks Like We Do!" Adams expresses how moved she was to know that her secret desires were heard and answered by others, to know that there was someone out there who did indeed listen to her. "'There Must Be a God . . . Somewhere'" reveals a profound loneliness and desire for community. And in *Dark Symphony*, this intense and romanticized longing for an ideal interlocutor (what I have elsewhere described as an "erotics of talk"[79]), takes the form not only of a wish that God would "walk and talk" with her (105), but also that the pain of a life "made up mostly of solitude" (187) might somehow be alleviated. Even Adams's violin playing is mediated by this desire to connect to others, a vision of "playing so that a listening audience might see" (64), a longing for the "joy sublime" of public performance (109).

Some of the weaknesses of Adams's writing style might be caused by just this desire for a responsive listener. The preciousness and artificiality of a stilted passage such as "Grandpa saw to that. Yes, Grandpa was what he wanted to be called—just plain Grandpa" (38) is an attempt at dialogic form, written as if the reader's own voice has just asked, "Oh, and is that what he wanted to be called?" and is now being answered. All too often, Adams's life reduced her to the role of being what sociolinguist Erving Goffman calls a "self-talker": one whose social position leaves her talking to herself, muttering, asking unanswered questions, or, ultimately, silent:[80] "I coughed. No one heard. I banged on the glass. But my . . . hands could not make much noise. I yelled. My voice was drowned out by a tidal wave" (8); "Once in a while Mother, hearing me mutter[,] would call out, 'Did you say something?' 'Just talkin' to myself, Mamma dear,' I would reply, with a sigh" (100). Adams's challenge, in other words, was not only to find her own voice, but to produce for herself a listener, someone who would recognize her voice, someone who would answer her back.

Given her unique circumstances as a middle-class, black Catholic woman and given what we can discern of her training in reserve and restraint, this was no easy task. Writing in 1945, Mary Scally predicts the day when "the future may produce a Catholic

Paul Laurence Dunbar or James Weldon Johnson."[81] Both Dunbar and Johnson faced difficult questions of audience and worked creatively to develop a double voice. As Johnson put it, the African-American author can't "just go ahead and write and not bother himself about audiences. That is easier said than done."[82] It was certainly easier said than done for Adams. There was no natural or ready-made audience for her. Negotiating both divided audiences and controversies over blacks and the Catholic Church must have sometimes felt like "marching" through land mines. No wonder that Adams's African-American contemporaries sometimes questioned whether she was truly up to the task and whether her voice came through, strongly and clearly, as her own. Certainly, for them, she fell short of being a Catholic Dunbar or Johnson.

Contemporary readers will judge for themselves whether Adams found her own voice and rose to her challenges. Certainly we can acknowledge that keeping her voice from being simply "drowned out by a tidal wave" and keeping herself from simply falling silent, or "self-talking," was no ordinary achievement. Even Adams's failures, in other words, offer extraordinary lessons in the challenge of negotiating conflict and attempting to find a "place." To whatever extent Adams succeeds in making us sympathize and respond to her story, she succeeds not only in telling a conversion story but in creating one as well: a narrative that can convert her reader into an interpreter of double voices, into someone who can recognize—and hence release—her voice.

NOTES

[1]James Mack, "12,500,000 Potential Catholics," *Torch*, vol. 30, no.1 (January 1946), 17.

[2]A few years after *Dark Symphony* was published, Harlem Renaissance writer Claude McKay wrote about his conversion to Catholicism: "On Becoming a Roman Catholic," *Epistle*, vol. 11, no. 2 (1945), 43–45. Nearly ten years after the publication of *Dark Symphony*, another African-American woman, Helen Caldwell Day, published her autobiography, *Color, Ebony* (New York: Sheed & Ward, 1951). See also Claude McKay, "Why I Became a Catholic," and "Right Turn to Catholicism," both unpublished, in the McKay papers, Schomburg Center

for Research in Black Culture, New York; Helen Caldwell Day, *Not Without Tears* (New York: Sheed & Ward, 1954); and Ellen Tarry, *The Third Door: The Autobiography of an American Negro Woman* (New York: David McKay, 1995).

[3]Sales and royalty figures are approximations, obtained from Sheed & Ward, personal correspondence and communications.

[4]*Torch*, vol. 26, no. 11 (October 1942), 27, for example, carried the following "Letter to Elizabeth":

> I have just read with great pleasure your most interesting book, "Dark Symphony." The broad, tolerant Christian spirit, the keen discerning grasp of the problems discussed, as well as the delightful literary style of which you are a master, make the book a very exceptional one. You certainly should write more; you can so well help both sides, that of your people and their difficulties and that of us of the White race who need enlightenment and growth of understanding and sympathy in our relations with our Colored brethren who are equally the children of God and for whom Christ died as much as He did for us, since He loves us all with an equal love.
>
> I am a convert to the Catholic Faith, of New England Puritan stock. Love for the Mother of Christ and the Real Presence in the Blessed Sacrament came to mean so much for me. I did not become a priest, but established a Catholic College, a preparatory school for boys.

[5]Edward Doherty, a Catholic journalist, published a story about Adams's humility and forbearance in dealing with racism in the office in which she worked; his story was nearly as popular as her own book. See "The Black Cross," *Torch*, vol. 28, no. 1 (December 1943), 13–15, 32. "The Black Cross" was reprinted, in a slightly shorter version, in *Catholic Digest*, vol. 8, no. 4 (February 1944), 25–28, under the title "Incidents in an Office" and was also reprinted in its entirety in Father Norbert Georges, O.P., S.T.Lr., ed., *With Blessed Martin de Porres: Favorite Stories from* The Torch, *1935–1944* (New York: Blessed Martin Guild, n.d.), 225–31. I thank Tara Hoover for locating the Doherty essay.

[6]*Torch*, vol. 26, no. 6 (April 1942). It was no small thing, moreover, to have this status in the Catholic press. About the time *Dark Symphony* appeared, the Catholic press had a combined circulation of 9,125,635, as reported by *Interracial Review*, vol. 15, no. 5 (May 1942), 79.

[7]*Torch*, vol. 26, no. 7 (May 1942), inside cover.

[8]John LaFarge, S.J., *The Race Question and the Negro* (New York: Longmans, Green, 1944); and John T. Gillard, S.S.J., *Colored Catholics in the United States* (Baltimore: St. Joseph's Society Press, 1930).

[9]Elizabeth Laura Adams, *Dark Symphony* (New York: Sheed & Ward, 1942), 124; 105. Hereafter cited in text by page numbers only.

[10]Virginia Lieson Brereton, *From Sin to Salvation: Stories of Women's Conversion, 1800 to the Present* (Bloomington, Indiana: Indiana University Press, 1991), xii.

[11]Brereton, *From Sin to Salvation*, xii.

[12]For further explanation of the commitments of a Tertiary in Adams's time, see *The National Catholic Almanac* (Paterson, N.J.: St. Anthony's Guild, 1942). The "Idea of the Third Order" is explained as follows in the first issue of the *Torch: The Monthly Bulletin of Dominican Tertiaries*:

> It is not possible for all Christians to withdraw from the busy cares of the world, nor are they, indeed, all called to do so. There are many, who, though not led to embrace monastic seclusion, still bear in their heart a holy longing for divine things. In the book of their life one may read the inspiring lesson of souls imbued with a lofty sense of greater than earthly goods and filled with a desire to be generous and unfaltering in the service of God. For such as these, it was the thought of St. Dominic, as it was also of his seraphic contemporary, St. Francis, in behalf of his following, to provide a means of regulating and of sanctifying life according to an approved rule and constitutions, of sharing in the work of a great Order in the Church, and of fostering and generally promoting its interests. . . . Tertiaries . . . are not monks or nuns, but they seriously pledge themselves to live according to a prescribed rule and to do their utmost worthily to fulfill its ordinances.
>
> J.R.V., "The Third Order of St. Dominic," *Torch*, vol. 1, no. 1 (August 1916), 4–5.

[13]See especially Alice Walker, "In Search of Our Mothers' Gardens," in *In Search of Our Mothers' Gardens: Womanist Prose* (New York: Harcourt, Brace, Jovanovich, 1983); and Tillie Olsen, *Silences* (New York: Delecorte, 1978).

[14]Elizabeth Laura Adams, "She Talks Like We Do!" *Interracial Review*, vol. 13, no. 10 (October 1940).

[15]Zora Neale Hurston, "The 'Pet' Negro System," in *I Love Myself When I Am Laughing and Then Again When I Am Looking Mean and Impressive: A Zora Neale Hurston Reader*, ed. Alice Walker (New York: The Feminist Press, 1979), 156–62.

[16]See the following reviews of *Dark Symphony*: Mary O'Neil, *Interracial Review*, vol. 15, no. 5 (May 1942), 81; John LaFarge, "One God for All," *America: A Catholic Review of the Week* (May 30, 1942), 215; Ted LeBerthon, *Los Angeles Daily News* (June 4, 1942); *Sign*, vol. 21, no. 11 (June 1942), 698; *Colored Harvest* (June–July 1942); reprinted in Rev. Michael J. O'Neil, S.S.J., *Some Outstanding Colored People: Interesting Facts in the Lives of Representative Negroes*, 116–18; Joseph Dwyer, *Torch*, vol. 26, no. 8 (June 1942), 27; *Liguorian*, vol. 33 (January 1945), 334; and George E. Keenen, Jr., *Ave Maria: Catholic Home Weekly*, vol. 56, no. 10 (September 5, 1942), 314.

[17]Ellen Tarry, review of *Dark Symphony*, *Catholic World* (July 1942), 504–5.

[18]See Bruce Kellner, ed., *The Harlem Renaissance: A Historical Dictionary for the Era* (New York: Methuen, 1987); and Arna Bontemps, ed., *The Harlem Renaissance Remembered* (New York: Dodd, Mead, 1972).

[19]Theophilus Lewis, review of *Dark Symphony*, *Interracial Review*, vol. 15, no. 5 (May 1942), 80–81.

[20]Elizabeth Laura Adams, "'There Must Be a God . . . Some-where,'" Part II, contd., *Torch*, vol. 25, no. 1 (November 1940), 19.

[21]Elizabeth Laura Adams, review, "The Art of Living Joyfully," *Torch*, vol. 27, no. 2 (December 1942), 29; and Elizabeth Laura Adams, review, "Children Under Fire," *Torch*, vol. 27, no. 12 (November 1943), 29.

[22]*The National Catholic Almanac, 1942*, 408; *The National Catholic Almanac, 1943* (Paterson, N.J.: St. Anthony's Guild, 1943), 427. A brief biography is included in Brother David Martin, C.S.C., B.L.S., A.M., *American Catholic Convert Authors: A Bio-Bibliography* (n.p., Walter Romig, 1944). Adams is listed in a number of the standard sources on African-American biography, such as: Russel C. Brignano, *Black Americans in Autobiography* (Chapel Hill: Duke University Press, 1984), 3; and Jay David, *Growing Up Black* (New York: William Morrow, 1968), 60–70 (including an excerpt from *Dark Symphony*). She appears in Mace Spalding, ed., *In Black and White: A Guide to Magazine Articles, Newspaper Articles, and Books Concerning More than 15,000 Black Individuals and Groups* (Detroit: Gale, 1980), 5; and in Geraldine O. Mathews, *Black American Writers, 1773–1949: A Bibliography and Union List* (Boston: G. K. Hall, 1975). There are useful discussions of her life and work in Sister Mary Anthony Scally, R.S.M., *Negro Catholic Writers 1900–1943: A Bio-Bibliography* (Detroit: Walter Romig, 1945),

19–23 (Scally provides a partial bibliography of Adams's work); and in Rebecca Chalmers Barton, *Witnesses for Freedom: Negro Americans in Autobiography*, with a foreword by Alain Locke (New York: Harper and Bros., 1948), 123–34 (Adams, interestingly enough, is included under the rubric of "The Experimenters," along with Hurston and McKay); there is a brief mention of Adams in Joanne M. Braxton, *Black Women Writing Autobiography: A Tradition within a Tradition* (Philadelphia: Temple University Press, 1989), 140.

Adams is not, however, even mentioned in many of the places one might expect to find her, such as: Kimberly Rae Connor's *Conversions and Visions in the Writings of African-American Women* (Knoxville: University of Tennessee Press, 1994); Jon Alexander, O.P., *American Personal Religious Accounts, 1600–1980* (Toronto: Edwin Mellen Press, n.d.); Virginia Lieson Brereton, *From Sin to Salvation: Stories of Women's Conversions, 1800 to the Present* (Bloomington: Indiana University Press, 1991); and Stephen Butterfield, *Black Autobiography in America* (Amherst: University of Massachusetts Press, 1974).

This too is a familiar story. As a Catholic, she falls out of Butterfield's gaze, and perhaps as a woman as well. As an African-American woman, she falls out of Alexander's and Brereton's vision. She falls out of Connor's, one would have to presume, simply because, by 1994, she has become too obscure to relocate.

I am grateful to Tara Hoover for checking *The National Catholic Almanac* for listings after 1943.

[23]Harper & Row Publishers, personal communication, July 16, 1996.

[24]Jacqueline Jones, *Labor of Love, Labor of Sorrow: Black Women, Work, and the Family from Slavery to the Present* (New York: Vintage, 1986), 199.

[25]In *Dark Symphony*, Adams thanks Mr. and Mrs. John Brown, "faithful friends" who, she says, "came to my rescue" when she suffered serious heart trouble during the Depression (187). In all likelihood, these are the same Browns mentioned in Adams's letter to Sheed & Ward dated September 26, 1952, asking for $375 in return for relinquishing all future claims to royalties.

[26]Zora Neale Hurston, *Dust Tracks on a Road.* (New York: HarperCollins, 1991; originally published 1942).

[27]Cyprian Davis, O.S.B., *The History of Black Catholics in the United States* (New York: Crossroad, 1990), 242–43. McKay's conversion might seem an obvious exception to this statement, since he was such a central figure in the New Negro and Harlem Renaissance movements. By the time of his conversion, however, the New Negro movement was long over

and McKay had retreated into virtual isolation from all his former political and artistic associates.

[28]Countee Cullen, *Color* (New York: Harper and Brothers, 1925).

[29]Elise Johnson McDougald, "The Task of Negro Womanhood," *The New Negro*, ed. Alain Locke (New York: Albert and Charles Boni, 1925); reprint (New York: Macmillan, 1992), 369–82.

[30]See especially, M. M. Bakhtin, *The Dialogic Imagination*, ed. Michael Holquist, trans. Caryl Emerson and Michael Holquist (Austin: University of Texas Press, 1981); and Mikhail Bakhtin, *Problems of Dostoyevsky's Poetics*, ed. and trans. Caryl Emerson (Minneapolis: University of Minnesota Press, 1984).

[31]Elizabeth Laura Adams, "Our Colored Servants," *Torch*, vol. 25, no. 10 (September 1941), 17.

[32]Elizabeth Laura Adams, "The Last Supper," *Torch*, vol. 27, no. 8 (June 1943), 12, italics in original.

[33]Elizabeth Laura Adams, "The Finding of a Soul," *Sentinel of the Blessed Sacrament*, vol. 33, no. 2 (February 1930), 99.

[34]Elizabeth Laura Adams, "'There Must Be a God . . . Some-where,'" Part I, *Torch*, vol. 24, no. 12 (October 1940), 4.

[35]Elizabeth Laura Adams, "'There Must Be a God . . . Some-where,'" Part I, *Torch*, vol. 24, no. 12 (October 1940), 5.

[36]Elizabeth Laura Adams, "'There Must Be a God . . . Some-where,'" Part I, *Torch*, vol. 24, no. 12 (October 1940), 4 (my italics).

[37]See *The National Catholic Almanac*, 1942, 401–2; and Felician A. Foy, O.F.M., and Rose M. Avato, eds., *Catholic Almanac* (Huntington, In.: *Our Sunday Visitor*, 1995), 302. I am grateful to Sue Houchins, now of a Catholic monastery in Baltimore, Maryland, for helpful discussions about Catholic publishing, imprimaturs, and African-American Catholic women.

[38]As explained in *The National Catholic Almanac* for 1942, those books "required by Church Law to have ecclesiastical censorship prior to publication" would include: "Books of Holy Writ"; "Books treating of Holy Scripture"; "Prayer-Books"; "all writings which contain anything that particularly concerns religion and morals" and "sacred images," 401.

[39]"Miss Conroy," Adams wrote to the manager of Sheed & Ward on June 2, 1947, "I am very anxious to know why the copies printed in Dutch do not have the official stamp of 'Imprimatur' as the book published in New York has and also the one in England. I do not like the idea of it being left out of the book. It was in the others and I wonder what reason there could be for it being omitted. I am not 'fault-finding' dear Miss

Conroy but I realize that the official mark of approval is essential in this type of book. Is there any way that future editions be published with it?"

[40]Elizabeth Laura Adams, "She Talks Like We Do!" *Interracial Review*, vol. 13, no. 10 (October 1940), 153.

[41]Georges, ed., *With Blessed Martin*, 19.

[42]See the special canonization issue of *Torch*, vol. 46, no. 6 (June–July 1962), 7. See also Mother Mary Aloysius, *History of the Dominican Sisters of the Perpetual Rosary* (Paterson, N.J.: St. Anthony Guild Press, 1958).

[43]Norbert Georges, O.P., S.T.Lr., *Meet Brother Martin!: A Little Life of Blessed Martin de Porres, Saintly American Negro, Patron of Social Justice*, 15th ed. (New York: Blessed Martin Guild, 1936); *My Pilgrimage to Lima* (New York: the author, 1958); *Meet Saint Martin de Porres: Patron Saint of Social and Interracial Justice: A Living Model of the Encyclicals* (New York: The Saint Martin Guild, 1936); and ed., *With Blessed Martin* and *The Fifteenth Anniversary Book of the Blessed Martin Guild: Articles from* The Torch, *1945–1950* (New York: The Blessed Martin Guild, n.d.).

[44]See Charles R. Auth, O.P., *A Dominican Bibliography, 1216–1992* (Washington, D.C.: Dominican House of Studies, n.d.), vols. I and II; and Rev. James Reginald Coffey, O.P., *Pictorial History of the Dominican Province of St. Joseph, U.S.A.* (New York: Holy Name Society, n.d.).

[45]Norbert Georges, "Whither Blessed Martin de Porres," *Torch* (January 1942); reprinted in Georges, ed., *With Blessed Martin*, 210.

[46]Barton, *Witnesses for Freedom*, 125.

[47]Adams's treatment of domesticity may be not just double voicedness, but genuine ambivalence. Because of historic attempts not only to deride but even to destroy African-American family life, the domestic sphere has an especially privileged status for many African-Americans. Building and celebrating the domestic sphere can be a form of resistance not only to white racist assumptions but also to demands for labor and participation in the public sphere, "a drain on their time and physical resources that might otherwise have been expended in the work force," as Jacqueline Jones puts it (Jones, *Labor of Love*, 4). Adams, at one point, puts her own love for her mother in interestingly racial terms when she declares that "I was not born in Africa . . . but my devotion to my earthly mother goes back to the devotion that black folk cling to." Elizabeth Laura Adams, "'There Must Be a God . . . Somewhere,'" Part IV, contd., *Torch* vol. 25, no. 4 (February 1941), 11. Adams's devotion to her mother is best seen in her letters to her publisher, which are much more concerned with the twists and turns of her mother's health than with her own career.

INTRODUCTION

[48]Cheryl Townsend Gilkes, "The Politics of 'Silence': Dual-Sex Political Systems and Women's Traditions of Conflict in African-American Religion," *African-American Christianity: Essays in History*, ed. Paul E. Johnson (Berkeley and Los Angeles: University of California Press, 1994), 103.

[49]See Zora Neale Hurston, *Their Eyes Were Watching God* (Urbana: University of Illinois Press, 1978), first published in 1937; and Nella Larsen, *Quicksand* and *Passing* (New Brunswick: Rutgers University Press, 1986), first published 1929.

[50]Her father objected, in part, because he was a Mason and Adams was to have become an Eastern Star. There is a long history of antipathy between the two groups. See also Barton, *Witnesses for Freedom*.

[51]Scally, *Negro Catholic Writers*, 21 (my italics).

[52]See "Juliette Derricotte," *Notable Black American Women*, ed. Jessie Carnie (Detroit: Gale Research, 1992), 275–77.

[53]Elizabeth Laura Adams, "'There Must Be a God . . . Some-where,'" Part II, *Torch*, vol. 25, no. 2 (December 1940), 10.

[54]Mack, "12,500,000 Potential Catholics," 17–19.

[55]W. E. B. Du Bois, letter to the editor, correspondence on "The Catholic Church and Negroes," *Crisis* (July 25), 121.

[56]As quoted in "Catholics Urged to Fight Race Bias," *New York Times*, March 9, 1936.

[57]Francis N. Wendell, O.P., "The Formation of a Lay Apostle," *Torch*, vol. 26, no. 11 (October 1942), 4–6; 29. In Part II of this essay (*Torch*, vol. 27, no. 1 [November 1942], 14–15; 28), Wendell lays out the program, responsibilities, and duties of a lay apostle, stressing the need for order and discipline. On the formation of an interracial lay apostolate, see also *The National Catholic Almanac*, 367.

[58]Foy and Avato, eds., *Catholic Almanac* (Huntington, Indiana: 1995), 397.

[59]Davis, *History of Black Catholics*, especially 196–256.

[60]Claudia Carlen Ihm, ed., *The Papal Encyclicals, 1939–1958* (Raleigh, N.C.: McGrath Publishing, 1981), 24–25 (my italics).

[61]John LaFarge, S.J., "The Conversion of the American Negro," *Epistle*, vol. 11, no. 2 (Spring 1945), 38.

[62]*The National Catholic Almanac* (1942), 366; 365.

[63]Mack, "12,500,000 Potential Catholics," 17.

[64]Norbert Georges, O.P., "Blessed Martin de Porres and the Conversion of the Negro," *Epistle*, vol. 11, no. 2 (Spring 1945), 52.

[65]John T. Gillard, "Blessed Martin de Porres—The Catholic Answer to Racism," *Torch* vol. 24, no. 3 (December 1939), 4–6, 29; reprinted in Georges, ed., *With Blessed Martin*, 175.

[66]Davis, *History of Black Catholics*, 239.

[67]See, for example, Gillard, "Blessed Martin de Porres—The Catholic Answer to Racism"; and Georges, O.P., "Whither Blessed Martin de Porres," *Torch*, vol. 26, no. 3 (January 1942); reprinted in *With Blessed Martin*.

Gillard writes: "No longer do black backs of slaves run red with blood, but the souls of black folks are assigned to servitude by those of us who vainly seek Heaven while making the lives of Negroes a hell. Rigorously excluded from a voice in a government which claims to be democratic, handicapped by a double wage standard in the battle for bread, and scandalized by sepulchral Christians whose whitened skins hide hearts hardened against human suffering, small wonder that these black and brown millions are growing restless . . . we are stirred to vociferous indignation at the cruel expression of racism in foreign countries, but we are strangely silent at its ugly practices in our own country" (177, 181).

Georges writes: "Pick up a Negro newspaper and you will find plenty of instances of the unbelievable hypocrisy of forcing Negroes, at one and the same time, to get ready to impose democracy on the rest of the world and to endure a merciless treatment from the hands of the *superior* race" (211).

[68]Davis, *History of Black Catholics*, 253.

[69]Davis, *History of Black Catholics*, 220–37.

[70]Davis, *History of Black Catholics*, 207, 219.

[71]John T. Gillard, S.S.J., Ph.D., "White Robes and Black Skins," *Torch*, vol. 21, no. 4 (January 1937), 14–15, 23; reprinted in Georges, ed., *With Blessed Martin*, 66.

[72]"When given their rights in fact as in law," Mack writes, "they will prize with us our national heritage and not lend ear to agitators whose real objective is not to improve but to destroy our way of living" ("12,500,000 Potential Catholics," 18).

[73]Georges celebrates Martin de Porres, in part, because he "found a way to perfect development and self-expression without revolution" (Georges, "Blessed Martin and the Conversion," 53).

[74]"Father McCann Praises Restraint of Colored People," *Catholic News* (March 30, 1935).

[75]Elizabeth Laura Adams, "'There Must Be a God . . . Some-where,'" Part V, *Torch*, vol. 25, no. 5 (March 1941), 23.

[76]"Popery among Southern Negroes," *Protestant* (Washington, D.C.: May 1922), 37.

[77]*Afro-American* (September 22, 1934), for example, tells the story of the mostly black Ascension Church in Bowie, Maryland, where "white persons occupy all the front pews" and "colored members . . . some of whom broke rock for the foundation . . . must take the row of seats behind the whites."

[78]"Catholics Put Father LaFarge on a Hot Spot," *Afro-American* (April 27, 1935).

[79]See Carla Kaplan, *The Erotics of Talk: Women's Writing and Feminist Paradigms* (New York: Oxford University Press, 1996).

[80]Erving Goffman, *Forms of Talk* (Philadelphia: University of Pennsylvania Press, 1981), 109 and passim.

[81]Scally, *Negro Catholic Writers*, 8.

[82]James Weldon Johnson, "The Dilemma of the Negro Author," *American Mercury*, vol. 15, no. 60 (1928), 477.

Elizabeth Laura Adams

The publishers tell us that *Dark Symphony* by Elizabeth Laura Adams and published about three months ago has already had a warm reception from the buying public as well as many excellent reviews. One of the best reviews, which appeared recently in *America,* said in part:

"There is simple truth, life and motion and a running current of shrewd observation of the great white world in which she grows up. There is the steady progress of a transparent soul toward God and the Catholic Faith."

Dark Symphony

by

Elizabeth Laura Adams

1942

SHEED & WARD

NEW YORK

COPYRIGHT, 1942,
BY SHEED & WARD, INC.

Nihil obstat
Arthur J. Scanlan, S.T.D.
Censor Librorum

Imprimatur
✠ Francis J. Spellman, D.D.
Archbishop, New York
March 4, 1942

MANUFACTURED IN THE UNITED STATES OF AMERICA
BY THE HADDON CRAFTSMEN, INC., CAMDEN, N. J.

✠

J. M. J.

Dedicated to Three Loyal Friends

MOTHER MARY ALOYSIUS
Sub-Prioress
Dominican Sisters of the Perpetual Rosary
Union City, New Jersey

REV. FR. NORBERT GEORGES, O.P.
Director *The Blessed Martin Guild*
New York, N. Y.

REV. FR. FRANCIS N. WENDELL, O.P.
Associate Editor *The Torch*
New York, N. Y.

in Gratitude for Your Faith in Me

ACKNOWLEDGMENTS

Special acknowledgment is due the editors of *The Torch* who, very generously, have granted permission to use extracts from: "There Must be a God Somewhere."

I am indebted to many persons for their encouragement and guidance. In particular I wish to express my gratitude to those whose sincere interest in the Negro race aided me in reaching my goal. . . . . Mr. and Mrs. John Steven McGroarty, Mrs. Conyers Pritchett Hedge, Mrs. Ella F. J. Tafe, Dr. Arthur Patch McKinlay, Mrs. Alice Hunnewell, Dr. Kenneth P. Bailey, Miss Adelaide Mernagh, Reverend Mother Agnes of Jesus, Prioress, Carmelite Monastery, Indianapolis, Indiana, Reverend Mother Emmanuel, Prioress, Carmelite Monastery, San Diego, California, Father Noel Dillon, Father Edward Wade, Father John G. Flack and The Father-Abbot of a Trappist Monastery and Miss Irene Cronkhite.

CHAPTER ONE

Dawn

My LIFE, as a very small child, was filled with happiness. I saw only the beauty of rose coloured dawns. No clouds were visible to darken my path.

Life was a simple matter. In the morning I was awakened by my mother or father. Then followed the general procedure of bath, breakfast, play, lunch, nap, play, dinner, more play—then bath again and off to bed. This was my daily routine.

One particular morning I peered through one of the living room windows and, to my amazement, beheld the yard next door swarming with children.

I pressed my face against a pane and watched them. They skipped, hopped, ran, galloped and pranced. Children. Large groups. Children. Small groups. Many, many children. Of course I could not count them because I did not know how to count. But the sight of their impish antics delighted me; and I was seized by a sudden desire to join their merry-making.

Joyfully I ran through the house calling my mother; wishing to share this great discovery with her—unconscious of the fact that she had been annoyed daily by the shrill screams long before the uproar attracted me.

Mother responded to my call. She defined the assemblage of skippers, hoppers, runners, gallopers and prancers as groups of school-children.

I looked a question.

Further information was offered:

"School is a place where children are sent to be taught."

Taught. That was a big word. I did not understand big words. I pondered. Questioned. The questions flew out, then circled back like a boomerang—unanswered. Mother had disappeared.

I trailed her. Questioned some more. Begged. Pestered. Tugged at her apron strings to make my cause more effective.

"You're much too young for school," she said. "There is plenty time yet before you start to kindergarten." Then without another word she dismissed the subject.

I ran back to the living room. Heretofore I had been too tiny to see out although the windows were low. Then all of a sudden I had chanced upon this strange, new exciting world.

My nose flattened against the pane. I coughed. No one heard. I banged on the glass. But my chubby hands could not make much noise. I yelled. My voice was drowned by the tidal wave of childish glee next door.

Disappointed, I turned away. Undaunted, I resolved to watch for the opportune time when the window would be opened.

The anticipated moment arrived the next day when Mother pushed aside the curtains and raised the window to let in warm air and unbound sheaves of golden sunlight.

I waited. Listened cautiously. Her footsteps retreated. . . .

Grabbing a doll, picture book and toy wagon wheel, I climbed as best I could on to a chair and looked out. More territory presented itself. There was a large building with many windows. A spacious yard. A high, high

8

fence. I had no idea that the world was such a great, big, place.

From my point of vantage the interior of one of the school rooms loomed clearly. The teacher (her back to the class) was writing across a blackboard.

I made a queer noise: a combination gurgle and cough. Nothing happened. I coughed again—this time omitting the gurgle. No one paid any attention. I coughed louder. A little girl raised surprised eyes as she looked in my direction. Then she turned away. I coughed once more. She raised her eyes again and saw me dangling a headless china doll in mid air. She put a hand over her mouth to keep from laughing out loud. Then she waved. I waved back. She next leaned forward and whispered to the child occupying the seat in front of her. Soon several children were laughing and waving at me. Those nearest the windows held up their books. Suddenly the teacher turned and saw me. Hastening over to the windows she placed her hands firmly across a sill.

"Stop disturbing this class!" she yelled. And then— Bang! Bang! Bangbangbang! The teacher closed all the windows. But I could still see her as she walked over to her desk, picked up a stick and shook it at the class. A year or so later I learned that the stick was called a "ruler."

The teacher's speech and actions gave me to understand that I should vanish. Frightened, I climbed down from my newly-found observation-tower; but from that day on my parents had no peace of mind until the time came for them to send me to kindergarten.

As all good things come to those who wait, the hour arrived when, with a handkerchief pinned to my dress and a note bearing my name, address, age, and the name of my parents (as if I could lose the way home with the

9

school right next door) my mother took me by the hand and said to my father:

"Well, Papa, we're ready for kindergarten."

Papa shook his head and made a funny noise with his tongue between his teeth. The noise was supposed to convey the idea that he was overcome with surprise as he asked:

"Mamma, do you think our little baby is old enough to go to school?"

Years later I found out that Papa was very indiscreet (as Papas sometimes are) when he asked that, because Mamma was living through one of the unforgettable moments of her life; an experience to be cherished in long after-years as a tender memory; to be spoken of with tears in one's eyes and a lump in one's throat. That was why she did not answer Papa's question but kept adjusting and re-adjusting the collar on my dress.

With an enthusiastic: "Well, well, well! Isn't this wonderful!"—Papa kissed me goodbye, reminding me to be an apt pupil.

It was Mamma who wanted to be reassured that I had not forgotten my identity. So for her sake I pointed to the identification tag ornamenting my dress; and staring blankly at both parents (as though they were total strangers) told them my name, address and age, as well as their names. But Mamma was not so sure that I remembered the "Thou shalts" and "Thou shalt nots" rehearsed days and days previously. Thus for her especial benefit I recited the parental commandments.

Mamma beamed as I began at the top of the list and named them one by one.

Summed up, the admonitions obliged me to remember: to be a perfect little lady; to walk and not turn; to remember not to sit with my feet crossed; to blow my nose *quietly* when it needed blowing; to sneeze in my handkerchief; politely to refuse candy, chewing gum and all other edibles by tactfully remarking that my parents would not permit me to eat anything between meals; to obey my teacher and always courteously address her "Yes, Miss-So-and-So" or "No, Miss-So-and-So" unless she directed me to resort to the old fashioned "Yes, Ma'am" or "No, Ma'am"; to remember to be unselfish with my playmates; to play at recess and have a grand, glorious and wonderful time without getting a speck of dirt on my dress; my right hand was supposed to be raised when I wanted to ask a question or when . . . .

My mind went blank. I pondered. There was so much to be remembered.

Mamma (ever to the rescue) saw my dilemma and bending down, whispered very, very softly in my ear lest Papa hear our secret. Her words revived my memory.

Final instructions were that I was to come straight home after kindergarten hours. Papa had paid a carpenter to cut a small gate in the fence which separated the school yard from home. I was to enter through it. Under no circumstances (including fire, earthquake, flood or hail storm) was I to go near the large school gates that led to the street unless Mamma, Papa or a teacher was with me. The street (my parents told me) was "out in the world" where big red electric cars whizzed by and automobiles ran rampant. Sometimes a little school girl ran out into the territory called "street" and a big red bus or an automobile hit her, and then she was never able to play any more.

When Mamma was thoroughly convinced that I comprehended all these details she took me to school.

Half an hour later my admittance to kindergarten was

11

Gramley Library
Salem College
Winston-Salem, NC 27108

seconded by the principal's approval and my name included on the enrollment list.

Papa had gone on to his work, so Mamma had to face the final ordeal alone.

She held me close to her heart; and I listened vaguely as she murmured something about life being a long road and her baby taking the first step up the something-or-other of progress. Then we kissed each other again and again; I devotedly clasping my arms tightly about her neck in the fond embrace that we called a cinnamon bear hug.

I was just about to ask Mamma why she was crying, when a freckled faced girl in a blue dress (a child about my own age) with stringy, taffy-yellow hair, came upon the parting scene.

She observed us quizzically. She grinned. A front tooth was missing. She beckoned to me.

"Wanna play?" she invited.

With an impulsive, wild-west whoop, I ran from my mother's embrace.

My new playmate clasped my hand tightly in hers and round and round the school house we ran.

Mamma stood on the steps waiting for me to throw her a fond, farewell gesture. But alas, I never paid any more attention to Mamma or even thought about her again until the end of kindergarten hours.

My freckled face companion in the blue dress, with the stringy, taffy-yellow hair and her winning front-tooth-missing-smile, had taken me with her into the happy, care-free kingdom of the first day at school.

CHAPTER TWO

The Word

Kindergarten (as it appeared to me) was a wonderworld, fairyland, dream-island, Elysian paradise, Utopia and the Promised Land combined. I had such a wonderful time playing with other children that had it been left to my decision I would have spent the rest of my life in the pre-beginner's class. However, the Board of Education intervened.

Now when I first heard the name "Board of Education" (like others classified in the category of big words) its definition was beyond my comprehension. But in due time I learned that it was made up of people who had a great deal to say about what went on in school.

Secretive as *The Board* tried to be, I discovered that it was this organization of distinguished intellectuals that snatched away my happy-go-lucky hours of kindergarten. Its members were the snakes-in-the-grass, the wolves-in-sheep's-clothing that decreed all games, laughter, drills, frolicking and joyous freedom give way to systematic routine.

I did not ask to be promoted. I did not want to be promoted. I was happy in the idyllic atmosphere of the little folk's class. However, the Board never consulted me or took into consideration my personal feelings about the matter.

I was not alone in my revolt against progress. My little

13

comrade with the stringy, taffy-yellow hair (Mary Carty by name) disliked the grades as much as I. She too yearned to turn time backwards in its flight and enjoy the tranquillity of kindergarten; for it was there that she had learned how to string beads. And Mary asked nothing more of life than to sit for hours slipping painted wooden beads on a piece of string.

One balmy day, as we sat in second-grade-class, she whispered to me.

"I *wisht* I could string beads!" she breathed.

She had to speak under her breath, whispering being one among the many inconveniences imposed by grades higher than kindergarten. One could never talk out loud unless asking or answering a question.

Now if Mary had not mentioned stringing beads, the thought of marching might never have occurred to me. But the oral expression of her heart's delight brought to my mind the inexpressible joy I experienced when parading.

"I *wisht* I could march, Mary," I whispered back.

Then I began to think about marching and its extraordinary advantages over ordinary walking; for when a person walked there was no music, but when one marched one stepped lively to a stirring tune. That was why, I reflected, kindergarten was so much nicer than first and second grades. Kindergarten-Teacher had played the piano and spoke in a singing tone:

"Heads-up-and-shoulders-back-and-look-at-the-flag!" And as she played and sang, a procession of children stepped "two by two." A flag-bearer walked alone, heading the procession. Every child had begged for the privilege of carrying the flag, and each child had a turn.

I kept thinking about marching and music until my feet automatically lifted themselves from the floor: and

14

before I realized what was happening I found myself standing beside Second-Grade-Teacher's desk.

Second-Grade-Teacher was not pretty like Kindergarten-Teacher. She was fat and wore glasses perched on the end of her nose.

"Why didn't you raise your hand before *marching* up here?" she demanded, looking down at me.

I beamed. My heart turned over with happiness. I thought it wonderful that she knew I wanted to march without my telling her.

"What do you want?" she asked.

I smiled; a friendly, winsome, cooperative smile.

"I wanna march," I told her.

Second-Grade-Teacher smiled back; but not friendly, winsomely, nor cooperatively.

"So you want to march?" she questioned, nodding as if contemplating the idea. "Why?"

Second-Grade-Teacher's voice scared me a little, the way the last inquiry boomed out. I gulped, then smiled again.

"I wanna march because I don't like this—" I answered truthfully.

"Don't like what?" she almost screeched.

I went back to my desk, picked up my book with the pictures of the C-A-T (cat) and the D-O-G (dog). I knew that a C-A-T cried "meow" and a D-O-G barked "woof-woof." Throughout the first grade I had heard about cats, rats, bats and hats. That was enough, I thought.

"I don' like this book," I explained to Second-Grade-Teacher, who glared at me.

She did not take the book. She simply folded her arms and half-spoke, half-questioned:

"So you don't want to learn how to read and write. You just want to march?"

I shook my head happily: glad that she understood at last.

"Yes, Ma'am," I replied.

"And where do you want to march?" Her voice became unusually sweet and low.

I remembered kindergarten.

"Roun' an' roun' th' room," I told her.

Somebody giggled. Then before I could bat an eye, Second-Grade-Teacher's voice rolled through the room like a peal of thunder.

"Suppose you march right back to your desk!"

The fury of her rage blew me to my seat like a tempest tossing a ship at sea.

Everybody laughed until Second-Grade-Teacher struck her desk with a ruler; that is everybody except Mary.

Little Mary Carty who had welcomed me my first day at school, who walked with me into class every day thereafter, and who now sat beside me—Mary, with the stringy, taffy-yellow hair and the winning front-tooth-missing-smile, looked at me with sad eyes. And as I sat down, my head hung in shame, Mary (the loyal comrade that she was) stuck out her tongue at Second-Grade-Teacher (when that target of her disapproval was not looking) and then handed me a token that bound our friendship with the bond of everlasting devotion—three sticky gum-drops.

"I love you, Elizabeth" she whispered. And she meant it. For it was Mary who stood by me the day that I first heard—the word.

It happened like this:

One day a stranger arrived at school. We called her the "new girl" because we had never seen her before. When Mary asked her to join our game she shook her head and refused. Pointing in my direction she declared:

16

"I won't play with her because—*she's a nigger*."

That was the first time that I had ever heard—the word.

I was a very small child when this happened, but I can remember the queer expressions that passed over the countenances of my playmates. A few backed away, a frightened look in their eyes. Others gazed at me—then at one another.

I think every Colored person in the world can recall the first time he or she was called by this uncomplimentary title. Countee Cullen, Negro poet, wrote a poem about it. He called the poem INCIDENT. The poet says:

"Once riding in old Baltimore
　　Heart-filled, head-filled with glee,
I saw a Baltimorean
　　Keep looking straight at me.

Now I was eight and very small,
　　And he was no whit bigger,
And so I smiled, but he poked out
　　His tongue, and called me, 'Nigger.'

I saw the whole of Baltimore
　　From May until December;
Of all the things that happened there
　　That's all that I remember."

In my case I wondered what had happened to change me so unexpectedly that my playmates would stare wild-eyed.

Mary Carty patted my hand and said, "Never mind, Elizabeth. I love you."

After school hours I marched home (yes, I say *marched*, because I usually hummed something like a tune to step to) and ran into the house and asked:

17

"Mamma, what am I?"

Mother was busy and replied nonchalantly. "You're Mamma's little girl."

I shook my head. This was the wrong answer.

She then informed me that I was Mamma's and Papa's little girl if it would make me any happier to have both parents included.

I shook my head again.

I asked: "Mamma—what's a 'nigger'?"

My mother was very tactful. She inquired first where I had heard the word. I told her. She suggested that we have a "little talk": and so we went into an adjoining room.

I remember that Mamma became very busy with her sewing as she began the conversation. She kept biting off bits of thread and seemed unable to find the eye in the needle. She told me that the word "nigger" was not a "nice" word. It was not complimentary. Next she hastened to add that perhaps the little white girl who called me that did not know any better. Then followed the admonition to love the little girl just the same, even though she refused to join a game in which I was playing.

Yes, Mamma wanted me to think kindly of her. No matter how many times she called me "nigger" I was not to strike her, it seemed.

"I do not want you to strike her," my mother said. "It is not that she is better than you that I ask this; but you must not strike at people. A lady never strikes back."

Then I was told that if any difficulties came up I was to tell mother; and she would see my school teacher. She next requested that I reveal the little girl's name. It was Lillian. How could I forget, when it involved so much explanation!

18

That night when I said my prayers before retiring, Mother demanded that I ask God to "bless Lillian." I did so because I had to obey. Of my own volition I would not have bothered to have told God anything about her. I did not hate the child. I was rather dazed over the affair; because for the first time the fact that my skin was dark had been brought to my attention. I had thought of myself as "Elizabeth" because my parents said that was my name. Mary Carty was "Mary Carty" because she said that was her name. I had never thought of her being different in color to myself.

"Don't worry about it any more," Mamma said as she tucked me in bed that night.

Of course I had no intention of worrying. I did not know what it meant to worry. After I had asked God to bless my parents, grandparents, my school teacher and everybody else far and near including my dolls and "Rags" (the pet who slept in a dog-house out in the back yard) there was nothing else to do but go to sleep.

After I was snug in bed, my parents held a council. The council was Mamma's idea. Papa wanted to read the evening paper and enjoy a good smoke.

Many, many years passed before I learned the details of that particular parental pow-wow. Mamma herself related the highlights to me when she was convinced that I had reached the age of reason; that age being, by the way, quite a number of years past seven.

It seems that Mamma became exasperated when she and Papa began their discussion about the word; as Papa immediately threw back his head and laughed and laughed and laughed. Between chuckles he kept saying:

"I know it's serious, darling. But when Baby asked that question her expression was so blank that it was comical!"

19

Provoked by this outburst, Mamma said that she looked very stern and addressed him thus:

"Daniel, this is no laughing matter. There's nothing to joke about. Absolutely nothing!"

I was told that at this juncture Papa apologized for treating such a grave situation so lightly. His apology accepted, the discussion went on to "higher heights and deeper thoughts."

"As Colored parents we have a grave responsibility," Mamma told him. "We can't let Elizabeth go through life hating people."

Respectfully Papa replied, "No, dear. You're right."

"There's no time to lose," Mamma went on. "We must begin right now to teach her that she must love her enemies."

Respectfully Papa replied, "Yes, dear. You're right."

"Only the grace of God can take her through the hardships of this world," the gentler voice continued.

"That's right," Papa affirmed. And then it seems that he began winding his watch.

"We must teach her to live and face life as our parents taught us," quoth the gentler voice.

"Mmnh," assented Papa.

Then Mamma said to him:

"Daniel—you and I—we know how hard these things are to endure. You know that the first time you heard the word it was only God's grace that kept you from bitterness."

"Mmnh," assented Papa.

Suddenly Mamma realized that he had never told her exactly what he had done the first time the word reached his hearing. So she asked him. He told her in the humorous, frank manner characteristically his own.

"Darling," he said. "I well remember the first white youngster that called me 'nigger.' And I am sure that he remembers me to this very day."

"What did you do, Daniel?" Mamma wanted to know. "How did you face the problem. I—"

"Yes, dear?" He noticed that she hesitated.

"I was hurt when I found out that the word was said to hurt me," Mamma confessed. "But I forgave, Daniel. I forgave."

She looked at Papa. "And you, dear—?"

He yawned and rubbed his eyes.

"I must get some sleep," he said, sighing. "Must be at work early tomorrow."

"Don't be evasive, Daniel."

Papa bowed his head and began taking off his shoes. He cleared his throat:

"I socked that white kid in both eyes and tried to kick the pants off him."

Mamma all but swooned.

"Daniel!" she commanded. "Don't ever let Elizabeth know."

Then with emphatic words and imploring gestures it seems that Mamma tried to explain to him that their offspring (being a girl) could not go about hitting people in the eyes or battering up other sections of people's anatomy; not even in self-defense.

Mamma was very religious. Not fanatical, but she had great faith in God and believed in the practice of forgiving those who trespassed against her. Papa believed in God, too, but he always gave Mamma credit for being on better speaking terms with Him than himself.

Years afterward (when these facts were revealed to me) I was told that she finally succeeded in getting him to admit that what he did once in childish ignorance he

21

would not do after having arrived at adult wisdom. Then, seriously reflecting, he said to her:

"When a Colored man is married to an adorable wife and they have a child to love and care for, he thinks twice before losing his temper. Anger sometimes leads to tragedy. And no worth while husband and father wants to disgrace his family. Therefore, believing as many other Colored men do, I would now accept such an insult without retorting, Lula—for my family's sake."

My mother knew that he was sincere. She felt a bit sorry, perhaps, that he did not give God credit for giving him grace to think of such things with a well-balanced mind. But religion was something seldom discussed between them. Nevertheless, because Mamma believed that every good wife should be a spiritual guide to her husband (without talking about religion until he became aggravated) she tried, diplomatically, to show him his responsibility as a Christian parent: for her sake he had permitted his name to be written in a church register. He always tried to please her.

Being of a thrifty and industrious nature, my mother usually crocheted in the evening while she and my father talked over the affairs of the day. So, while she lectured him on the duties of a Christian parent, she sat crocheting: her eyes fastened on her needlework lest she lose a stitch.

Of a sudden, she claims, she heard a queer noise in the room.

"Daniel!" she called.

But Daniel, her dearly beloved husband and my devoted father, did not reply. In the midst of a family crisis, a time of peril and turmoil, Papa had fallen asleep! He was peacefully and contentedly snoring.

22

CHAPTER THREE

The Awakening

THE awakening of race consciousness wrought a series of bewildering revelations in my life.

I discovered (to my surprise) that Lillian's contempt for dark people influenced several playmates, which resulted in my loss of their friendship. Nevertheless, there were other white children who (like little Mary Carty) remained ever faithful and tried to amend the wrongs of the easily-persuaded-to-become-prejudiced of their own group by engaging in fierce word-battles with them; and who imparted to Colored children petty ways and means of revenge. Thus it was that while my mother saw to it that I implored the Omnipotent to bless Lillian, Mary Carty conscientiously instructed me as to the proper procedure of turning up one's nose at an enemy.

"Doncha be scared a-her," Mary consoled whenever we talked of Lillian. "I'm with you!"

Hence there were mornings when we two (silhouettes in black and white) strutted hand-in-hand past my adversary. And Mary (to whom had been bequeathed an aquiline nose by right of inheritance from Anglo-Saxon ancestors) sniffed and turned up her nose as a gesture of indignation. I tried to imitate her. But alas, I (to whom had been bequeathed a short, stubby, button-like covering for the anterior part of the nasal fossae by right of inheritance from African ancestors) could only sniff disdainfully—my nose (being not of stream-line design) proved a blunt weapon in snooty combat. But I sniffed. I could not strike Lillian without having upon my conscience the guilt of disobedience to my parents. But I could sniff.

It worried my little white companion considerably that my nose (unlike hers) could not be upturned. She was puzzled. So was I. But there was nothing we could do about it. So after numerous disheartening lessons, Mary, exasperated, lost hope and ceased coaching.

"You'll just hafta be happy sniffin' at everybody what makes you mad," she concluded.

Unfortunately Lillian addressed a few of the other Colored children by the word and they made plans for her to be torn from limb to limb. Then extremely troublesome times ensued for me when the dark group *demanded* that I join their ranks.

"We're goin' to beat her up!" they informed me.

The idea astounded and stunned. Helplessly I sought to evade the issue.

"I can't fight," I told the ring-leader, a very pretty Colored child with the face of a cherub and the fists of a Goliath.

"Why not?" she wanted to know.

"Because my mother says I can't. My father says I can't," I replied.

"Beat her up and don't tell them," she suggested.

Fully awakened to the realization that the word was specially devised to carry degrading implications, a conflict began within. If being called "nigger" was supposed to make a person fight, then I wanted to fight. But my hands were tied by the invisible cords of obedience: for my parents having told me that all things done in secret would be witnessed by God, I imagined the Deity peering down at me through the fleecy clouds; and presumed there was some secret method of direct communication between God and my elders so that He could let them know at once if I disobeyed.

The ring-leader threatened to "beat me up" if I failed to comply with her wishes.

That night when I began the recitation of bed-time prayers I decided not to mention Lillian. This white child was a burden on my soul. So I avoided asking that she be showered with toys and made a good girl.

My mother, noticing the omission, demanded a repetition of the prayers. Repeated they were. But again she heard no audible plea for Lillian's share of blessings. Then in no uncertain terms Mother commanded that I incorporate in my heavenly petitions the name of this child who humiliated me. Reluctantly I acquiesced.

Every night my mother led the forgive-thine-enemy campaign.

Once or twice I wondered how God would like it if someone called Him "nigger"; then remembered that according to my Sunday-school teacher no one dared to question or wonder about the Creator.

Finally, owing to Mother's blessed patience, I ceased battling. Of my own volition I asked the Great Unseen Giver of Gifts to give my enemy bountiful treasures from His storehouse of supplies.

I now look back on this part of my life with mingled emotions—mostly smiles. Whenever there is reason to refer to it in the presence of Caucasian friends someone invariably asks with solemn, hesitant voice:

"Isn't it difficult for a Colored child to be really happy after finding out that he or she is a victim of racial prejudice for life?"

But in fact the child-victim of racial prejudice, though

shocked on becoming aware of the disreputable intention of the word "nigger," regards it merely as a strange happening, a baffling mystery and in time something to fight over; he is too young to have the slightest perception of the many complexities that make up the problem of Negro life.

I particularly recall how my curiosity became aroused as I began to notice the racial differences in my schoolmates. Some were white, red, yellow, brown, black. There were marked distinctions in features and texture of hair. Wondering about these things led me to seek knowledge from the oracle of oracles—Mother.

How did it happen, I wanted to know, that I was born Colored instead of Chinese, Indian or another race? Why had I not been given stringy, taffy-yellow hair like Mary Carty's? Why were my eyes brown instead of blue? Why did I have round eyes instead of slant ones like Kim, my little Japanese playmate? Why? Why? Why? Oh, yes: why was I born anyway? Where had I come from? Where did everybody come from?

Mother volunteered information: and that was how I first heard of the stork.

"An' th' stork brought me as a present to you and Papa?" I queried.

"That's right," Mother responded.

"An' flew right over our house an' dropped me down the *chimmbly*?"

"That's what I have just said," remarked Mother-Oracle. "But the word is chimney, dear, chimney."

The stork-story held me spell-bound. With the vivid imagination with which the majority of normal children are endowed, I visualized the white bird circling over our house-top. According to Mother I slumbered peacefully in a large black satchel which the Bird of Travel

26

held securely in his bill. Then he placed satchel and me right into a cradle.

The idea fascinated me. But if my Mother thought the telling of the story thus far would suffice she was mistaken. My mind was a bit hazy concerning a few items which I considered important.

"Where did the stork get me?" I asked.

"From heaven," remarked Mother with an air of intense conviction. "There are trillions, billions and millions of little babies there," she went on as though answering my thought. "And God, being busy, sends them to earth by the stork."

She next proceeded to describe the sales-tag on the satchel in which I reclined, saying that it read:

"Please Deliver To—
    Mr. and Mrs. Daniel Henderson Adams,
    Santa Barbara, California,
    One baby-girl to be named,
            Elizabeth Laura."

"Why didn't the stork leave me at Mary Carty's house or Kim's house instead of giving me to you and Papa?" I demanded suspiciously.

Ah—that was a brain-wrecker for Mother! All she had to do was to explain to me in simplified language why I, a Colored child, had not been presented as a gift of joy to our white neighbors, the Carty's, or to Kim's family, our Japanese neighbors.

Mother coughed a couple of times and then continued.

"The stork is very wise," she said in a low voice as though sharing a secret. "He has a wonderful eye for color. Likes to see everything match. So he gives white babies to white mothers and fathers and red babies to red mothers and fathers and so on and so on until all the different colors of parents have babies to match. Isn't that wonderful?"

I mused. Smiled. Grinned. Yes, it was wonderful! That explained everything—why Mary Carty was white, Kim Japanese, and I Colored. God had painted us different colors—then the stork selected us to blend harmoniously with the bodily color-scheme of our respective families.

I was almost convinced when one other thought popped into my mind.

"But," I faltered, "how does the stork know Mammas and Papas want the babies?"

Mother cleared her throat and coughed again.

"They pray to God, asking Him for their children," she said. "Then He orders the stork to deliver them to earth."

Then with the dramatic air of an actress, Mother leaned back in her chair and a sad, sad look crept into her eyes.

"All children should love their parents, dear," she sighed. "For they have to work hard, save their money and have a nice home all ready for the little baby when it arrives. And the poor stork," she said pathetically, "goes from house to house, country to country—all over the world. As soon as he delivers one baby he has to fly right back to heaven for another to take to some other family."

That explanation settled all doubts. I needed to hear no more. My sympathy rested with the stork. I pictured the poor bird weary and hungry—his wings rain-drenched one day and scorched and sagging from the heat of the sun on a bright day.

I threw my arms about my mother's neck: glad, glad indeed, that the over-worked bird had remained constant in his fidelity to duties of transportation and had not collapsed from exhaustion while en route to our house.

Even as a very small child I believed that good news and the meritorious achievements of others should be

28

shared, that was why I started for the door to pass the word along to Mary Carty and Kim.

"Where are you going?" Mother demanded.

When I told her she caught me quickly and sat me down.

"Now listen," she said positively. "You must never, never tell others the story about the stork. It's our secret!"

A secret! I looked at her.

"Maybe—maybe Mary an' Kim don' know about the stork," I murmured regretfully as my mother's restraining hand continued to rest upon my shoulder, and indications of my opportunity to be publicity-agent for the stork began to fade.

"Their mothers will tell them," came the response. "Listen, dear—" Mother's tone softened. I looked at her and she whispered:

"We must keep this a family secret. The stork wants all families to keep the story of his coming to themselves. He wants to surprise everybody."

Surprise! I understood that word. A surprise meant something one did not expect and it always brought happiness (so I believed)—unexpected happiness such as rice pudding for dinner, a new doll, a new dress.

I had but one more request to make.

"What now?" Mother inquired.

I whispered loudly:

"May I tell Papa when he comes home?"

A few weeks later, there stood in my mother's room a dainty basket-shaped bed decorated with pretty blue and white ribbons, and in it was a baby. A real, live baby!

"It's your Baby-Brother," the lady in the white uniform told me.

I did not like the lady in the white uniform. She was

29

Colored, but even that did not make us congenial. I thought her impatient and very, very cross when she slapped my fingers as I slyly started to poke them into Baby-Brother's eyes to see if he would squeal. Another grievance held against her was that she would not let me see Mother until late in the afternoon, and then for only a short time. And she always spoiled my visits by beginning to speak as soon as I crossed the threshold of Mother's room, saying: "*We* haven't long to stay, Mother. *We* must hurry along."

I did not like the idea of her calling my mother "Mother" —and I did want to stay a long time in Mother's room. I wondered: what right did she have anyway, trying to talk for both of us?

Then something strange happened about the third day after I first saw Baby-Brother. I went over to the fireplace. No fire burned, and no one was looking. I tried to catch a glimpse of the stork.

Alas! Only the black, sooty channel of the chimney was visible.

I sought the lady in the white uniform, knowing that Mother-Oracle was not available.

"Where's the stork?" I asked.

She snapped at me.

"Stork? What are you talking about?"

"The stork that brought Baby-Brother!"

"Questions! Questions! Don't you ever think of anything else but questions?" she snapped again.

"Please, Ma'am," I persisted. "Where is he?"

"He's flown!" she said and walked out of the room.

And though it is true that I disliked the lady in the white uniform (and seldom had one confidence in a believed-to-be-enemy) nevertheless Baby-Brother's existence being a visible sign of the stork's arrival—could I do aught else but believe she spoke the truth?

CHAPTER FOUR

The Invader

Our house was a large, roomy place. In the living-room the chairs and divan were upholstered in olive-green. An old grandfather clock stood in one corner, chiming away the hours. A brightly polished mahogany piano occupied a space of prominence. Small tables and shaded lamps were artistically arranged.

The lamp shades were exceptionally pretty, I thought, especially at night when the beaded fringe sparkled like the precious gems described and illustrated in the story books Mother read to me.

To my mind the grandest bit of living-room furnishing was the carpet—the soft, soft carpet. There were times when I imagined it the magic rug upon which the Thief of Bagdad sat; and when no one was near by to observe, I would ceremoniously seat myself in the center of it and make a wish to be carried up to the moon. Why the selection of the moon for my destination I cannot say, except that it was so far distant I presumed a ride there would be of longer duration than anywhere else.

Footsteps were barely audible whenever one walked across the carpet: I came to believe that that was the reason why no one heard a sound when one night Death came for Baby-Brother.

There followed the strange day when all noises about the house were muffled. The privilege of going out into

31

the back yard to play was denied me. But indoors it seemed I got in everybody's way.

"Go sit down," someone suggested.

Immediately I thought of the living-room carpet—the soft, soft carpet. I decided to sit there, out of everybody's way, and pretend it was the Thief of Bagdad's magic rug and imagine I was sailing way, way up to the moon. But two men walked into the living-room and began unfolding chairs which they set up row-by-row. After they left the shades were partly drawn, and everytime I went to sit even on the edge of the carpet someone whispered: "Stay out of here, Child."

Toward afternoon groups of people came and seated themselves in the semi-darkness of the room. They talked in low tones. Father was home for a while, too. He sat beside Mother who wore a dull black dress, and held one of her hands in his.

The unusual gathering mystified me. Grown-ups declared that Death had taken Baby-Brother away, but I could see him with my own eyes. He lay in a small white box with wreaths and bunches of sweet-smelling flowers on and around it. Grown-ups had a name for the small white box—"casket" they called it.

The strangest thing was that Baby-Brother lay so still. Very still. His tiny fingers no longer clutched at the air, nor did he murmur "goo-goo" or any of the other peculiar sounds he used for words.

A lady whom I had never seen before played the piano, but touched the keys so lightly that the music could hardly be heard.

When the music faded away a man with a black book in his hand rose. Everybody followed his example, except that they remained in their places while he walked over

32

and stood behind the small white box. All eyes were turned in his direction.

Slowly he opened the book and began reading. His voice was deep, vibrant, distinct.

He said:

> "The Lord giveth,
> The Lord taketh;
> Blessed be the Name of the Lord."

Simultaneously the grown-ups answered back just as if he had asked them a question.

They bowed their heads and said:

> "Blessed be His Holy Name.
> His will be done.
> Amen."

Then the people sat down again. The man with the black book began to talk. But he, like most grown-ups, used "big words," and I grew quite tired of listening to that which I did not understand. Suddenly the thought popped into my mind that it would be great fun to swing my feet just a "teeny bit" and make believe I was marching while I talked inside myself saying, "Left, right, left, right. . . ."

But the instant I moved a foot Mother placed a gentle, detaining hand on my knee. She never turned her head, moved her eyes, or uttered a sound. I wondered how she knew what my intentions were. With a sigh and stifled yawn I sat quietly through the rest of the ceremony.

I had no chance to ask questions of Mother until bedtime.

I wanted to know why Death had come, where he had taken Baby-Brother and if he would ever bring him back.

Mother appeared reluctant to talk that night, but she

33

did tell me that Death came at the command of God: that it was his duty to take Baby-Brother back to Him: that the infant would never return but someday we would go to see him.

The explanation proved somewhat confusing. I wondered why God sent the Stork to earth with babies to make mothers and fathers happy, then ordered Death to bring them back to Him.

I wanted to make more inquiries, but there were tears in Mother's eyes, and her voice had cracks in it and sounded like it might break into pieces any minute as she said:

"Let's not talk any more tonight, darling!"

When she kissed me goodnight, she held me close— close, close to her heart as if she did not want to tuck me under the covers. And I, according to custom, put my arms about her neck, giving in return that extra special embrace defined in a preceding chapter of this book as the cinnamon bear hug.

Somehow the false impression that the Invader came to earth only for children implanted itself in my mind. Consequently I was vaguely surprised when, three months later, another funeral service was held for that white-haired old lady, Great Grandmother Josephine Kellum— my mother's grandmother.

The people did not come to the house that time. We saw them at a big building which grown-ups referred to as "church."

Mother explained that Great Grandmother Josephine Kellum (being an old, old lady) had grown tired, and God realizing this, had sent Death to show her the way to His home in Heaven that she might rest. But the minute I insisted on knowing why she could not rest just as well at home with Grandma and Grandpa Holden (my mother's parents) Mother's voice changed, and I heard the cracks in it again. So the question remained unanswered.

Three weeks passed. Only three weeks.

Grandmother Laura Holden had just cleaned up her kitchen. She took great pride in her home, Grandmother Laura did. She had washed and ironed the dainty, ruffled curtains hanging at the windows. The floor had been mopped. Everything was spick and span. The other rooms were neat and clean. Her house was in order. . . .

But the door ——

Someone had left it ajar. Grandfather Holden, of course, as since the death of her mother, Great Grandmother Josephine Kellum, no one else shared their home.

An open door meant a standing invitation for an invasion of flies, dust, a draught ——

Grandmother Laura stepped across the smoothly polished surface of the linoleum.

She fell. . . .

The afternoon of the same day our door bell rang. The telephone whirred. Confusion. Sobs. People came in. People went out. Short, sharp, insistent door bell ringing again. Messengers. Prolonged, imperative telephone whirring again.

Then another day of silence—intense, depressing silence. Orders to tiptoe about the house. No play. No laughter. Overhearing half-subdued voices mumbling unfinished sentences:

"Three deaths in a little more than three months ——"

"Heart trouble ——"

"So much sorrow at one time ——"

Back again to the big building called "church." Organ music. A slow, steady march down an aisle. Another long,

35

narrow box—dove-grey with long, slender silver bars. Flowers. Sweet-smelling flowers. Singing. The man with the black book—slowly fingering the pages and saying in deep, vibrant, distinct tones the same words I had heard twice before:

> "The Lord giveth,
> The Lord taketh. . . ."

That night as I lay in bed the desperate quietude about me merged into an indefinable sensation. With the imagination of a frightened child, I thought the darkness of the room became intensified. Momentarily I waited for a sound. Organ tones kept roaring in my ears. Roared. Rumbled. Growled. Wailed. Whimpered plaintively.

I sat up in bed—terrified.

Perhaps—perhaps the mysterious invader Death was right in my room. The thought seemed to shut out the air—choked me.

Death—what was he like?

Perhaps like the pirates in my story books. Powerful. Tall. Taller than our house, maybe; taller than a telegraph pole, a mountain. His laughter a loud, loud roar. Perhaps, like a pirate, he carried a sharp, gleaming knife between his teeth ——

Pirates were *thieves*.

Death was a thief. He had stolen Baby-Brother, Great Grandmother, Grandmother. . . .

Perhaps ——

My teeth began to chatter.

Perhaps he was right in my room—ready to grab me and take me away from my mother and father—ready to cut off my head. . . .

I screamed!

For several weeks thereafter a light was left burning in
36

my room at night. But during the day the fear of being taken away from my parents haunted me. I imagined Death following me to school. That was why on a certain day when the teacher asked me to spell the simple word "bird" my mind went blank. I grew cold. My body trembled. I began to cry. . . .

The teacher sat in our living-room talking to Mother and Father. I was supposed to be playing, but curiosity prompted me to peek through the keyhole. I was afraid that I had done something dreadful by failing to spell "bird." The keyhole was small. I saw nothing. Voices were inarticulate. I heard nothing. So I went out to play.

In years to come I found out that the conversation between the school teacher and my parents went something like this:

Teacher: (timidly) Of course I don't wish to interfere, but I think it detrimental to take the child to funerals. . . .

Father: (politely) We appreciate your interest. But Elizabeth must learn to face the cruel realities of life.

Teacher: Yes, but ——

Mother: I guess our method does appear rather crude, but we believe it a wise course to take.

Teacher: Yes, but the child is so young. . . .

Father: She might as well learn of sorrow now as to wait until she is older.

Teacher: Yes, but ——

The teacher's entreaties fell on ears of stone. No doubt she left the house thinking them the strangest Colored people she had ever met.

Only one person dared defy my parents on the subject. Only one. He dared, defied and was not defeated.

37

The victor?

Grandfather Holden!

After Grandmother Laura's death, Mother and Father persuaded him to live with us. So when we moved to another location, a new house where the rooms were not darkened by the shadows of sad memories, he came to stay.

Life changed for me then. Grandpa saw to that. Yes, Grandpa was what he wanted to be called—just plain Grandpa.

The approach of summer brought the end of a school term and the beginning of vacation, giving me more time at home. On warm summer evenings Grandpa and I used to sit, side by side, on the back porch steps. Grandpa had a strange way of asking questions, then answering them himself.

"You need sunshine, fresh air and other children to play with, don't you?" he half-stated, half-asked one time as he drew whiffs of tobacco smoke from his pipe.

I looked up at him wonderingly.

"Sure you do," he answered as if an adequate reply from me were not expected. "You need to get out of that starched-stiff dress and hop into a pair of rompers."

A gleam twinkled in his eyes.

"Ah-ha!" he exclaimed as though he had thought of something important.

I regarded him in mild astonishment.

"What's rompers, Grandpa?"

"Never mind, never mind," he commented with a laugh fore and aft. "Just forget I said anything."

The latter part of the week we went on a picnic, we two, Grandpa and I, to a place described by him as "way out in the country."

When we reached the place I thought it an enchanted

38

land! Grandpa shaded his brow with his palm and looked about. I imitated him.

Sunlighted landscape. Green hills. Wild flower paths. Trees laden with ripe fruit. Whitewashed fences. Barking dogs. A pasture. A stream. . . .

From beneath his coat Grandpa took a package. Unwrapping its contents, he turned and faced me.

"See that tree over there?"

I looked in the direction indicated.

"Well," said Grandpa, "while I turn my back you skip over there and jump into this suit. Pretty nice, eh?"

With a critical eye I observed the garment he held up.

"What is it, Grandpa?"

He chuckled amusedly at the question.

"A romper suit!" he boomed. "And you don't have to worry about getting it dirty."

That day was a great day. I ran. Romped. Yelled. Made mud pies. Rolled on the grass.

Grandpa sat under a tree, watching me for a while, then read newspapers and magazines.

We ate lunch.

Lunch was wonderful. No spinach. No carrots. No milk. Sandwiches, ice cream, soda pop, pickles, candy and chewing gum.

"Let's have a gum-chewing contest," Grandpa suggested. "See who can chew the faster."

He made a tremendous effort to chew a stick of gum. He failed, intentionally of course. The prize, a pipe with which to blow soap bubbles was awarded to me.

While I "oh-ed" and "ah-ed" over the new treasure Grandpa mentioned the subject that secretly worried him.

"Are you happy, Tootsie?" he asked. Before I could answer he continued. "I want you to be happy. You mustn't be afraid of anything—ever." He sighed. "It

39

makes Grandpa feel badly to know that you're afraid to sleep in your room without a light."

He paused.

"Don't you know that Ol' Death can't hurt you?" he half-laughed. I became attentive—alert.

"He's took most everybody at home," I challenged. "That's why I'm scared he'll come an' take me away too."

Grandpa looked at me tenderly. He did not speak for a few seconds. When he did, he spoke reassuringly. No doubt his words were prompted by the sense of protectiveness the aged have in their hearts for the young.

"Death can't ever hurt you or take you," Grandpa said solemnly, "because *I'm staying at the house now.*"

I stared.

"Oh, I know what you're thinking," he added. "You're wondering why I didn't stop him before. Well, I've been pretty busy. But now I've got this ——"

From his hip pocket he drew forth a gun. And it is not unlikely that at that moment he mentally prayed: "God, forgive me for the lie I'm going to tell. But somebody's got to chase her fears away."

"A—a—a gun!" I stammered. I had seen guns in a picture book in which bandits were illustrated.

"It'll stop anything that's mean," he said.

I did not know why Grandpa's eyes were scanning the sky, but in a few seconds his face beamed at the sight of a hawk flying from a tree in pursuit of a bird.

"There's a hawk after a poor, little helpless bird," exclaimed Grandpa. "We won't let him get away!" And he shot the hawk.

The noise of the fired gun scared me almost silly. *But the hawk ceased flying after the firing of the gun!*

"Now," said Grandpa. "I'll be watching when you're asleep. And if Ol' Death comes I'll shoot him down—like I shot this hawk."

40

At those words Grandpa became the most wonderful, the "grandest an' bestest" grandfather in the whole, whole world.

Fear vanished. I had nothing to worry over. The Invader never could catch me. Grandpa would "shoot him down."

Time came to go home.

Grandpa folded up the rompers and fastened the buttons down the back of my dress.

"Suppose we don't say anything to Mamma and Papa about the romper suit," he suggested.

"A secret?" I asked.

"Er—a—a—yes, a secret!" he chuckled. "And suppose we don't say anything either about my sitting up to shoot Ol' Death. That should be a secret, too."

I promised.

That night I slept—my dreams undisturbed.

Great times followed: days spent in the company of Grandpa and the "boys at the office."

"The boys" were five elderly Colored men whose days of active employment had ended; "the office" a room with five dusty desks, five squeaking swivel chairs, five spittoons and a table. Here the old gentlemen sat, smoked, philosophized and viewed the panorama of their younger days. Here they waited for financial returns from an oil well investment in which they had purchased shares with their hard earned savings. They waited and waited and waited. . . .

On entering the office Grandpa always sat me on his desk. Then with salutations and laughter the other four old cronies rose from their chairs, looking like bow-legged bull frogs climbing over the edge of a pond, and croaked their homage:

Crony Number One: This child's sure growing, Holden. (Here, Baby, have some cough drops.)

41

Crony Number Two: 'Tain't right to raise one child by itself, Holden. You oughta tell your daughter and son-in-law they should have more'n one. (Here, darlin', take a peppermint.)

Crony Number Three: Holden, you're the luckiest man. Wish I had a grandchild. (Want an orange, Baby?)

Crony Number Four: She looks kinda delicate to me, Holden. My six grandchildren are healthy lookin'. (Help yourself to a cookie, Little Doll!)

Grandpa and the four old cronies showered me with devoted attention. A Park Avenue debutante never received more flattering gestures of admiration.

Meals eaten at "the office" were supposed also to remain a secret between Grandpa and myself. But there came a day when the menu of ice cream, dill pickles, candy and soda water made me ill, and Grandpa carried me home limp as a rag doll.

Mother revealed her anxiety. "I never let Elizabeth eat anything between meals," she said. "I hope you didn't break the rule, Father."

Grandpa snorted.

"Do you think I'd break one of the iron rules for which this house is famous?" he puffed. But after that he saw to it the rations portioned out by "the boys" were curtailed.

Sometimes Grandpa told me stories of his travels; travels enjoyed in the early days before his marriage.

A man of the sea, he had been. And he never wearied telling the myths, legends and traditions connected with those who sail the ocean waves: of ships in stormy waters; foreign ports nestling in a haze of fog; peasants dressed in colorful garments; jungle territory and chattering monkeys swinging from the branches of trees; the seamen's mascot—the talking-bird known as the parrot; lands where dark-skinned natives go proudly, balancing upon their

42

heads baskets of tropical fruits; islands of wind-swayed palms, drum dirges, garlands of exotic flowers. . . .

I used to hurry home from school, eager to hear the re-told stories of his adventures.

In the new neighborhood the school was three blocks from home. I missed the companionship of Mary Carty, but found another playmate, a little Colored girl named Louella Allen, a child whose excellent home training revealed itself in her speech and decorum.

Louella Allen and I were chattering at a great rate of speed one afternoon when, as we neared my house, I stopped—literally petrified.

"What's the matter?" she asked.

When I failed to reply, she shook me.

"Elizabeth—what's wrong?"

I never answered, but broke loose from her grasp and ran—ran—RAN!

A dead-wagon stood at our front door.

I ran up to the house—breathless.

A neighbor met me at the door.

"Ssh, Child! Quiet! Your—your Grandfather's dead!"

A lump rose in my throat.

I made my way to the back of the house and sat down on the porch steps.

I clenched my fists. Hot tears stole from beneath my eyelids, and rolled down my cheeks.

The loss was hard to bear.

The truth was bitter—bitter—bitter.

I knew at last that no one—or any power on earth could ever impede the approach of death.

Nothing could stop Ol' Death!

Nothing—not even Grandpa Holden's gun. . . .

CHAPTER FIVE

Home Life

Tʜᴇ prose-paintings of my home life are not fake replicas of life scenes portraying a back-ground of cultural pretence. They are genuine.

I describe my mother.

In word-etching the radiant light within her eyes, the sad sweetness of her smile, her natural grace and poise, gentleness and soft speech, my admiration for her is like that of a sculptor for a masterpiece of statuary: a sculptor who, at the unveiling of an African Madonna in bronze, sees in the dark image the same maternal loveliness that is graven in the Medici Madonna chiseled out of marble by Michelangelo or an Andrea della Robbia statue-symbol of motherhood.

I extol the beauty of her soul.

So doing I feel like a lapidarist on beholding the brilliance of a jewel from one of the world's finest collections of rare stones.

As a girl, my mother was educated in the public schools of Los Angeles. Her talent in drawing cultivated, preparation for an art career was advanced under the able tutelage of Josephine Williams, one of California's prominent artists who found in her Colored student an eye for color and aptitude of unlimited scope in painting flowers, landscape and still life.

At the conclusion of six years' study, Miss Williams sug-

44

gested that she try to gain admittance into the Los Angeles School of Art and Design, a private institute of art attended almost exclusively by young people of wealthy families.

Miss Williams, a Caucasian in whose heart no racial prejudice lodged, exerted her influence and the application was accepted.

The foundress of the school explained, however, that the acceptance of a Colored student would be an experiment.

"It is up to you, Lula Holden, to make good," she said.

The young Colored woman's efforts to succeed attracted the attention of two internationally famous artists: the French artist, Paul de Longpré and Henry Koch of Germany. These two urged her to make a specialty of flower paintings in oil.

Lula Holden painted—painted—painted. Meanwhile she dreamt of completing her studies abroad. She planned to spend several years in foreign countries. She would study, study in Paris. Of course, Paris! The dream-city of every artist!

She pictured herself in an atelier splashing colors on canvas. Masses of color that would take shape and bloom into buds and open blossoms.

Lula Holden worked hard. The Los Angeles School of Art and Design never had cause to regret accepting her; and in time her ability merited promotion to a teaching position.

Then—upon an evening at the home of friends came the introduction to a guest. A man whose deep, mellow voice and magnetic smile made him the central figure in the gathering.

A very dark Negro. Seated, the dignity of his repose

45

suggested an Ethiopian Ruler contemplating the destiny of his people.

A patient listener, the dark man. He gave undivided attention to Lula Holden as she spoke (at the request of her hostess) of studying art in Paris. He even nodded approval when the enthusiastic artist declared that no power on earth could persuade her to give up the dream of winning one of the coveted European awards of merit.

Then he smiled.

And I have been told that, when he smiled, Lula Holden lowered her eyes and looked away as was modestly becoming to an unmarried woman of that time.

He was not young—this dark man. On the contrary. He was quite a few years older than the ambitious artist with whom he conversed.

A year later Daniel Henderson Adams proposed marriage to Lula Josephine Holden. Her parents approved the match and they became engaged.

And so they were married.

For a wedding gift he gave her a home in Santa Barbara, the plans for which she designed. In this home I was born. Shortly after my birth Mother and Father moved to Los Angeles where they would be near her parents in their declining years.

Mother, an adherent to the old-fashioned teaching that the most essential requisite of a loyal wife is willingness to make any sacrifice that benefits her family, presided over the home with her husband's and child's happiness foremost in mind. She loved us both devotedly.

My father's love for Mother was like that which a curator of a museum has for the possessions entrusted to his guardianship. He values them and exercises extreme caution to insure the protection of each treasure. He cherishes

46

the treasures and is pleased when others can appreciate their worth, but he rarely takes them away from the security of the museum to be placed on display in the homes of friends. And so likewise was Father's love for Mother. He surrounded her with every luxury his income afforded, but he preferred his wife to have no interest in civic affairs. A wife's place, he believed, was in the home—to be adored by her husband, worshiped by their child.

Unlike many husbands, he never failed to remember their wedding anniversaries. He always sent a gift to bespeak his love. Christmas, New Year, Valentine's Day, Easter, Thanksgiving, Mother's birthday—none of these occasions slipped his memory.

Mother suffered the trial of being a much envied woman. People who based this couple's happiness upon Father's attentiveness to Mother considered her an exceptionally fortunate wife. Sometimes women openly voiced their opinion that they believed Father an ideal and perfect husband—a man without fault. However, according to Mother, had any of these "worshipers-of-another-woman's husband" been married to him the illusion of his being without fault would have faded.

He was not unkind: do not misunderstand. He was kind, affectionate, goodhearted, congenial; but exacting.

As a boy his education had been thwarted as after his father's death he helped provide for his mother. This he did willingly and unselfishly. But no amount of privation stifled his inbred tendency to accumulate a share of the best of life's goods.

Though schooled in higher education solely in the University of Hard Knocks, he came to a high degree of appreciation for everything beautiful. The skilled craftsmanship embodied in an exquisitely carved table was to him a prayer in wood. And in a rug, he saw a poem asleep

47

upon the floor. A white cloud floating in a sky of blue was a lone sailboat a-drift a turquoise sea. And in the wing-fleetness of the winds he heard music. A dreamer, my father, yet a realist in his firm conviction of the impracticality of dream-materialization without hard work.

As a boy he earned money running errands, sweeping walks, shining shoes. In his early twenties he was employed as a valet. Desiring to travel he next obtained employment with a railway company hiring Colored waiters.

His neat appearance, efficient service, obedience to orders, non-complaining attitude, cool, calm resourcefulness exercised under provoking circumstances, attracted the attention of passengers who took the trouble to write their praise of him in letter form to railway executives. And so one day he received an order to report at the office of one of the managers as soon as the train pulled into the station.

The manager cordially greeted the young Colored waiter who stood before him, waived formalities and said:

"Dan—it would be an unwise policy for the company to exalt its young employees too much. They might get big-headed. But I don't mind telling you that you're the best waiter we have."

Father is reported to have merely replied:

"Thank you, Sir. I try to do my best."

The manager continued.

"As a manager it's my duty to look after the company's best interests first by encouraging competent help to remain with us. But as a white man who believes it also his duty to help ambitious young people of minority groups succeed, I'm giving your future first consideration. Do you plan to spend your life on the road?"

The waiter reflected.

"After I've traveled more I'd like to remain employed

48

steadily in one city. Settle down. Own a home of my own. Marry."

The manager then went on to explain that the owner of a large hotel was looking for a courteous, trustworthy young Negro to wait table in his hotel; one worthy of being advanced to the position of head-waiter. The majority of head-waiters being white, the man wanted to prove his theory that there could be found a Negro capable of supervising a Negro crew with tolerance and understanding and be obeyed by them.

Father accepted the offer.

He struggled diligently through trials and discouragements: training waiters with the same efficiency, power of command and vision of uniformed men in unison of action as an army officer in command of a regiment. He established a system of daily uniform inspection before each meal. The waiters stood in line, and he criticized a crooked tie, stooped shoulders, an unbrushed suit, a frayed cuff, uncreased trousers, unpolished shoes: allowing no one to begin work until these flaws in attire were corrected. But never once was he known to humiliate a waiter for threadbare clothing if he knew him to be circumscribed by poverty. If the man *could* not afford to purchase a new suit, he bought one for him, and never exacted or accepted payment.

What some Colored men looked down upon as being a lowly domestic job he successfully elevated to the ranks of a "position," by instilling in the waiters' minds the necessity of banishing the thought of table-service as a "cast off job" handed down to poor, despised Colored servants; suggesting that instead of visualizing themselves doomed to drudgery, that they achieve as perfect as possible a synchronization of light tread, courtly bow and gracious manner.

49

Needless to say some Colored waiters refused to put on rose colored spectacles and view the long hours of serving in the light shed by his idealism. However, their disgruntled remarks never lessened his emphasis on the subject. He gave each man a fair trial; weeded out aggressive trouble makers, retaining only those willing to fit in with his system.

Time spent training waiters was not in vain. Guests' compliments upon the excellent service and exceptional courtesy of the waiters became widespread, and "Dan" Adams recognized as the best qualified Colored headwaiter from the Pacific to the Atlantic coast.

Dignity and courtesy were not masks worn by my father at work and discarded at home. They were a part of him. I never saw him sit down to the dinner table without first seating Mother. He taught me to do likewise.

"You have no brothers," he said, "so it becomes your duty to seat Mother in my absence."

I saw very little of my father. He left early in the morning, returned at two o'clock in the afternoon and rested until five, then resumed his duties at the hotel. When he came home at night the hour was late and I asleep.

Father always looked forward to Sunday afternoon; Sunday dinner being the only time he ate at home except during his vacation. His meals were provided at the hotel where he sat in the waiters' dining room—alone, a waiter serving him. So only Sunday afternoon was ours to enjoy for a while. We would sit, a family of three, and discuss the happenings of the week. I would prattle enthusiastically, relating incidents that had occurred at school while Father listened attentively, sometimes exclaiming: "Now what do you think of that!"—or "Well! Well! Of all things!" Time, it seemed, passed all too quickly, for at five o'clock he had to leave.

The week preceding Christmas, however, the special privilege of remaining up until after Father came home was granted me. I would greet him with hugs and kisses, perch upon his knees and sit entranced while he described Santa Claus!

Santa! Red cheeks. Long whiskers. Fat. Jolly. Santa Claus, who dressed in a red suit trimmed with white fur, lived (so Father said) up in the Arctic where he managed the largest toy shop in the world—a big factory made from ice blocks. And because the shop belonged to the grand old gentleman who spent his life making children happy *it could never melt!* Its dome was of icicles. Inside, the walls painted in fresco shaded from orchid-lavender and plumbago-blue to apple-blossom pink—pastels taken from the rainbow. The windows were cut out of sheets of transparent ice.

Here dolls and toys of various sizes and descriptions were made by Santa's assistants—an industrious race of tiny creatures called elves and brownies. Some stood (according to Father) only a foot high. Thus thousands and thousands of them worked comfortably as they sat cross-legged on window ledges, shelves and in cubby holes.

"They always sing when they work," Father told me, "especially the shoemakers. They tap out rhythms with tiny hammers." And taking a pencil Father proceeded to tap rhythmically on the arm of a chair and hum until he was sure I had a mental picture of the scene, saying: "Close your eyes and you will see long benches—miles long. On both sides elves and brownies are working and singing."

Father's voice was deep, mellow and convincing. Therefore as he talked, the picture was threaded on the loom of my imagination and scenic patterns woven. And I, con-

51

fident that I saw every single elf and brownie, would squeal for joy.

Usually at this juncture Mother interrupted. Whenever she did, she put "steps" between her words. For a long time the steps made it impossible for me to grasp the meaning of her speech, which was something on this order:

"Daniel—don't take S-O-M-E-B-O-D-Y we know too high up in the sky. If ever she R-E-P-E-A-T-S all this, people may think our C-H-I-L-D somewhat *C-U-C-K-O-O.*"

Then Father would stop humming and tapping long enough to grunt and place steps between his words and reply:

"Don't worry about people, dear. I'd rather have a C-H-I-L-D somewhat C-U-C-K-O-O on this subject than one too W-O-R-L-D-L-Y W-I-S-E."

Mother and Father used this code every year until I progressed in spelling to the degree that I could spell CHILD and CUCKOO. After that Mother resorted to spasmodic coughing spells.

And when she began to cough Father reached for his watch and looking at me asked: "Do you know that it's getting late? Why it's way past time for you to go to slumberland!"

Tucked in bed I would think about the little creatures at work in Santa's toy shop: the elves and brownies whose duty it was to tabulate children's names and addresses correctly in order to spare Santa's valuable time by avoiding delay in reaching their homes: elves and brownies whittling sticks and painting toys; writing, illustrating and binding story books; cutting cloth and designing doll's clothes; shelling nuts and packing sweetmeats. And then, as my eyelids grew, Oh, so heavy, I ceased trying to see the toy shop and listened instead, hoping to hear the

52

strains of special music that Father said Santa ordered played for children during the holidays. And sure enough (exactly as Father predicted) of a sudden the tap, tap, tapping of tiny hammers came to a standstill. The hum, hum, humming of elf and brownie choruses faded into oblivion—and then, I was certain that I heard it, the sweetest of all music, the tinkling tunes played by a music box. And it tinkled . . . tinkled . . . tinkled . . . until I fell asleep.

As a child, the busiest day of the year for me was Christmas Eve. As I was not inclined to care for my dolls (disliking to wash, iron or sew for them) Father told me that, beginning the first of December, Santa Claus commissioned the brownies to make an investigation and check on the condition of children's toys and books.

"Nobody can fool the brownies," Father informed me. "They won't accept parents' reports about their children. They come to see for themselves and then go back to the Arctic and tell Santa."

This caused me no end of concern. And conscious of my negligence I hauled out discarded play things. And so, Christmas Eve found me washing, ironing and mending a year's accumulation of dolls' wardrobe. I straightened up the toy box. Polished doll furniture. Swept the play house, spurred on by the thought that my every action was spied on by the dwarfs who were supposedly watching around the corners of the house and hiding behind garden foliage. I became as "good as gold"—helped Mother every way possible with the housework. She would commend me and give assurance that Santa never let such efforts go unrewarded.

Both parents believed that one kindness should always be returned with another. Therefore I was taught to set the table for Santa (while Mother prepared a meal) as my offering in return for the anticipated gifts.

"Poor old Santa," Father lamented the first Christmas I was old enough to offer my services in exchange for the presents. "Think of all the snow drifts his reindeer will have to plough through before he arrives at our house. He will be *cold—tired—hungry*."

And when Father said "cold," he shivered; "tired," he slumped down in his chair exhausted; "hungry," he looked about as though looking for something to eat.

Watching him my heart became sympathetic. It never dawned upon me to question the number of hours it took to drive a reindeer-drawn-sleigh through the sky from the Arctic to California, or to doubt the possibility of such a miraculous feat. Observing Father caused me to imagine that I could hear the ch-ch-chatter of poor ol' Santa Claus's chattering teeth; the whee-whee-wheezing of his icy breath; and the drip . . . drip . . . drip . . . drip of melting icicles falling from his frozen whiskers on to the floor. And with the vivid imagination with which most children are endowed, I pictured poor old Santa Claus shivering in his boots until the red and white of his suit revolved so rapidly that the resemblance was like the red and white stripes of a barber pole in motion.

Christmas Eve night (while I slept) Mother and Father devoured a "scrumptious menu" leaving the soiled dishes as evidence of Santa's visit and appetite.

Christmas morning found me up about five o'clock. I would jump off the bed and tiptoe to the living-room. The sight that greeted me overwhelmed. I gasped! Oh-my-ed! Oh-dear-ed! Called mother! Called father! Clapped my hands! Jumped up and down! Laughed aloud! Ran around the room! Exclaimed! Shouted!

Why not?

54

There in the center of the room stood a green, pine scented tree! Star-studded! Glistening with flakes of artificial snow! Bright with sparkling ornaments! Shining tinsel! Blinking candles! Swinging bells! And piled high at the base of the tree, presents galore! Christmas was a joyous day!

After the Yuletide followed Easter.

I never saw the Easter Bunny who Mother said placed the red, yellow, orange, purple and green candy eggs in baskets for me. (Nice Rabbit that he was.) But Mother said his fur was as downy as the powder puff on her dressing table, and that he had pink-tipped, floppy ears.

From one holiday to another I was showered with gifts. For besides those given by my parents and their friends, hotel guests who admired Father and knew of his love for me would often pay duty on novelties purchased in foreign countries if they thought it would please him and make me happy. Of the many imported toys my favorite was a woolly lamb on rollers. The animal was fleecy white when he came into my possession, but watching mother apply a poultice to my chest during a siege of whooping cough gave me the idea of putting a mud pack on "Scootie" (so named because he scooted easily on the rollers), at which time Scootie became a black sheep.

No child ever received more love from parents than I. But they were not indulgent in gratifying my whims. Both Mother and Father had an abhorrence of "spoiled children." So when the death of Baby-Brother left me their "only child" they agreed not to pamper me; to squelch the first indications of selfishness in my disposition with the promptness of a forest ranger extinguishing sparks from smoldering brush.

The necessity of alluding to their methods of child training forces me to reveal publicly my defects of character.

55

And I admit, candidly, that it wounds my pride to be compelled to confess that I was just an ordinary child—a very ordinary child; for in most autobiographies that I have read autobiographers (recounting personal reminiscences of childhood days) have made mention of unusual talents that made them prodigies or of supernatural graces that made them saints in infancy.

The earliest recollection of punishment for my misdeeds was that of standing (for a brief period) in the corner of a room, on one foot, *denied the privilege of kissing mother*. And while I wailed Mother pretended to be indifferent, saying: "Only thoughtful girls deserve to kiss their mothers. You were careless and left the dust cloth on the serving table. You banged a door and neglected to feed the chickens."

Ah! My sins of commission and omission! I can see myself now as I stood in the corner, my face to the wall (denied the privilege of even looking at mother) and sniffed and sniffed and sniffed, pleading to be allowed to kiss her *"just onest"* and promising to "never, never be bad again."

Impertinence was not tolerated.

"We give you a good home, good food and good care," my parents told me. "We will not tolerate impertinence. We are your parents!"

And they *meant* what they said.

They wanted me to obey them not because of fear of punishment, but because they were kind and deserving of loving obedience given in return for their love.

I, like the average child, disliked systematic routine and discipline and tried to dodge the responsibility of household chores. I despised dishwashing and took at least two hours to wash dishes for Mother and myself, leaning against the sink, lazily dipping my fingertips into the

56

soapy water, stirring up lather until the dishpan and sink overflowed with bubbles.

None of my haphazard ways escaped my parents' notice.

Father said: "She needs discipline. We must enforce it."

Mother said: "The scripture reads, 'Spare the rod and spoil the child.'"

Corporal punishment was meted out by mother. Father disapproved of a male parent whipping his daughter.

"A man is physically stronger than a woman," he argued. "When he strikes he strikes with an overabundance of energy."

However, as I meditate over the times Mother wielded the "rod" and then think about Father's point of view, I wonder—and wondering makes me realize that the weaker sex can have an overabundance of energy at whipping-time.

Whenever the "rod" needed to be not spared, Mother would pluck slender peach tree switches. A just woman was Mother—taking time to ask me if I understood the graveness of the offence for which I was about to pay penalty.

With the solemn countenance of an executioner, she would stand beside the pantry door.

Why the pantry?

Because it was on the side of the house nearest the school and my wailing attracted the attention only of school children, whereas on the opposite side of the house broadcast cries disturbed occupants in the apartment next door.

Before Mother whipped me, her manner was somewhat like that of a judge who clears his throat and requests that the prisoner at the bar arise to hear sentence passed. How clear the tone of her voice as she stated:

"After this whipping you will retire to the seclusion

of your room, there to remain. The hour for dinner shall come and pass, but you will partake of no food until breakfast. Do you understand?"

"Yes, Ma'am," I would answer meekly.

The cold formality of Mother's address bordered on that of a *lettre de cachet* issued during the reign of Louis XV. Samuel Bannister Harding's *Essentials in Medieval and Modern History* has a sample one in which the monarch expresses his concern over a prisoner as follows:

"Monsieur ——. I send you this letter to tell you to receive in my Château of the Bastille Monsieur —— and to hold him until further orders from me. And I pray God to have you, Monsieur ——, in his holy keeping. Written at ——.

Louis."

So, as Louis XV sent transgressors of the law to his "Château of the Bastille," Mother escorted me to the "Bastille of the Pantry."

There were times, however, when I permitted myself to be influenced by the suggestions of other children on the subject of how to escape a whipping. One school child told me that when her mother started to whip her she caught the switch and snapped it in two. I tried her method. But my Mother caught me and almost snapped me in two. So that did not help matters. Then another child declared that the best thing to do would be to stretch out on the floor and pretend to be dead. I tried that; stretching full length on the floor, one eye half open and breathed laboriously as I heard my mother's approaching footsteps when I did not answer her call. She looked down upon me and said: "Oh—so you are dead, are you?" Well, to make a long story short, suffice it to say that my resurrection was a memorable one. One more method was tried out.

58

"Run when your mother stands at the pantry with the switch in her hand," somebody told me.

I did. I ran through the house and down the front steps. When I looked back Mother was standing in the doorway. I looked at her. She looked at me. We looked at each other. Then she called me.

"Come here," she said.

I did not move. I looked at her. She looked at me. We looked at each other. Then she spoke with calm deliberation:

"I am not going to run after you. You are coming here to me. *I am your Mother!*"

And my ankles hinted to my feet that under the circumstances a walk in mother's direction would be the proper steps to take. So I started walking. Mother's eyes were focused on mine with the steady gaze of a lion tamer concentrating on an unruly cub. Finally she said: "Never will you run from me again. You shall remember this day to the minute you die."

What happened after I entered the Bastille of the Pantry need not be divulged in public testimony except the fact that my Mother's words left an impression on my heart, and the switch its impression.

The purpose of my parents' strict training was to prepare me to work purposefully that I might face undismayed the perplexities and disappointments of life.

When I swept a floor and hid the dirt under a rug Mother demanded that the entire room be swept again. After I washed and dried dishes she inspected the chinaware and if she found soap-scalloped saucers and plates weeping water, every dish had to be re-washed and re-wiped. When I tumbled into bed leaving my clothes scattered from one end of the room to the other she waited

59

until I was sound asleep then woke me, made me rise and neatly fold each garment.

They did not ask me to do what they themselves did not practice. Mother and Father were extremists in their convictions about tidiness. Father never walked into the house without first scraping his shoes on the door mat. His toilet articles bore his monogram and he never allowed anyone to use his comb or brush. His things were his things. They belonged to no one else. It was not that he was selfish but he simply would not tolerate borrowing even from his own family.

I had my own room—my own closet. Everything had to be kept in order. If not, Mother expected an explanation.

By the time I was nine years of age my parents had trained me to respond to their commands by a gesture. If they had placed me in a circus I would have won out in competition with a well-trained seal without the slightest effort.

Whenever they called to see friends and spent a pleasant evening (which was seldom, because of Father's hours at work) they expected me to sit like a statue. I was not supposed to annoy the hostess by taking the books out of her bookcase, or running about the house. I was supposed to "sit" and remain "*sitted.*" If I even stretched my cheeks to yawn my Father's sharp eyes noticed it, and I "unstretched my cheeks" into a smile. If the hostess noticed me and asked: "Are you sleepy, dear?" I was expected to reply: "No, Ma'am. I am not sleepy. I have been admiring your pictures." That was, of course, if there were any pictures. If not, then I was supposed to substitute books in the bookcase (though I could only sit and look at them). The reason for these lovely phrases being that my parents' hostess should never be concerned

60

about me at all. It was very, very dull listening to grown-up conversation. But there I would sit, my hands folded in my lap, smiling, and wishing I could play with other children. If, though, there was a child at the house I could play. But if in our games I gleefully raised my voice above the pitch my parents maintained as suitable and not too hard on the ears, Mother coughed. Automatically I lowered my voice. She did not have to call me. I knew the code. Her cough said: "Lower your voice. Too much noise. Be thoughtful. Shrieking may disturb others."

When it was time to leave I was expected to drop the toys as if they had been hot cakes in my bare hands. I never dared yell out: "I don't want to go home. Wait a while." No! No! The "Honorable Parents" would have objected.

When friends came to our house I waited upon them as though I were a servant. My parents conversed while I brought in small glasses of juice or a refreshing drink. At first I was quite nervous, for had one drop spilled out of a glass my Father would have reprimanded me severely. But practice enabled me to serve with ease.

I can remember the first time my Father asked me to bring him a glass of water. Filling a glass I took it to him. I might as well have offered him poison. He took me out into the kitchen and said: "I will show you how to prepare a glass of water. Remember it all the days of your life." Here is the method he prescribed:

(1) Obtain a small tray
(2) Place a dainty tray cloth on the tray
(3) Put a small plate on the tray cloth
(4) Place a lace doily on the plate
(5) Place a glass of cool water on the doily

(6) If flowers are in season, a tiny flower should be beside the glass to indicate to the guest that the server esteems it a joy to wait upon the guest.

Father said there was no other correct way to serve a glass of water; that prince or pauper was entitled to the same service. And that was that!

Other parents who witnessed my knee bendings and head bowings and gracious service lauded me to the skies. Their praise never made me vain because I thought all the parents in the world were teaching their children the same thing. But I discovered to my amazement that children hated me. For a long time I did not know why. Finally one child confided her reason: "I hate you 'Lizabeth Adams because my Mother's always trying to make me be like you."

Alas! That was the source of my trouble. Parents singled me out as the "ideal child" and children yearned to throw brickbats at me.

Yet, notwithstanding strict methods, my parents raised me according to the honor system. And I enjoyed a certain amount of freedom that other children were denied. Neither Mother nor Father hid valuable things from me. They were within my reach to take or leave. They never put candy out of reach. Mother said: "You have had enough for the present." And she left the box right on the table. If I took an additional piece my own conscience was the reminder and when I said my evening prayers I invariably confessed the deed. She would listen calmly and reply: "Nobody is going to keep reminding you. Eat too much and you will become ill. The suffering will be your own fault." And that also was that!

I used to wish that I could eat ice cream and candy while walking along the street, for I saw other children licking the smooth, creamy paste or smacking their lips before taking a bite out of a candy bar. Father prohibited this. He said it was not proper to eat on the street at any time or for any reason. Sometimes when I was with Mother she would buy me an ice cream cone and then pretend that she had to find a bill or letter in her purse. Then suddenly she would remark: "Oh, dear! How could we forget what Papa says about not eating on the street!" And I, knowing the cone was devoured, looked blank but happy.

Though it may appear to a reader that my parents' method of child training was too severe, future chapters will bear testimony to the profound influence it had upon my life.

Father loved music. My appreciation of it may be attributed to his untiring zeal in showing me the path that music makes leading to a Dream-World for all who wish to dwell therein. And so at an early age I was entrusted with a violin.

I can remember the day it came into my possession—the Gift-of-the-Singing Strings; for my father told me that the bow that went with it was like a magic wand. He said:

"Remember—this bow will make the strings sing. And then there will be music. Music will let you see stars in a star-less sky . . . sunlight on a cloudy day . . . moonbeams in the darkness of a stormy night. Remember."

And Father bought music for me. Sheets of music. And when I took them to the German professor who taught at Von Stein's Academy of Music he laughed and cried out: "Not yet! Not yet! Four years, five years, six years maybe. Then you play these. And someday even greater compositions!"

The German professor, like Mother and Father, was

goodhearted, but strict. When I played a false note he took the bow that belonged to the Singing Strings and whacked my fingers until the skin broke. I complained to Mother—complained several times. But each time she merely replied, "That is good for you!" And I could tell by her attitude that she was not the least sorry for me.

But sometimes he spoke tenderly—the German professor—particularly when he heard no discords. He would walk about the room, his hands behind him, and talk in low tones. And as the half-notes escaped from the undertow of his breath, he would say to me:

"Today, the tones, they are not so bad. But practice. Practice. Practice. Someday, perhaps, you will become a great violinist."

And so the dream of becoming a concert violinist was my first great dream: that of standing on a stage with the Gift-of-the-Singing Strings under my chin and the magic-wand-like-bow in hand; and playing so that a listening audience might see stars in a star-less sky, sunlight on a cloudy day, moonbeams in the darkness of a stormy night.

Mother piloted me to the Academy twice a week for lessons. Father labored to pay the tuition.

In raising me, my parents had but one grave difference of opinion. They did not entirely agree on religious training. And because Father was indifferent as to necessity of church attendance, Mother saw to it that my first steps to Glory were marshaled by religious workers in a Methodist Episcopal Church.

CHAPTER SIX

Steps to Glory

MOTHER, a devout Methodist, firmly believed in church attendance. Father went occasionally only to please Mother. He had his own philosophy of life. He despised the theological wranglings caused by denominational differences over biblical interpretations, and maintained that a high percentage of the world's suffering resulted from the intolerance of bigoted and contentious-spirited Christians. Often he said to Mother:

"My dear—you understand God better than I. Go to service every Sunday if you wish. But I cannot comprehend the meaning of Christianity as practiced by most of the so-called Christians." Then he would smile (smiling no doubt to soften the harshness of his statement) and add, "I see some of the white Christians turning hungry black men from their doors, and black Christians so filled with hatred that they will refuse needy white men bread. You go to church, my dear, and pray for Baby and for me."

And so, when Sunday came, Mother took "Baby" to church. But it seemed that I inherited my father's dislike for religious service. Mother spent Saturday giving me religious instruction which invariably slipped my memory by Sunday morning.

I was the chief dunce in Sunday-school. The only two outstanding memories I have retained of this period are: first, the joy of receiving holy pictures (especially the ones

65

wherein Jesus was pictured blessing little children and healing the sick); second, my admiration for my first Sunday-school teacher. Bitter were the tears I wept the day promotion elevated me to the ranks of first grade religious class. The requirements demanded that I learn more Bible verses. In my childish opinion this was more punishment than honor.

"Every little boy and girl must learn a new Bible verse for each coming Sunday," our teacher announced one morning in the sing-song tone so many religious teachers use—why, I do not know.

I knew four verses:

(1) "The Lord is my Shepherd, I shall not want."
(2) "Suffer little children to come unto Me and forbid them not, for of such is the kingdom of heaven."
(3) "Jesus wept."
(4) "God is love."

Generally a race took place between boys and girls to inform the teacher that "Jesus wept" and "God is love." The instructress, however, objected to repetition. Her objection was supposed to inspire us to memorize new verses.

I discovered that the child seated nearest the teacher had the advantage over others. So I cleverly arranged to greet "Teacher" at the classroom door. Poor "Teacher"— a gentle, God-fearing woman—never realized that I spoke sweetly to her, placed one hand in hers, and carried her Bible so that I might obtain the "first seat." Such loving devotion was prompted solely that I could have first choice of the four best known Bible verses.

Yes, I am ashamed of myself, now that I think about

it. But she should have heeded the word "watch" as well as "pray."

As I grew older—old enough to leave the primary class, I soon came to the conclusion that the quickest way to cultivate patience was to attend a Colored Methodist church. After spending an hour or more in Sunday-school, service began at eleven o'clock. It lasted until about one thirty or two in the afternoon. Children grew weary. Some drew pictures in hymnals, but alert teachers or very particular parents (such as Mother was) would not permit this. There was nothing for a child to do except sit throughout the hours listening to a clergyman spiritually froth at the mouth while he preached a "mighty and powerful sermon."

Why is it most clergymen like to preach from the Book of Revelations? Until this very day I can fall asleep whenever a minister of the gospel announces: "My text is taken from such and such a chapter of Revelations." As a child I heard such wildly descriptive scenes of the destruction of the world, and watched so many ministers hold up imaginary blue-prints upon which hell was supposedly outlined, that I failed to develop a pietistic-fearful view of religion, for the description always sounded to me as though it had been memorized and was used for no other purpose than to scare people. Because of the pastor's graphic interpretations of hell, I grew to detest church attendance—except for the music.

Music always aroused me from lethargy to spiritual alertness. When the deep tones resounded and a robed choir sang, I sat up and took notice of what was happening. Now and then bass voices would proclaim the Unseen Creator "King of Kings" and the sopranos add, "Lord of Lords." Then, suddenly, the trend of service would change. Choir-members seated themselves. The

67

minister stood silently before his congregation. His eyes were closed. The congregation became motionless. The silence filled one with awe and reverence. The hush that fell over the vast number of Negroes was almost indescribable. Now as I recall its effect I know it was like the pause following a prelude—those moments of profound quietude during which a music master sits with upraised hands over a piano keyboard before continuing to play a great composition; the silence of evening awaiting the approach of night; the silence of the desert awaiting the sunrise. Then someone in the congregation (usually an elderly white haired and wrinkled character) began to hum the first notes of an old-fashioned hymn or spiritual. Slowly, other voices joined in.

Negro voices!

If you have never heard hundreds of Negro voices singing you have missed a great concert.

In my memory I can hear the sweet mellow voices of my people. Sometimes the tones were almost inaudible —seemingly afar off like the distant murmuring of the sea pounding against a rock-piled shore. The soft tapping of their shoes made accompaniment not unlike the beating of drums. Dark bodies swayed slightly to the rhythm. Sometimes the sacred song depicted the saints marching up the "stairs of glory" or Daniel walking about the lions' den unharmed because God's protecting power overshadowed him. I admired Daniel's faith, but continued to be afraid of lions and other wild animals when present at a circus. It took me a long time to realize the symbolical significance of God's protecting love in the midst of temptations.

Shouting frightened me. It became the principal orgy of church-going. One dear old lady used to proclaim her devotion by screaming aloud, walking up and down the aisles, embracing people and knocking their hats off. I lived in constant fear lest some day she knock my hat to the floor.

A Sunday-school teacher informed me that the Holy Ghost "came down" upon Sister Hartie (as she was called by all) at such times. I was informed also that every individual should look forward to the descent of the Holy Ghost.

"It will happen to you, my dear child," the teacher explained, "if you are a good girl and pray." From that moment I feared conversion.

I thought of God as the Divine Creator. His home, I believed, was somewhere "way up" in the sky. He made the earth, set out the brown hills and green valleys, streams and rivers—erected the purple mountains and placed the sun, moon and stars in the blue sky. He had a great golden throne, glittering with jewels and beautiful angels with golden trumpets surrounding it, always faithfully carrying out his commands. God was far, far away. How impossible it was to imagine Him interested in a little girl! My mother was shocked when I told her that I loved her much more than I did God. Horrified, she hastened to explain that parents were supposed to watch over their children, but they should always love God first and adore *Him*.

I remained unconvinced. I believed it was proper to love God, but when a door closed on my finger it was "Mamma dear" who kissed the pain away and made the finger "all well again." My own "Mamma dear" tucked me into bed and told me stories. God had other things to do. He had to light up the moon and the silver stars. He had to keep the waves of the ocean rolling. The sun had to be reminded to shine the following day. Millions, billions and trillions of sick people had to be healed. Why, then, should God be concerned about me?

"Don't question God!" religious people exclaimed. They spoke seriously. It seemed as though a person had to be afraid of God for Him to be happy. It was evident that an individual could not tell Him the things one liked or did not like without His becoming offended. Yet they said He knew one's thoughts.

Brought up in a home where courtesy was emphasized as an essential to proper home training, I had no desire to be converted if it meant the descent of the Holy Ghost making me fling my hat to one side, or causing me to run up and down church aisles shouting. And I thought it very impolite of the Holy Ghost to impose Itself upon people, to make them do unsightly things.

"Don't contradict the Almighty!" teachers warned if you said you did not believe something they stated to be a fact. God was a God of wrath. It seemed to me, though, He grew offended very quickly to be so wise.

I reflected that I never had a chance to ask God about being a Methodist. I did not think it fair for Him to send a child to earth, permit parents to have that child christened Methodist, and then not let the child have its "say so" about conversion.

"Repent and Believe!" was the church-cry.

When I did wrong I admitted it to my parents. They said that if I disobeyed and failed to tell them I would be untrue to myself. When I admitted wrong-doing they punished me. I reasoned that God being all-wise knew about it, that He expected them to punish me when I did wrong. Therefore I did not understand why conversion meant I had to wail repentance. I was only a child. Why would God want to see a child cry?

Secretly I decided that perhaps if I did not think about

the Holy Ghost, the Holy Ghost would not think about me. We could avoid one another.

Multiplying religious perplexities caused me to develop a spiritual sense of inferiority. I thought everybody in the world knew more about God than I could ever attempt to learn even in little ways.

During service I saw children of my own age testifying: "Jesus walks and talks with me." I listened to them, but I had an analytical mind. I knew that these same youngsters played many pranks and told me confidentially they never intended telling their parents of their misdeeds. I did not consider myself a perfect child; but I knew that I did *try* to obey my parents. So I concluded that Jesus evidently selected certain people to "walk and talk" with. I wondered: why had He slighted me? Then I decided it was because I feared conversion.

Teacher explained the mystery of the Holy Ghost. I grasped the idea that God the Father, God the Son, and God the Holy Ghost were One. But I did not understand the reason all three were one and one all three. I respected God the Father "way up in heaven" as Manager of the world. God the Son was Jesus; and Jesus, the Man painted on holy cards Whose eyes were kind. I cannot but smile now when I reflect and realize that within my own childish heart I thought Jesus "very pretty" in the picture blessing little children. But God, the Holy Ghost, I thought best to shun. That was to become my biggest problem: always to evade the Holy Ghost. I told no one of my plans.

Strange though it may seem, as much as I loved my mother (whose advice and answer to all problems I sought) I hesitated to speak to her about religion. I feared she might be ashamed of me because I could not boast of "walking and talking with Jesus."

71

The church we attended seated hundreds. It had stained glass windows. Carpeted aisles. A grand organ. A great choir. Back of the pulpit a painting. For a long time I wondered why the painting had no frame. Then Mother told me that it was a mural of the Ascension.

I knew the Ascension had something to do with Jesus going up to heaven. But I liked it because when most of the people began to scream, the painting took my mind off the shouting. I could sit and watch Jesus gliding up, up, up and up among the fleecy clouds. Sometimes I thought He looked as though He were smiling right at me. And when I thought this, even my fear of the descent of the Holy Ghost abated for the time being.

I heard many sermons in that church, but only one minister's words impressed me. And the words he said that reached my soul were not said in a sermon. He spoke directly to me. It happened like this:

One Sunday morning, after Sunday-school, my class was taken in to see the pastor. And the teacher called out our names and remarked concerning each student. I can see her now, with my mind's eye. I can hear her voice, sharp and harsh.

"Reverend, this is Johnny. He is a very good boy. Always says his prayers. Always reads his lessons over carefully. He knows many Bible verses."

Johnny was her son.

The pastor nodded and shook hands with the intelligent disciple-in-the-making.

A little girl followed, next in line.

"Agnes is a dear child," quoth the teacher. "I know Jesus loves her. She knows all the commandments by heart."

The pastor nodded and shook hands with Agnes, dear and blessed little Colored cherub that she was.

72

And then, I stood facing the pastor.

The teacher grunted before she made her remarks.

"This is Elizabeth Adams. Her grandfather and grandmother helped to build this church. They were wonderful Christians. Her mother is a good Christian. Her father a fine man."

Of course, I now know that she mentioned father because he always gave a liberal donation whenever he was called upon to give one. However he only merited being referred to as a "fine man."

Then staring coldly at me and biting her words, she added:

"But Elizabeth does not know the commandments by heart. She couldn't even remember her Bible verse this morning!"

I wanted to run away. But had to stand there.

The pastor spoke. The sound of his voice made me lift up my eyes. He said: "Come here, Elizabeth."

Slowly I walked over to him.

He spoke again, saying: "Look at me, child."

I obeyed. And when I looked into his eyes I thought about the painting behind the pulpit, because the pastor's eyes were filled with kindness and were smiling eyes.

I heard him say: "I'm glad to see you, Elizabeth." And he shook hands with me, but held one of my hands between his palms as he added: "Lots of little girls and boys can't remember Bible verses, but Jesus loves them just as much as those who can."

And then I smiled. And the pastor's study seemed to be flooded with all the sunlight in the world. And I felt like marching and singing at the same time.

After that, whenever Sunday service ended, I disappeared down the aisle, shoving my way through the crowds to where he stood, shaking hands with members. Some-

73

times a grown-up said: "Stay back, child. Wait until I get a chance to speak to Reverend." But I paid no heed, I clutched skirts and trouser legs trying to shoo grown-ups out of my way until I reached the pastor. And it mattered not how many tall people were ahead of me, somehow he would catch a glimpse of the child who sought to greet him.

"God bless you!" were his words.

That was all I wanted to hear. And away I went, back to Mother who would be conversing with friends.

But there came a day—an unforgettable Sunday when a new pastor preached to the congregation.

Mother said that the former pastor had to go away for his health. But Father said: "You might as well know the truth, Elizabeth. That man was a good man. He worked hard to support his wife and children. He did more than just preach on Sunday. He visited the sick. He helped the poor. He acted like a Christian. He lived like a Christian. But this church is a big one. It wants a man who can talk the money right out of people's pockets instead of good into their souls."

Mother said: "Ahem! Ahem!"

But Father looked at her and replied: "Well, Lula, that's the truth of it. And you know I'm right!"

The new pastor was different. When the Sunday-school teacher lined us up for a visit to his study he told boys and girls that those who did not remember Bible verses were not pleasing to the Lord.

I did not like him.

74

CHAPTER SEVEN

Little Lessons

I NEVER loved a teacher as I loved Miss Marlowe. It was a horrible blow when I learnt, as the school year drew towards its close, that she was to be married in the late summer and would return to teach us no more. One morning my friend Natalie, whose mother knew Miss Marlowe, had a wonderful piece of news.

"Now we can't tell the other girls," she said. "But I happen to know that Miss Marlowe's aw-ready chosen the flower girls for her wedding, an' they're the four girls she likes best outta our class." Natalie clicked her tongue. "Guess who they are?"

Peggy Ann became almost hysterical. "U-u-u-US?" she stammered.

"Us!" Natalie nodded. "Meanin' Patricia, Elizabeth, Peggy Ann and me. Us four an' no more! But my mother says we're not to let Miss Marlowe know that we know. She's gonna ask us herself, later on."

That afternoon I went home, ran into my closet, switched on the light, looked about. Rows of dresses hung within easy reach.

For every-day: gay-ginghams—plain piques—printed percales. . . .

But for Sundays and parties: fluted-voiles—ruffled-organdies. . . .

I looked at my shoes.

75

For every-day: plain shoes (dull black and dark brown) with broad toes. . . .

But for Sundays and parties: beautiful sandals! Shiny patent leather with imitation silver buckles—soft white kid with silk tassels. . . .

I had thought each dress and shoe splendid finery. But now—for Miss Marlowe's wedding—?

I sought Mother. "Please—may I have a new dress," I begged. "Som'pthin' fancy—awful, awful fancy."

"Why?"

"I'm gonna be one-a the flower-girls at Miss Marlowe's wedding!" I exclaimed, jumping up and down gleefully.

Before Mother had a chance to reply I supplied the details of the event exactly as Natalie had said.

Mother, as usual, maintained her poise. "Well," she said, "let's not get too happy until Miss Marlowe lets us hear from her."

Then Mother mentioned something about the fire in the stove being too high under the potatoes, and went out into the kitchen.

I pitter-pattered to the kitchen. My new dress? What about my new dress? Evidently Mother had forgotten it. I shadowed her as a reminder, calling her attention to my request.

Mother caught her breath the way she sometimes did when thinking of something she had almost forgotten and suddenly remembered.

"Well, dear," she began slowly, "when we hear from Miss Marlowe you may have a new dress."

That promise won Mother three cinnamon bear hugs and two kisses which I bestowed with all the fervor of my heart.

Throughout summer vacation, every time the telephone rang I waited close by while Mother answered it.

76

"Who on earth are you expecting to hear from?" she asked one day.

"Miss Marlowe," I told her. " 'Cause Natalie said she'll call 'bout the wedding."

Whenever I wanted to talk over the wedding it seemed that Mother was always rushed for time.

For days I tra-la-ed wedding marches and measured my steps. I had witnessed many wedding ceremonies, Mother had taken me with her to many. But this one, I knew, would be the grandest of them.

Closing my eyes I imaged the setting. Church. Many, many people. A flower-decorated altar. Music. Flower girls. . . .

Peggy Ann, dressed in light yellow, led the procession. (I was sure that she would lead because she was the "cutest an' littlest").

Patricia followed, dressed in rose; a rose ribbon in her hair.

Next Natalie who liked gold; in a golden dress and golden sandals to match.

And then "me-my-own-self" in blue; wearing my party-best sandals with silver buckles.

Patricia! Natalie! Peggy Ann! Elizabeth! Four flower girls—"us four an' no more"—showering rose petals all the way to the altar.

Late summer passed with its warm star-lighted evenings. And as the fall school term approached with no word from Miss Marlowe I concluded that she had wisely changed her mind; that perhaps she realized life would hold nothing for her without the four little girls who adored her; that perhaps we would find her at school, eager to welcome us back.

Not knowing where my little pals lived there was no way for me to contact them until we met at school.

77

When the last days of the summer season ended, I took up my books and started back to school.

Patricia, Natalie and Peggy Ann stood at our trysting place, waving to me.

I was just about to ask if Miss Marlowe had returned when Peggy Ann exclaimed: "We cried when Miss Marlowe said you couldn't come to the wedding 'cause you were sick."

Sick? When? I had not been ill.

Suddenly, as I stood there, every sound in the world seemed to die down.

"Sh-sh-she married?" I stammered.

"Uh-huh," piped Peggy Ann, "an like Natalie said we were the flower girls!"

I ate sparingly at dinner that evening.

"No appetite?" Mother inquired.

"I'm—I'm not very hungry," I choked, and asked to be excused.

Mother looked surprised. "No dessert?"

"No, thank you."

"You may be excused," said Mother. "But I guess a dose of Castor Oil will be in order tonight."

Blindly I made my way out to the back porch steps and sat down. The steps were like a shelter. I could cry there—unheard—unseen. . . .

I was not hungry. Never again would I be hungry: of this I was sure. Furthermore, all the Castor Oil in the whole, wide world could not make me want to eat: of this I was sure also. Unhappy as I was I did not care if Mother mixed Castor Oil, Epsom Salts and Sassafras Tea all together in the same glass and asked me to drink it with one swallow.

I was disappointed. I had been deceived.

Mother's voice reached my hearing. "Elizabeth—where are you?"

I brushed the tears back. "On th' back porch steps," I answered.

"Suppose you come inside, dear. Mother wants to talk to you."

I wiped my face on the hem of my dress; opened the screen door; closed it; latched it; walked into the living room.

Mother's arms were outstretched toward me. I ran to her.

Cuddled in protecting-arms I sobbed out my anguish. Why, oh why, I wanted to know had Miss Marlowe deceived me.

I was surprised to hear Mother say that I had not been deceived; that she, Mamma, had known all the while that I would not be a flower girl at Miss Marlowe's wedding.

I sat upright. "You—you knew?" I asked.

"Certainly, darling."

Then I wanted to know "how-come-so" that Mother knew it.

She replied, smiling: "Because I'm older than my little girl."

"Did Patricia an' Natalie an' Peggy Ann know that she wasn't going to ask me?" I inquired.

Mother shook her head the way that meant *no*. "I'm quite certain they didn't," she said.

Then Mother explained. . . .

She said the world was a great, big patch of ground divided by fences: that red people were fenced in; white people fenced in; yellow people fenced in; black people fenced in. I was told that the fences were erected to

79

separate the races and thus prevent one race from trespassing upon another's territory.

"Each race has its own customs," Mother explained. "The ancient ceremonies of the yellow race might appear strange to those who are white. The ways of the white, foreign to the red. The life of the black, a puzzle to the red. And so forth and so on."

Mother concluded the subject by saying that the fences were built also as a protection against ridicule and argument.

"Races mingle only on special occasions," she said. "At school, lectures, theatres, at work, and now and then at a public banquet. But when hallowed ceremonies take place such as weddings or social affairs in homes—people of different races rarely mix."

"Miss Marlowe loves you," Mother went on, "but she could not let you be a flower-girl because many of her friends do not like little girls who wear black dresses."

Black dresses? I shook my head hopelessly. Mother was getting all mixed up. People wore black to funerals. Light colors to weddings. I asked her if she had forgotten that.

"I'm not speaking of dress-goods," Mother answered, "but the little black dress known as your body, which covers up your *soul*—your real-self."

Then I wanted to know "how-come-so" that some of Miss Marlowe's friends did not like black.

"That's a long story," Mother told me. "But for the present let's say they don't like black for the same reason you don't like spinach and carrots."

"I sure hate spinach and carrots!"

"Why?" Mother asked.

I shrugged my shoulders. "Jus' don't like them. Dunno why."

Mother laughed. "Nevertheless they are good. Well, that's the same attitude some of Miss Marlowe's friends adopt. Some don't like little Colored girls for the same reason that you don't like spinach and carrots. They 'dunno why'!"

"Why'd Miss Marlowe tell a story and say I was sick?" I demanded.

"Because she loves you," Mother replied. "And she didn't want Patricia, Natalie or Peggy Ann to know why you were not invited. Did you tell them that you were not ill at that time?"

"No, Ma'am!" I admitted truthfully.

"Well," Mother continued, "there's a lesson in this for you. Remember—never take a supposition for granted."

The following afternoon when father came home to rest before reporting again for duty at the hotel, and learned of my disappointment, he offered (as balm for my disillusionment) to buy a wedding veil for me as lovely as Miss Marlowe's.

"Daniel!" Mother interposed. "That's absurd! A waste of money! A half-yard of mosquito netting will be ample."

Father protested. He said money was minted to spend and that if buying a real wedding veil would make up for Baby's disappointment, well. . . .

"Cheap mosquito-netting, Daniel!" Mother opposed with finality. "That or nothing!"

"Mother wins," Father laughed, winking at me. "So I'll have to obey."

For a couple of weeks thereafter mock-wedding ceremonies took place in our back yard.

Swathed in mosquito-netting and stepping daintily in a pair of my mother's old shoes I "tra-la-ed" and "make-believed" I was Miss Marlowe marching to the altar.

Happy? Of course I was happy!

81

Does a wee bird cease chirping because its frail wings will not lift it beyond a high fence?

There came a time when successive controversies engulfed me.

That was why, one day, quite inevitably, an incident occurred which caused me deliberately to ignore my parents' Forgive-Thine-Enemy commandment and venture publicly in pugilistic combat.

Trouble began for me when the school bully, an overgrown, fat, red-headed, brown-freckled, white boy, scrambled out of class, hid behind a door and awaited my exit.

As I tripped merrily by, he emerged, and blowing a blast of talcum powder in my face, mischievously jeered: "Ho! Ho! Ho! This'll turn you white!"

Before I could catch my breath the culprit had swiftly and laughingly taken to his heels.

A crowd of children gathered. Some among them offered to go in a body and tell the teacher. But I, attempting to be noble, refused to accept justice through intercession of tattlers, and hastened to the Girls' Washroom. My Loyal-Sympathizers followed me; ably assisted in washing my face; and soon the chalky traces of talcum were brushed from my hair save for a few streaks.

Back in class, I tried to concentrate on the blessedness of practicing divine forgiveness. But, unfortunately, the Bully occupied the seat directly in front of mine. And the desire to "get even" tempted me beyond human endurance.

I found a pin.

A split-second later, to the astonishment of teacher and class, the school-bully yipped like a mistreated puppy and "riz up" from his seat.

Wheeling about he glared ferociously at me. . . .

At that moment I became the most unconcerned member of the class—innocently staring up at the ceiling.

The boy stubbornly refused to reveal the source of the disturbance when asked to do so. The teacher continued the lesson.

Maliciously the boy turned to me and hissed threateningly: "I'm gonna beat you up, Smarty, right after school!"

After class I hurried down the main hall to the nearest exit. But the school-bully caught up with me, and as soon as I stepped outside the building he hit me on the arm. I returned the blow. He hit me again and ran. I gritted my teeth, clenched my fists and ran after him. Fight! Fight! Fight! I wanted to fight!

Now it so happened that of all the afternoons out of the three hundred and sixty-five afternoons in a year, that *particular* afternoon, my father (home on his vacation) decided to accompany me to my music lesson. That was how he reached the school just in time to be scandalized at the sight of his daughter sprinting over ground trying to catch an overgrown, fat, red-headed, brown-freckled white boy, and fight a battle-royal.

Of course, the boy (who was much stronger than I) would have won. Providence sent my father. The boy saw him, and realizing that he had violated the school rules by running on the Girls' side of the yard disappeared before a teacher could lay hands on him.

I am unable to express in few words my father's indignation. I tried to avoid the look of severity in his eyes as he led me home.

At home I faced trial before the parental-tribunal.

With spiritless acquiescence I plead guilty. I explained that the fight had begun "this-a way" and "that-a way"—only to discover that my parents were not interested in

83

"what-a way." They refused to listen to an elaboration of motives.

My parents took counsel. Wagged their heads. Discussed my escapade. They did not know, they said, how they would survive the scandal. I was led to believe that my actions had disgraced the family name forever.

"We've told you," my father said sharply, "that should anything of this sort happen, you're supposed to go directly to a teacher or speak to us. There is nothing more disgraceful than a common brawl. We expect you to behave as a little lady should behave."

I made a terrible mistake by attempting to explain that the fight was "jus' a little fight."

"No impertinence, Elizabeth!" Father snapped.

I apologized; for whenever Mother or Father called my name in that tone instead of referring to me as "Baby" I knew that my faults or misdemeanors were exceedingly displeasing.

I sighed. I reflected. . . .

Secretly I regretted losing that fight. But as in the case of many a would-be-conqueror attempting conquest, I had not only lost the battle but sacrificed my reputation. Shamefacedly I bowed my head and looked down at the toes of my shoes.

Many years afterwards I found out that after my parents had dismissed me from their presence Father said to Mother: "Well, thank God, she has spunk enough to fight for herself!"

In response Mother murmured something about "He that controlleth his temper is greater than he that taketh a city."

The next controversy that caused my submissive spirit to exert itself and rise once more took place when a White child with skinny arms and spindling legs told my Colored chum, whose name was Louella Allen, and me that all colored people were supposed to be poor, wear rags and live in shacks.

Louella and I disbelieved, disputed and argued. But Skinny-Arms-and-Spindling-Legs demanded proof on our part.

Children "took sides." The majority joined ranks with our opponent. The minority championed our cause.

The long and short of the controversy resulted in Louella and me strutting down the street, a line of White children parading behind us.

Louella's mother was not at home. So my little colored chum raised the front door mat, found the key and made unbelievers welcome.

As I now look back upon that six-room-excursion, I am forced to pause for a bit of laughter. It all seems so ridiculous!

From front to back our curious opponents explored the Allen home. They felt the heft of the rugs. They bounced up and down upon the upholstered furniture. Opened book cases. Skidded down the hardwood floor of a narrow hallway. Peered into linen closets. Rummaged in clothes closets. Snooped about the pantry to ascertain the food supply.

Skinny-Arms-and-Spindling-Legs was not convinced.

"Didn' you say your father drives-a automobile for rich folks?" she questioned.

"What's that got to do with my house?" Louella asked in an injured tone.

Skinny-Arms-and-Spindling-Legs sucked her teeth. "I betcha he stole all these things from the folks he works for!" the child declared vehemently.

Louella, thinking her mission an apparent failure, gave

85

up and began to cry. *But not I.* I led the expedition to my own home.

Mother was with Mrs. Allen at Parent-Teachers meeting.

I secured the key from its hiding place. . . .

I opened the china-cabinet. Displayed cut-glassware, a pretty dinner set, handpainted china. Then awaited our chief-opponent's verdict.

Skinny-Arms-and-Spindling-Legs looked dubious.

"Didn' you say your father works in a hotel?" she inquired.

"What's that got to do with my house?"

Our chief-opponent grinned satanically. "I betcha your father stole this stuff from the hotel!"

Opening a drawer of the serving-table I took out the silverware. Showed them the engraved "A" on knives, forks, spoons. Without a word I brought forth a silver tea-set. At sight of it the children gasped. Their eyes marvelled.

Triumphantly I faced our chief-opponent. We were attempting to glare each other out of countenance. . . .

My mother walked into the room.

With a single bound the children headed for the front door!

Mother pointed to the display. "Why were you showing these things to those children?" she asked.

I told her.

Immediately after my explanation she began to talk. She talked rapidly; not even pausing to take a breath. And what she said sounded just like words borrowed from one of the Methodist preacher's Sunday sermons.

She said: "Vanity—false pride—vainglory." And then: "Do you hear me?"

Before I could answer she had added up everything

86

she was thinking and made a step-ladder of thoughts for me to climb.

She said: "Now, young lady, from this day forward remember—fine clothes, costly rugs, pretty dishes, hand-painted china, engraved silverware, none of these things or anything else material is more important than character."

And then she asked: "Do you hear me?" But before I could answer she went right on talking and acting like the Methodist preacher except that she did not bang her fists, stamp her feet, or pray.

She said: "And furthermore, young lady, from this day forward remember—whoever has to use material possession to prove that she or he is somebody, that she or he is nobody!" And then she asked: "Do you hear me?"

I was too bewildered to answer. Tears rolled out of my eyes. Trickled down my cheeks. My tongue stuck to the roof of my mouth.

And then I forgot about keeping quiet and said that I only wanted to prove something.

"You proved something all right," mother replied, "your ignorance!"

And then she said: "Your punishment is—to bed without supper."

Next day when I encountered Louella she informed me that when *her* mother saw their house she was "maddern'n ever—so mad that ——"

Well—while telling me Louella did not sit down.

For a while the deportment of the two little colored girls, Louella Allen and Elizabeth Adams was fairly commendable. But alas and alack! We became involved in another controversy when a white child whom we called

The-Girl-With-The-Pretty-Brown-Eyes asked us if our mothers would "take in washin'" for her mother. . . .

We told The-Girl-With-The-Pretty-Brown-Eyes that our mothers did not run laundries. The girl laughed at us. Instinctively we resented that laugh. Then Louella whispered in my ear: "Let's make fun-a the way she talks."

We did. But the little girl's speech was mellow with the dialect of the South; and my Colored chum and I had never before heard dialect. So we ridiculed the girl's speech, telling her that she could not "event speak plain Englush."

The girl reddened quickly. And her pretty brown eyes flashed, and tossing her thick braids back over her shoulders she told us that her great grandfather owned slaves and that all those slaves were colored.

And though Louella and I knew that many people employed servants, slavery, as explained by the girl, was new to us.

The little white girl from the South said she could be proud of her ancestors because they were great. But colored people, she said, had no famous ancestors—theirs were only slaves.

Louella began to cry. But my anger welled up. Quick. Consuming.

"Louella an' I have got famous ancestors. Greater than great."

The-Girl-With-The-Pretty-Brown-Eyes smiled sarcastically: "Name them!"

"Sure I'll name them!"

The girl raised her eyebrows haughtily, and asked me to tell her who my great-great-grandparents were.

I squinted my eyes. "Sure I'll tell you!" I yelled defiantly. "They were ——"

I stopped—mouth wide open. Confused, I licked my

88

lips, closed my mouth but left one end of my tongue hanging out a corner.

Almost I became frantic. Ancestors! Ancestors! My ancestors—who were they and why were they hiding out on me? I needed ancestors!

A colored child, just behind me, whispered in my ear: "Tell her your grea' grea' gran'maw was a queen."

I whispered in the colored child's ear: "How'd you know my great, great grandmaw was a queen?"

The colored child whispered back: "There's white queens so there mus' be colored ones."

My whole aspect brightened. Out of the depths of nowhere ancestors were being supplied.

But alas and alack—my adversary doubted me, contending that she had never heard of a colored queen. A word-battle raged.

The Mexican children claimed kinship to a certain Queen Isabella. But up to now I do not in the least know whether it was Isabella *la Catolica* of Castile, or Isabella II, born in Madrid. But I do know that the Spanish children resented this and told their Mexican playmates (in no uncertain terms) that they had no right to claim Isabella, but should confine themselves to praising Mexican rulers. Chinese and Japanese children squabbled. White children bragged of grandfather-senators, uncle-generals, cousin-majors and so forth and so on. Colored children, determined not to be "out-ancestored" boasted of grandfather-and-father-Presidents of the United States.

All went about as well as could be expected of such a controversy until a colored child announced that her great grandmother's cousin had at one time been a lady-in-waiting to Queen Victoria of England. A child of English descent objected. And in defense of the colored child's ancestry the rest of us stamped our feet, crossed and re-crossed our hearts on the right side, declaring at the same time that all our great grandmothers' cousins and nieces had been ladies-in-waiting to the same queen. Not to be outdone, one little colored cherub caused the English child to denounce us as "guilty of untruths" when she attempted to convince the antagonistic audience that one of her "great granduncles" was a "real-true-an'-honest-t'-goodness English Lord"—emphasizing that "mos' importan' of all" he was *half* English, *half* Indian, *half* Spanish and *half* Colored.

For a few minutes I withdrew from the rebellious discussion. As the others debated divergent views I searched the remote corners of my memory trying to find a mental-photograph of an ancestor.

Suddenly an image—a beloved image flashed before my eyes. . . .

Grandpa Holden!

Grandpa Holden and the stories of the sea that he had so often told to me—I remembered them vividly—all the old Colored seaman's stories of roving voyages.

I smiled to myself as a synopsis of each story projected itself upon my mind's screen.

The ships in stormy waters. . . .

The foreign ports nestling in a haze of fog. . . .

The peasants dressed in colorful garments. . . .

The jungle territory where chattering monkeys swung from the branches of trees. . . .

The seaman's mascot—the talking bird known as the parrot. . . .

The lands where dark skinned natives strode proudly balancing baskets of tropical fruits upon their heads. . . .

The islands of wind-swayed palms, drum dirges and garlands of exotic flowers. . . .

I reflected: surely Grandpa Holden must have owned

that ship that sailed to those far lands. Why not? And if he owned it—he must have been the captain. Why not?

I rejoiced! I could now prove there was a famous somebody in my family; that I too, had a great ancestor!

Thus it was that I told the children that my grandfather had been a "real-live" sea captain and owned a "grea' big ship."

I entered our house "tra-la-ing" and laughing.

Mother wanted to know what was so funny.

Echoes from the controversy bounced from my lips and hit the walls like a rubber ball.

" 'Course we don't believe her ——"

"Grandpa Holden ——"

"His ship—the one he bought ——"

"Colored people slaves ——"

My mother raised her eyes. "Well," she said, "when you have finished laughing let me know. I have something to tell you."

I did.

And mother kept her promise.

She said: "Your grandfather did not own that ship. It belonged to the United States Navy." She went on: "Your grandfather was not a captain. He was what is known as a cabin steward." I was disappointed on learning that a cabin steward does not stand at a ship's helm and direct its course; and amazed to hear that my greatgrandmother on my mother's side of the family had been a slave and could not read or write.

Staidness and sobriety temporarily fastened my jaws. For the rest of that afternoon and evening I sat in a huff.

Just before bed time Mother had a suggestion to make.

"Of course," she said. "I am sure you intend to keep your part of the treaty and tell the little girl that you were mistaken today."

91

I kept right on sitting in a huff and told her politely that I had no such intention.

My mother said that she was of the opinion that it was my intention to have no such intention. And undeterred by the fact that I would be subjected to ridicule and humiliation right then and there commanded that I must keep my part of the peace treaty.

I hopped out of my huff. My eyes flashed. I clenched my fists. I wanted to talk.

"I shall have no way of knowing whether you carry out my order," my parent reminded me. "Only God will know——"

What happened the next day was a bitter dose. But I swallowed it. It was a bitter dose for Louella too. But she swallowed it. So the whole affair was climaxed by jeers, two bitter doses and two swallows.

That afternoon my mother asked me if I had obeyed her.

Meekly I said, "Yes'm."

My mother thereupon proceeded to say: "Concerning slavery—I shall say little now. That is something to be discussed later—when you're older. But this you may now know. The Colored race has been enslaved, but so have other races. It is wrong to make slaves of other people. But remember—if poor, despised slaves were honest, industrious and trusty their descendants for generations to come will be endowed with good heritage. This vexation is not unusual. It happens to thousands of colored children. Somebody tells them their ancestors were 'nobodys' and they borrow ancestors from other races or make-believe-them until they learn this is not necessary. Understand?"

I nodded vaguely. The subject was a bit over my head. But I promised to try and remember all that had just been

92

said and to stay away from these terrible things called controversies.

It seemed that controversies would not stay away from me.

A little Mexican girl cried one day. Somebody had called her a "*greaser.*" . . .

Two little Chinese children bowed their heads and stood huddled together. Somebody had called them "*chinks.*" . . .

One little Japanese girl sat on a bench and blinked and blinked and blinked. Somebody had called her a "*jap.*" . . .

A chubby little Italian girl looked scared. Somebody had called her a "*dago.*" . . .

And a little Jewish girl screamed and screamed until a teacher hurried across the yard and took her in her arms. Somebody had called her a "*kyke.*" . . .

In time I asked my parents to tell me why the words "greaser, chink, jap, dago and kyke" made my playmates cry, bow their heads, blink, look scared and scream.

My parents asked: "Have you forgotten the day you learned the meaning of—*the word?*"

I told them that I had not forgotten.

And they said: "There are other words that hurt other people just as much as the word now hurts you. Do you understand?"

This I understood.

And they said: "Hereafter whenever you hear *the word* think of the *other words* that hurt *other people* and you'll realize that you are not the only hurt person in the world."

After that—I went out to play.

One afternoon I went home, and because my father

93

was there I asked him some questions instead of asking mother.

I said I wanted to know if it were true—the things some of the white children had said.

He listened while I repeated their argument.

He asked: "Now what is it you want to know about General Lee and General Grant and the part they played in the Civil War?"

I told him a group of white children said General Lee was the greater leader: a group of colored children claimed General Grant deserved more praise.

My father looked at me thoughtfully and then said: "In my opinion neither man was greater than the other. I have heard that General Grant had a cultivated mind and possessed moral and physical courage. Both men were great. Each man fought valiantly for the cause he believed in. The end of that war set Colored slaves free. Today General Grant is a national hero because the side he represented won that battle. Today General Lee is a national hero because the side he represented lost—and it takes great moral courage to lose a fight for what we believe is right."

And then my father closed the discussion by saying: "One man was a Northern gentleman. The other a Southern gentleman."

The next day at school I tried to settle a controversy by repeating my father's words.

A group of colored children almost scalped me. They said: "To think you ain't got no thanks for what General Grant's done for you. It's awful!"

A group of white children said: "You ain't got no right standin' up for General Lee! We're the only ones s'posed to belong on his side."

And the very next time I had a chance to talk to my

94

father I wanted to know which side was right and which side was wrong.

He laughed at me, then said: "Child—a battle is always right and always wrong. Because when we fight for what is right we cannot escape hurting those who have done no evil, and by hurting them we do wrong. So go back to school and stop worrying over grown-up problems. They'll be yours soon enough."

I promised to obey. But—I heard of more strange happenings.

A colored child said that she had heard that some grown-up white people were "awful, awful mean" to colored people.

A white child said he had heard that there were schools where white teachers would not teach colored children. . . .

When I refused to believe the accusations, both white and colored playmates suggested that I go home and *"ast"* my mother and father to *"learn"* me these things.

I did. I went home angry. But this time two surprises awaited me. . . .

Surprise Number One: My father became angry at me.

Surprise Number Two: My mother became angry at me.

Father bellowed: "Up to the present—have grown-up white people been mean to you?"

"No, sir," I replied.

Father bellowed again: "Then what have you to complain about? Answer me!"

And I answered, admitting that I had nothing to complain about.

Then mother raised her voice: "Has any white teacher ever refused to teach you? Answer me!"

"No, Ma'am," I replied.

Mother raised her voice higher: "Then what have you to complain about? Answer me!"

I answered, admitting that no white teacher had ever refused to teach me.

Then Father said: "Young lady—I may as well tell you now that I don't propose to stand by and see your mother work herself to death while you waste time and energy fighting the Civil War all over again. Now stop wagging your tongue over adult problems. Do you hear me?"

Politely, meekly, reverently and resignedly, I breathed: "Yes, Papa dear."

I was ready to leave the room, but Mother called me to attention.

"Stand still, you fidgety little maggot!" she said, "and listen to what I have to say. I don't propose to stand by and see your father work himself to death while you waste time and energy taking part in controversies. Do you hear me?"

Politely, meekly, reverently and resignedly, I breathed: "Yes, Mamma dear."

Meekly I asked for permission to be excused.

"You may be excused," Mother snapped. "And I'll excuse myself too and find some extra chores. You don't have enough work to keep you busy!"

The next day I was surprised to find a pile of wood stacked high in the back yard. My parents ordered me to appear before this wood-pile every day after school and neatly stack a few armfuls at a time in the tool house, in readiness for use in the fireplace during winter months.

For a long, long, long time thereafter I lost interest in controversies!

But, controversies, like "the goblins" will sneak up and "catch you if you don't watch out!"

Thus one day I was astounded by the unbelievable information a little white girl whispered in my ear. . . .

" 'liz'beth Adams," she said, "there ain't no stork!"

Up to this time I had been so busy resurrecting great-great-ancestors and investigating causes of the Civil War that I had not particularly thought about the stork since the time Mother had described him to me.

All the way home the little white girl's words jangled in my ears like a jiggety tune.

I recalled the time the stork was supposed to have brought Baby-Brother.

Had I not run to the fireplace and looked up the chimney to watch the bird fly away?

Yes.

Had I seen the stork?

NO! There was no doubt about that!

By the time I reached home I had made up my mind to question Mother, though I had not the least idea how to lead up to the subject. After all, I reflected, I could not just blurt out: "I don't believe there is a stork!"

Dinner bolstered me up. While washing dishes I hummed.

"You seem unusually happy!" Mother commented.

Happy? Oh, yes, I said that I was very, very happy. The day had been such a pretty day. So nice and warm. I remarked that after a while I guessed the weather would turn cold. Very, very cold. So cold that all the birds would stay in their nests to keep warm.

Mother, who had to remind me every day to put bird seed in the canary's cage, looked up. She had an uncanny way of reading my thoughts.

"Why this sudden interest in birds?" she asked.

Sudden interest? I shrugged my shoulders. I said that I was just wondering about the poor, little helpless birds

97

out in the cold (when it was cold) out in the rain (when it rained) out in the wind (when it was windy) out in the storm (when it stormed). I felt sorry, I said, for all birds that had to fly in cold, rainy, windy, stormy weather —"'specially" the poor birds with pretty, pretty feathers "like-a ostriches." . . .

I paused.

Mother offered no comment.

I continued: "Like-a ostriches ———"

I paused.

Still Mother offered no comment.

Boldly, with one breath, I continued and concluded: "Like-a ostriches an' storks!"

A moment of tense silence followed. Then Mother spoke.

"Stop washing the dishes, Child," she said with gentle decision, "and sit down."

Past experiences had taught Mother always to command me to be seated before shattering my illusions.

She had not forgotten (and declares to this day that she shall never forget) my behavior the time she told me that the Easter Bunny was a fable; for when I found out that (instead of a rabbit) my parents had placed the red, yellow, orange, purple and green candy eggs in a basket for me, I jumped up and down in disappointed revolt.

But now—back to the story of the stork. . . .

Mother began by saying: "My dear—there *is* a stork— and there *isn't* a stork!"

Secretly I thought to myself that Mother's explanation failed to make sense.

"The story of the stork," my parent informed me, "is told to children while they are very, very little. That is why, to them, the Patron Bird of Births is a reality until they are old enough to reverence and highly evaluate holy

98

knowledge relevant to the creation of human beings. This knowledge, pure and beautiful, is called The Sacred Story of Life."

Mother spoke slowly and quite simply. The spiritual convictions within her soul lent tremendous power to her words, which made a profound impression on me—an impression that has lasted unchanged throughout these years.

She affirmed that the love of a man for a woman—and the love of a woman for a man—though a human love, becomes *divine* when God sanctions their marriage through religious ceremony. . . .

She spoke of matrimony as a holy state of life. . . .

She spoke of the transition from matrimony to parenthood as a blessing bestowed upon husbands and wives. . . .

One fact in particular she indelibly impressed on my heart and soul: that to womankind only God granted the privilege of Motherhood. And Mother admonished me to regard all Expectant-Mothers as worthy almost of adoration. . . .

Thus I was taught that my soul should be mute with spiritual veneration whenever in the presence of a woman whose form was draped in the mantle of Motherhood.

Concluding, Mother said: "Avoid the little girl who told you that there is no stork. If she attempts to discuss the subject you must not pay any attention. Shut your eyes. Muffle your ears and run away from her. Do you understand?"

I understood. That was why, the next day, when the untrained child hailed me, I shut my eyes, stuck a finger in each ear and ran pell-mell.

That evening Mother said: "Elizabeth—I want you to realize now that should you marry, your wedded life will not be a path of orange-blossoms. You must learn how to be self-sacrificing, patient, tolerant and industrious or you will be a frivolous wife and make your husband's life miserable as well as your own."

Each evening thereafter I had to place Father's smoking jacket and slippers beside his chair as preparatory training.

I can recall how peeved I (not quite eleven years of age) used to become when compelled to put aside an interesting book to perform this service.

Who would want to get married, anyway, I asked myself, if it meant waiting on someone else the rest of one's life!

If Mother was occupied elsewhere I took my spite out on the slippers—sometimes banging them against the chair or beating them with my fists, muttering:

"Crazy husban'."

"Silly husban'."

"Hateful husban'."

"When I marry I won't wait on my husban'! I won't! I won't! I won't!"

Once in a while Mother, hearing me mutter would call out, "Did you say something?"

"Jus' talkin' to myself, Mamma dear," I would reply, with a sigh.

And so the season of controversies and learning little lessons passed.

One day, Father, usually in good health, came home complaining of illness.

Mother sent for our family physician.

Morning came.

I awoke. I sat slowly upright in bed. The room whirled before my eyes. I sank back. I called out: "Mamma!"

Mother answered. Came into my room with halting steps. . . .

100

An epidemic had reached our house—Influenza!

Influenza wrought a wave of terror everywhere. Health authorities issued warnings and advice through newspapers:

"BOIL WATER BEFORE DRINKING IT!"

"GAUZE MASKS TO BE WORN IN PUBLIC"

"SCHOOLS CLOSE TEMPORARILY"

The populace tried to flee from the epidemic—but in vain. Limbs gave way beneath the strongest of the strong.

Homes were quarantined. Hospitals filled to capacity.

And then Panic—despairing—almost indescribable—terrorized the city as many doctors and nurses were assailed by the disease.

Physically I had never been a strong child. The Influenza depleted what little strength I possessed and weakened my heart action. Knowing this, Father decided to gratify my every whim. So happy was he to have his lambkin spared, that my bleating became a welcome sound in his ears.

One day he asked me: "What would you like to have more than anything else in the world?"

I told him.

He told Mother.

But Mother said that I was too young to own a wristwatch. I did not know it then, of course, but learned later that Father, disagreeing, said to Mother: "Lula, if Baby dies we'll never forgive ourselves for not giving her the desire of her heart. She wants a watch. Let her have it. The poor child's suffered so ——"

But Mother remained resolute, saying: "If she dies—she'll not need a watch. Let it be a gift to her upon graduation from Junior High School. She'll be old enough then to appreciate it."

That settled that! And the very next time that I howled

and bleated, Mother said sternly: "Elizabeth—I've had enough of your foolishness. SHUT UP!"

And I shut up.

I know now that her words, like strong arms, reached out, picked me up and placed me within the fortress of disciplined limitations.

After many weeks the epidemic abated.

My father recovered completely. But Mother's health and mine caused the doctor grave concern and he recommended a change of climate.

Santa Barbara with its peaceful, health-restoring atmosphere was decided upon as the ideal place to recuperate.

And so Father accompanied us there to the home wherein I was born; saw us safely settled; then returned to Los Angeles to resume his work at the hotel.

Mother and I resigned ourselves to his absence, knowing that he would spend every other week end with us. We began to formulate new plans for an existence by ourselves. No—not exactly by ourselves; almost I have forgotten to mention that there was one other to keep us company—a tiny kitten which had been given to me.

After Father's departure I meandered about the back yard.

It was a big yard; walled in by a high fence overhung with thick masses of Moon-Plant. Clusters of purple grapes interspersed with Flaming-Tokays covered an arched arbor. There were trees: walnut, almond, peach, plum, apple, fig, cherry, nectarine. There were berry-bushes: blackberry and raspberry growing riotously over fan-shaped trellises. There were flowers: lilies, chrysanthemums, larkspur, and choice roses in a separate garden-spot. There were potted plants: ferns and fuschias.

There was a swing!

102

I jumped in it. Swinging I thought of Louella. The miles that lay between my little chum's home and mine seemed countless.

"I think it's going to be *awfully lonesome* here," I confided to the kitten. "Don't you?"

CHAPTER EIGHT

Stars

Santa Barbara was an ideal place in which to spend adolescent years.

It was quiet. Only two street car lines were routed throughout the town. Neither privately owned automobiles nor taxis caused grave traffic disturbances. Unlike a large city it was void of clatter, shrill factory whistles, dense smoke screens and raucous cries of peddlers.

It was picturesque. A crescent-shaped strand where in summer the sea sprayed the sands with filmy mists and in winter heavy wave swells crashed upon the beach. Moss-matted were some of the hills; winding the paths that led to mountain peaks.

It was quaint. Historic landmarks perpetuated the era of early Spanish colonization in California. In some localities old adobes with thick walls bordered the streets. Oak, camphor and grevillea trees shaded the sidewalks.

For four years my Mother and I lived in this small town so dream-like in reality. Whenever I look back on these years I think of two people walking down a lonely road in the light and shade of sunlight and shadows.

Forced by ill health to become a recluse, Mother seldom went anywhere except to church. Voluntarily I shared her exile: that was why the prospect of an occasional picnic or automobile ride thrilled me.

One evening friends invited us to accompany them to

religious service at the historic Santa Barbara Mission. But as church did not interest me (except for its sacred music) I dreaded going.

It was Good Friday.

The car in which we rode was driven up the wide driveway in front of the Mission and parked to one side. Then we got out, went in and seated ourselves.

With wonder like that of Alice in Wonderland I looked around. Members of the congregation were prayerfully kneeling. I noticed that those nearest me were not distracted by my impolite staring. Some were reading devoutly from small books; others fingered strings of beads. I did not know, at that time, that the small books were prayer-books, and the beads rosaries. I beheld the altars. I listened to the voices of the priests. I heard the words *Ave Maria*, not knowing the meaning was *Hail Mary*. This was a new world.

While sitting there I thought to myself: "If this is church —why have I disliked it so?"

Conversion is defined in Webster's dictionary as: "*A change from one state, or from one religion, to another.*" Chocarne, speaking of it says: "*Conversion, that phenomenon of light to the intellect and persuasion to the heart, is not ordinarily produced in the way of sudden illumination, like a flash of lightning in a dark night, but rather under the form of growing daylight, like that which precedes the sunrise.*"

In my case, the Great God knew that I, a little Colored girl, *feared conversion* because of a Sunday-school teacher's prophetic description of the descent of the Holy Ghost. The Great God knew also that deep down within the soul of this same Colored girl was a simple wish that the Son of God would "walk and talk" with her as the Colored Methodist children described Him walkin' an'

105

talkin' with them when they testified in church on Sunday mornings. And so conversion came to me quickly and quietly—like the slumber that gently closes an infant's eyes. I experienced no emotional reaction other than the desire to attend service at the Santa Barbara Mission forever.

At home that night I wrote a letter to my father telling him that I planned to "join church at the Old Mission." On receiving it he telephoned long distance to Mother, wanting to know if I had lost my mind.

"Why did you write such a letter to your father without telling me!" Mother exclaimed.

I became frightened. I had had no idea that my letter would cause confusion. It was at this time that I learned that Father, affiliated with the Masonic Order, expected me to join the women's auxiliary (to which Mother belonged) on my eighteenth birthday. This proved a mystifying bit of news. And on finding out that it was against the rules of the Catholic church for its members to join secret orders I was in a dilemma.

On Father's next trip home he and I discussed this all-important matter. Sternly he reminded me that I was very young and did not know what I wanted, stating emphatically: "You cannot become a Catholic!"

"What is so bad about becoming a Catholic?" I asked.

"There is nothing bad," he replied. "It's just that I will not permit you to become one."

Within I rebelled. Mother and Father had always told me: "We will not prohibit you from accepting anything good in life!"

I reasoned: since Father said there was nothing *bad* about being a Catholic; then it was evident that to join the church was *good.*

106

"Never discuss the subject again," Father concluded, and I was silenced.

Although the permission I sought was not granted by my father, I want to make it clear to readers that it was not denied because of any slanderous or derogatory gossip circulated in the world to prejudice people against the good Religious of the Church. My parents were too strong-minded to be swayed in opinion by evil hearsay. They respected the clergy of all denominations.

I knew that I would never forget that Good Friday service, and the small books from which some of the congregation read, and the beads and the altars, and the voices of the priests and the words *Ave Maria*. As a mirror reflects images, so the memory of the old Santa Barbara Mission and its ancient form of worship were always to be reflected in the mirror of my soul.

Father's decision left me no alternative. I dismissed the idea of becoming a Catholic, and gave undivided attention to my school work.

It was at this time that the cycle of events brought into my life a great teacher—one who taught me how to see the brilliance of the stars shining through sunlight—Mr. J. Defray Silvia, principal of Lincoln Grammar School.

Before meeting him I had somehow formed the opinion that all principals were to be feared by children; believing it was their sworn duty to whip school-bullies with a big, thick strap, and punish boys guilty of "playing hookey." These things I firmly believed until, as I have already said, I met this principal.

Almost twenty-two years have passed since he stood before the particular assembly of which I now speak and requested that boys and girls interested in forming an orchestra meet him in the Music-Room. Joyfully I thought of the Gift-Of-The-Singing-Strings—my violin.

107

Two boys and two girls waited for the principal.

A White girl, very like a Dresden China doll, said she played the piano. Her name was Ruth.

A Mexican boy, seated on a rickety chair, impatiently tapping first one foot and then the other upon the floor, said he played the cornet. His name was Serifo.

A White boy with unruly hair, his hands thrust into the pockets of his knickers, whistled nervously. He played the snare and bass drums. His name was Iyme.

An eager, smiling Colored girl waited also. She played the violin. Her name was—well, you should know it by this time.

Mr. Silvia, an accomplished musician, zealously trained us. He was born with the aptitude for teaching. He understood how sensitive and impressionable our adolescent minds were, and realizing that we were at the age to be instantly crushed by adult disapproval and lack of faith in us, he never failed to encourage our efforts to become good musicians. He never made us feel abashed by harshly censuring our spontaneous and sometimes impractical suggestions. Tactfully he avoided harping on our failings and magnified our virtues while developing the talent of each boy and girl.

I can see the room in which we practiced.

Ruth—seated upon an old fashioned piano stool before a square piano, her hands in position over the keyboard.

Serifo—a brass cornet pressed to his lips.

Iyme—holding the drum-sticks obliquely over the snare drum.

And I—violin under my chin, and bow in hand.

Mr. Silvia—a wavy fold of dark hair framing his brow; his eyes smiling as he rapped twice with his baton and asked, "Ready?" after which he gave the signal to play.

Sometimes Ruth missed notes. Serifo blew blasts from

the cornet that almost cracked the plaster on the wall. Iyme hit the snare drum so hard that it sounded as if it were about to burst. I drew the bow across the violin with such rapidity that the notes squeaked and played hopscotch on all four strings. Meanwhile we marked time with our feet, and looked inquiringly at our director whenever he was forced to rap loudly and continuously for us to stop!

But times there were when we were so enrapt in the "bitter-sweet" discords of unauthorized transcriptions of melody that we failed to heed the raps and played inharmoniously on until Mr. Silvia, exasperated (but ever hopeful) took a handkerchief from his pocket and wiped the perspiration from his forehead. Observing him, we, the orchestra, were puzzled as to why he grew so tired.

Day after day we rehearsed. In time our playing improved. Other boys and girls joined the group. And then, as a reward for perseverance we were allowed to play in public.

O joy sublime and sublime joy! What anxious moments were experienced before a public performance! Boys appeared with hair slicked back (pasted down with water) faces and hands scrubbed, clean white shirts and Sunday-best-suits. Girls wore their hair curled; flaunted about in ruffled dresses, gay sashes and Sunday-best-shoes.

Mr. Silvia walked back and forth back stage with quick, nervous steps, anxiously looking at his watch and counting heads bent over instrument cases. Now and then he had to grab a boy who insisted on poking his head out from behind the curtain "just-a t' see how many folks are fillin' up the seats."

Tuning-up-time put the director's patience to a test. Sometimes violinists tightened strings until they snapped. Occasionally a cornet player decided to sound Taps. The pianist practiced scales. The drummer took a notion to imitate savages beating tom-toms. Invariably somebody who did not belong to the orchestra sneaked back stage, picked up the triangle and struck it until it clanged like a fire-alarm. But our director's patience was unlimited. After a series of "Sh-Sh-SH-SH'S," he managed to quiet us. Then we scrambled to our chairs, watching him with absorbed eyes. The curtain went up. Lincoln Grammar School orchestra played!

Mr. Silvia's heart and soul were in his work. No form of race-prejudice blinded his vision—he saw the soul of a child and not the color of the skin. That is why one concert has always lingered in my memory as outstanding. . . .

The auditorium was crowded that night. The house-lights dimmed. Footlights brightened. The curtain went up. A pianist rippled opening chords. A violinist and an aspiring-violinist played. The violinist Mr. Silvia, and I the aspirant. The principal played second violin part, a largo-movement. To me had been given first violin part, a sparkling movement-allegro.

The selection ended. The audience applauded. We smiled and bowed. I left the stage—but Mr. Silvia remained, violin and bow in hand.

Applause! Applause! Applause!

I returned. We played an encore.

That concert gave me an opportunity for expression and provided an impetus to inspire me from one degree of attainment to another until I should reach my life-goal. At every orchestra rehearsal thereafter whenever Mr. Silvia raised the baton it seemed to me he pointed toward the sky and at a star.

Regardless of race or color, children are easily flattered,

110

and achievement won at an early age often causes the best trained to become self-centered unless parents wisely check the first indications of egotism.

My Mother deserves credit for my training in this respect, for as soon as she heard me boasting of my part in that concert she pointed out to me that it was Mr. Silvia who was great and not I.

"Do you know why you were encored?" she asked.

Child-like I thought it was because of my manner of playing.

"Be not deceived," my mother corrected, "you were encored only because Mr. Silvia never left the stage."

It was after this explanation that I realized that the principal's presence on the stage was like a voice pleading silently: "This is my pupil. Have faith in her as I have faith in her. Applause is encouraging. Applaud, audience, applaud!"—and apparently the audience understood.

I learned the lesson of humility taught by my Mother. Yes—I know full well that I learned it because the next time I saw Mr. Silvia it seemed to me that he had grown several inches taller, and I, in my estimation, had shriveled several inches shorter.

Lincoln Grammar School shared the same educational curriculum as other accredited grammar schools—but only the study of music and the fascinating stories from a book of classical myths interested me.

Music and Greek Mythology affected me as a Hindu fakir's weird music charms a snake—they held me spellbound.

In arithmetic, geography and history classes I daydreamed about the gods. . . .

I admired Jupiter whom the Greeks called "Father Sky" because they believed he commanded the snow to fall,

111

rain to drop, winds to blow; and thought the roar of thunder and flash of lightning expressions of his wrath.

I was enchanted by the story of Aurora, beautiful goddess of the dawn, who swung wide the gates of day and hid the stars to clear the sky-way for the chariot of the sun-god, Apollo, which was surrounded by lovely maidens known as the Hours.

I felt sorry for Pan, little god of the country, because the Nymphs ignored him. He was described in the book as playing music upon pipes, sleeping in caves at night—and in the daytime dancing in the forests with fauns and wild creatures, blowing the pipes as he skipped over hills and through glades. And it was written in the book that whenever shepherds lost their sheep or goats, Pan found them. And in gratitude for his kindness the grateful ones built altars to honor him and brought offerings of milk and honey.

I was awed by Pluto's habitation—a black region under the earth, supposedly inhabited by the souls of men after death. Here, the book said, Pluto, god of the Lower World, dwelt and reigned supreme.

I spilled tears over the tragic love story of Hero and Leander—two lovers forbidden to see each other. Poor Hero (an attendant upon the shrine of Venus), how I mourned her loss when Leander (who swam across the straits each evening to tell her of his love) was drowned in the tangling whirlpools of the sea and his body washed upon the shore.

I reverenced Diana, an unmarried goddess, who, as Greek maidens believed, exercised watchful care over them, her to whom they looked for guidance and protection.

But the time came when I had to leave the book of

classic myths and the orchestra. Grammar school days were over.

On entering Junior High School I noticed a drastic change in the attitude of some of my White classmates toward me. They became aloof, indifferent and evasive. Their action seems inexcusable, our friendship having been established in grammar-grades. But my experience was not singular. Other Colored students shared the same fate.

It is at this stage that many White youths, influenced by relatives or friends, assume an air of superiority over the Colored. Resenting this, the youth of my race resort to various means to conceal injured feelings and sometimes complete character transformation takes place. The gentle become aggressive; the quiet, loud-voiced; the even-tempered, rebellious; the shy, sophisticated.

Fortunate are the Colored whose parents dissuade them from bitterness which might develop into consuming hatred.

My parents advised me not to take part in racial arguments anywhere at any time. They told me that life was far too precious to waste energy trying to prove race-equality; that cultured White people never debased themselves by ridiculing or unjustly condemning the Colored, never boasted intellectual supremacy or arrogantly bragged of race-purity. They classified the White people who advocated segregation and unfair discrimination as White Pygmies, because, they said, though the fair of skin were not small of stature like the Black Pygmies of Africa, they were dwarfed in mind and soul.

It was my father who told me that every person in the world had "a place"—that that was why bankers counted money in banks; teachers taught in schools; motormen

113

ran street cars and chefs cooked in kitchens, but made it clear to me that White people of refinement never scorned domestic labor or designated it as a field set apart for Negroes.

My mother's advice to me was: "If you plan to cram your head with knowledge just to show-off and spite White-oppressors of our race, you may as well give up school now, because those who gain knowledge without wisdom are failures. The wise use education to enlighten and uplift humanity. They do not stoop to petty retaliations."

So I resolved to try to win the respect of the prejudiced students, to do all within my power to prevent my color from being a barrier, hoping to make friends instead of enemies.

Lighthearted I carried on my school work with diligence and perseverance.

Briefly I mention in this book the recognition I won in General Science. Instructor, faculty and student-body alike acknowledged that none of the other amateur scientists (irrespective of age, sex, race or color) could excel the record I held for stupidity.

Aimlessly I wandered around the laboratory watching everybody else experimenting with chemicals, and when in doubt as to how to conduct an experiment of my own, idly mixed liquids without a formula, content to make "pretty color combinations." I had a formula, of course. Everybody had one. But mine did not seem to make sense.

Though I lacked ability in some studies, I never lacked ambition. I always liked school and enjoyed it.

Music continued to be my favorite study. Besides the regular school program and additional hours of orchestra practice, I received private violin instructions twice a week.

Time slipped by.

Health failed. My heart was weak, the doctor said, and demanded that I leave school for a while.

I became a shut-in. Classmates, White and Colored, came to see me. They brought flowers, candy and magazines. They promised to stop by every day and cheer me. Their intentions were good, but they were healthy and strong, and the out-of-doors beckoned them. Gradually their visits became less and less frequent. Finally I heard their gay laughter only, as they hurried to and from school—and it saddened me.

Weeks passed into months.

It was during the dull days of convalescence that I discovered a world seldom explored by the youthful until suffering or sorrow comes to them—the World of Solitude.

Propped in a Morris-chair I gazed out the living-room windows and counted passers-by; watched the shadows of camphor tree boughs upon the front walk, a lame cat limping across the street, smoke coiling from a chimney; listened to the song of a bird, the hum of rising winds, the plaintive murmur of the sea.

But I was unhappy because hidden in the deep recesses of my mind were thoughts of school, my violin, the orchestra.

I read books, magazines and newspapers until I grew weary. But one day Mother called my attention to a column in the local paper, The Morning Press. The editor of the column, Grace May North, criticized stories sent in by boys and girls, accepted the best and the paper published them.

"Why don't you try writing an interesting story," Mother suggested. "It will make the time fly faster."

But I did not want to try to write stories. I wanted to take my violin out of its case and play.

"There's nothing to write about," I sighed. "I can't go anywhere and see interesting things."

Mother feigned disappointment. "That's too bad," she said, shaking her head. "There's a prize of one whole dollar for the boy or girl who sends in the best story. I thought you might like to earn money yourself and surprise your father by saving it to buy the new violin strings you'll need when you go back to school. But of course if you're not industrious ——"

Thoughts raced through my mind.

One whole dollar? New violin strings? Not industrious? I asked for paper and pencils.

That was how I began to create plots, to perceive beauty in simple things, to see more of the supposed-to-be invisible, to hear more of the seemingly inaudible.

The next time I observed passers-by I wondered: Where were they going? Why should some walk with heads held high while others plodded along dejected and slow of step? The next time I watched the shadows of the camphor boughs upon the front walk, I visualized puppets performing a fantastic dance. The next time I saw thin grey smoke coiling from a chimney, I imagined it a stray spiral of silver-grey fog. And when again I chanced to see a lame cat limping across the street, I magnified its size until it became a wounded jungle lion escaping capture by a hunter. I learned to interpret messages from the song of a bird; to hear an anthem in the hum of rising winds, a dirge in the plaintive murmur of the sea.

I submitted a child's story and was awarded a prize. This encouraged me. Thereafter, every time I won a dollar Father gave me five to put in the bank.

At last I was able to go back to school. However, strenuous exercise having been forbidden, I could not take part in games or athletics, and I found myself set apart from

116

the other students. Recreation-periods were lonely. It seemed as if my companions had travelled ahead of me during my absence—far down a long, long road—too far to hear should I call.

Quite unexpectedly gates leading to happiness were opened for me; swung wide by the teacher who taught the preparatory-High-School course in Music Appreciation.

This is how it happened.

This teacher was a dreamer. She sang songs and taught students how to sing them. Sometimes she played accompaniments on a guitar. Sometimes she put records on a phonograph, telling us to concentrate our listening power.

One day she played a recording that we had never heard before. Our lesson assignment was to describe the pictures impressed upon our minds by the inspiring music. Many White students complained. It was not easy, they said, to see or hear imaginary things.

My turn came. In the quick ascending succession of a harp's harmonic tones I had seen and heard the flutter of wings as birds sought the shelter of their nests before a storm; and in violins playing pizzicato had heard not an ordinary hail-storm, but a White rhapsody in frozen raindrops.

After this, the teacher taught me many wonderful things about music. She began by teaching me the art of playing a phonograph, saying that it was not as easy as some people thought, and taught me to listen for the breath-marks in vocal selections so that if compelled to cease playing a record before it was finished the song would not be abruptly interrupted. She taught me to lift a phonograph needle gently so as not to mar the surface of a fine record. She gave me books to read—biographies of great composers.

117

Once she said: "Come—I have friends whom I want you to meet."

I wondered where she planned to take me. But we did not go any place. She just took me by the hand, walked round the room and directed my attention to pictures bordering the walls—the likenesses of men and women of music genius. They represented various nationalities and spoke different tongues, but she said music was the one language they all understood.

"These are my friends," she told me. "I want them to be yours. The voices of the immortals will speak to you through the compositions they play and the songs they sing. But you, Elizabeth, must be willing to shut your eyes and ears to the distractions and disturbances of the world and patiently listen."

I took her advice.

Pictures and recordings of composers, operatic singers and other musicians became my companions and my friends.

Every noon hour I spent beside the phonograph. Had the teacher not been such a dreamer she would have insisted upon my staying out in the fresh air and sunshine, instead she granted me the special privilege of playing recordings throughout the entire lunch-period.

By combining music and imagination it became increasingly easy for me to see the room transformed into old music-masters' studios, opera-houses and concert-stages.

That is how I found new channels that led to old worlds wherein Beethoven, Mozart, Bach and Haydn composed masterpieces ordained to live forever. I listened to the singing of Caruso, Schumann-Heink, Galli-Curci, Farrar and other operatic stars. I imagined I saw the Pyramids and Temples of Memphis in Verdi's opera *Aïda*, the Temple of the Grail in Wagner's sacred *Parsifal*, the chapel scene

118

in the operatic miracle play, *The Juggler of Notre Dame*, in which the Holy Virgin blesses the youthful monk of humble piety. My favorite opera being *Il Trovatore*, I used to play the *Miserere* repeatedly to hear the solemn tolling of the bell and the deep-toned chorus of priests chanting a prayer that Heaven show mercy to the doomed prisoner, Manrico.

Almost before I knew it I had lost sight of the modern world. When girls of my own age chatted incessantly about the latest fashions, their language was foreign to me. So far as I was concerned my current interests dated with young Schubert home on a visit from the school of the court-choir, quartet-playing with his father and brothers about the year 1809; Chopin, at the age of eight, playing a Gryowetz concerto in 1818; Liszt, as a boy, giving concerts in Vienna in 1822.

Occasionally I spent Saturday afternoon at the home of a Colored classmate. Other afternoons and evenings Mother and I enjoyed together. Sometimes we made candy or popped pop-corn. On retiring I went to sleep with the echo of the recorded strains of the violin-mastery of Jascha Heifetz, Fritz Kreisler, or Mischa Elman in my ears.

My fifteenth birthday was a happy one. Father celebrated it with us.

"Just a few weeks more," he said, "and I'll be home to stay."

Morning dawned . . . the morning Father was to come home. The March sky was cloudless. The sun shone brightly. The air was crisp and permeated with the salt of the sea.

Mother and I busied ourselves here, there, and everywhere about the house.

Father's favorite books were on a table within easy

119

reach of his big chair. A new smoking-jacket, a surprise for him, hung in his clothes closet.

Lunch was ready. How homey it looked to see the table set for *three*.

The ringing of the telephone annoyed us. It was almost train time.

"Of all the times for somebody to call—" I began, picking up my hat as I went to answer it.

I removed the receiver. A friend's voice could be heard speaking in short, jerky, unfinished sentences, saying something about Father: *illness—sudden—come at once.*

Shocked we began nervously packing.

Somebody rang the door bell. Mother signed for a telegram. Opened the yellow envelope. Read silently.

Her face betrayed the truth . . . the long-distance telephone call had come first to soften the blow.

My father was dead.

The funeral over, Mother and I returned to Santa Barbara.

We tried not to speak of Father—just to remember that he had gone to sleep one night, and while he slept the phantom Death anchored its ship for a few seconds, then lifted anchor and sailed away carrying him as a passenger to the Land Beyond the Horizon.

The table was set again. I sat in Father's chair at one end of the table just as he had sat when on visits home.

I was accustomed to silences. But now—the silence of the house had a different quality from other silences.

Scarcely had one week elapsed after our sorrow before Mother had a confidential, practical talk with me. I cried because her words sounded cold, down-to-earth, matter-of-fact.

"We are alone now, my dear," she began as if stepping forward to assume grave responsibilities. "From this day

120

forward you must become self-reliant and prepare to face the world. If I should die ——"

I flung my arms about my Mother's neck and clung to her. I could not bear the thought.

Mother, unyielding in her determination to speak frankly, continued:

"If I should die before you are grown, you would suffer much because you are a dreamer. You have had the affection of parents—the protective seclusion of a home. The world would be cruel—relentless ——"

"We—we have friends," I stammered.

Mother sighed. "We have friends," she confirmed. "But circumstances have been such that we have not had to ask favors, therefore their friendship has never been put to a test."

The next day she took me with her to see the family attorney. She signed papers. He explained the data on the papers in simplified terms to me, then asked:

"Now, do you understand that in the event of your Mother's demise you're to notify me at once?"

Mother never troubled friends with her burdens. She lived through crucial experiences and sorrows silently.

"Learn the value of silence," she advised me. "It keeps friends friendly, and enemies never know where to strike."

And so when people began making inquiry as to what would become of me if anything happened to her, I said nothing. No one other than the attorney and ourselves knew that I would have been sent to a Colored girls' boarding school, there to remain until I was of age.

Facing life together united Mother and daughter in mind, heart and soul. Sometimes we sat by the hour watching the surf beat upon the beach until the sun, like a coppery-disc, sank from sight; then turned homeward, walking slowly in the soft light of a lavender-iris eventide.

121

One day we saw a star fall. Believe me, it was day—not night: the day the doctor said that I had developed a "rhythmic heart"—that it might be years before I outgrew the condition—that I should give up the idea of a strenuous concert career.

Strange that even while the doctor gave his report I should hear music . . . but I did . . . wild, weird music that gathered tempo and reverberated like thunder and burst into a crashing tempest of sound . . . stopped abruptly . . . then was heard no more . . . like a fragment of an unfinished symphony.

I put my violin away, and the dream of becoming a concert violinist followed the trail of the fallen star.

Dreary days followed.

On graduation day Mother gave me the wristwatch she and Father had promised would be mine at that time.

I left Santa Barbara Junior High School with friends among faculty and students.

Two teachers other than the one who taught Music Appreciation, remain outstanding in my memory: Mr. Curtis Stewart, an advocator of classic literature, who suggested that I study to become a writer, and try to make known to the world the unrealized dreams hidden in the souls of the people of my race; and Mr. John Hall, director of the orchestra who said, on learning of my unhappiness in giving up a musical career: "When one star falls from your dream-heaven—do not despair, for another will appear."

And so I waited and watched, and gradually began to glimpse a new star twinkling faintly in the distant heavens. I have learned since that this same Star shone centuries ago . . . and that Three Wise Men followed it to a manger in Bethlehem.

CHAPTER NINE

The Quest

I BEGAN to consider religion seriously. Memories of the one Good Friday service that I had witnessed at the Old Mission still lingered with me. I knew I wanted to be a Catholic. But as Mother was grief-stricken I would not burden her by mentioning that which Father and I had disagreed upon.

I tried to content myself by finding another church as a substitute, and eventually found one similar to the Catholic; a quiet edifice with candle-lighted altar, and stained glass windows.

Though I had always been identified with a Colored congregation, this one being White did not make me self-conscious, as my thoughts were not centered upon its members but upon the religious service. I never spoke to anybody. However, the clergyman noticed that every Sunday morning at seven o'clock a dark lamb knelt in the midst of his fleecy white flock. One morning as I was leaving he addressed me.

"You come alone to church every Sunday, Child, have you no parents?"

I had never talked much to ministers, not even those of my own race. I told him that I liked the quietude of the church. He smiled kindly and offered to give me two books to read which I accepted; one a book of prayers—the other entitled *The Holy Eucharist*.

I read both books from cover to cover, then asked

123

Mother's permission to join the "new church." I became a member of it and succeeded in interesting Mother to do likewise.

Dogmas meant nothing to me, and I never gave any thought as to who founded a church or why. I only wanted a quiet place in which to pray, believing the serenity would assuage our grief.

Shortly afterward we moved to another town, located a church of the same denomination, and presented our letters from the former pastor.

Determined to be steadfast in the faith, I faithfully observed Sunday worship. In his sermons the clergyman often pictured Jesus Christ hanging on the Cross.

"Jesus died to save all mankind!" he preached zealously.

He laid stress upon the terrible sin of missing Sunday worship unless hindered by serious causes: and his sermons convinced me that I had committed grievous wrong by not wanting to attend church in the past. I even decided that I had something to repent over, and often closed my eyes, prayed, and told God that I was sorry that I had not loved Him sufficiently to go to church some mornings instead of staying at home to read the "funny papers." And when I heard the clergyman tell the congregation that it was wrong to visit other churches, I decided to believe that too. No human being ever tried to be more sincere in adhering to church rules than I.

Mother and I never attended any social affairs at the church or had any desire to, because the group was White. If there had been a Colored church of this particular denomination we would have worshiped there. In order to have social contact with our own race Mother suggested that we visit the Colored Methodist church gatherings on Sunday evenings.

Conflict tortured my soul. How could we be faithful

members if we wandered from the fold? The clergyman had said that God disapproved of such infidelity. Believing this, the only solution of the problem was to abandon the idea.

One Sunday morning, the sun's rays blazed against the stained glass windows, the organ played soft music, white candles burned on the altar, and Mother and I knelt at the altar-rail to receive Holy Communion. As I looked up to gaze at the cross and thank God for the gift of Communion I beheld a strange sight. The clergyman was wiping the Chalice where my lips had touched it, briskly polishing it as though it were tarnished. Then turning the Chalice round he served the White communicant kneeling beside me.

Thoughts are like birds; they can wing their way speedily. The thought came to my mind like a newspaper headline: "RACE PREJUDICE AT THE ALTAR!" Then I became terrified: how could I think such a thought at such a holy time and in such a holy place? I begged God to forgive me. I spent the following week asking forgiveness.

Next Sunday, the same thing happened. In serving Communion from White to Colored the Chalice was not wiped, but from Colored to White he paused, polished it briskly as before that all might see and then proceeded.

I did not say anything to Mother. She did not say anything to me. But during the next week the White clergyman called to see us. He stated his mission, tears filling his eyes and streaming down his cheeks. He informed us that White communicants did not wish to kneel at the altar with Negroes . . . he regretted having to tell us . . . he hoped that we would not hate him . . . but he had to make a living. . . . White people contributed so

125

much to the church . . . he had more White parishioners than Colored.

Mother told him she was sorry that our presence had caused disturbance and assured him that we would not attend the church again, and reassured him that we would not hate him.

After delivering his message he went his way.

In a meditative fashion Mother said: "We must not think unkindly of the minister—or the congregation." She next added that since the incident had occurred, so far as she was concerned, I could use my own judgment in selecting a spiritual path.

I wondered: What about God—dogmas and creeds? What about the theory that God was displeased if a member of one denomination visited another church? What about the theory of regular church attendance? There were no Colored churches of that denomination in the town: what then was a Colored person supposed to do? What sort of a God would lay down' a lot of rules and then not make a way for them to be observed?

Lost in a maze of retrospection, I recalled that some of the Colored students who were neither Methodist nor Baptist had, from time to time, told me stories of race-discrimination that I had refused to believe. One girl had said that she joined a church and the White parishioners refused to recognize her as a member and asked her to leave. Another girl had said that she knew some Colored people who had had a similar experience. Both girls had laughed about the incidents. But I had responded angrily: "You are mis-judging White people. They do not do such things." And the girls had sneered: "Go on taking up for White people. Someday they'll show you what's really in their hearts."

Now that I had experienced being turned out of the

126

House of God, I had reason to believe there could be truth in the girls' stories.

Doubts crept in from the blind confusion of my thoughts. I doubted God's justice, I doubted His love for the Colored race.

I can remember shrugging my shoulders, thinking: "Oh well, I never liked church anyway—guess I made a mistake bothering about religion."

I never set foot in the church again. I passed by though, a couple of Sunday mornings, and heard the congregation singing, singing hymns of praise to the Almighty.

Mother had planned to spend fall and winter in Santa Monica, a beach town; and as fall was almost upon us, my trend of thought was infused with the joyousness of registering in Santa Monica High School.

For a long time I tried to avoid thinking of religion or mentioning it. But I found this an impossibility. . . .

As I was a stranger in the community the Colored students invited me to visit their churches. And, believe it or not, so did some of the White.

Never once did I refer to the race-discrimination endured in the past. Whenever anyone made inquiry about my church affiliation I casually remarked: "I do not belong to any church." But I soon stopped this because some students tried to "convert" me. I listened patiently to their impromptu lectures. I never argued. Because I had nothing to say they thought me a "stubborn, rebellious sinner."

One White girl told me that I could never expect a blessing, never expect any good to come to me until I "repented and believed" and went faithfully to church, adding that without going to church no one could be "saved."

Where, I asked myself, had I heard that before?

Realizing that the Colored students would consider me

127

unfriendly unless I accepted their invitations to go "unto a house of worship" I had to visit their churches. This of course brought on the ordeal of living through older people telling me to "get salvation."

After a while I grew weary of going to some church just to be "in vogue spiritually."

I made up my mind to find out everything I wanted to know about God if it took me the rest of my life. I was dissatisfied with the opinion I had formed of God. I certainly considered Him a God for the White Race—and decided that unless I could be convinced that His Son's death for the redemption of all people included the Colored, I could put my time to better use than praying to One Who heard only the fair of skin. If God was just and did love the Colored race—then by not trying to solve the problem of how to serve Him I would miss the benefit of His help.

While looking up some reference data at the public library I found some books written by a priest named Father Finn. They were children's stories but one in particular attracted me because it bore the title: *By Thy Love And Thy Grace*. Reading it revived the thought that the only church I had really ever wanted to join was the Catholic. It also gave me information about something I knew nothing of, the confessional.

A confessional, I learned, was built like a little closet. It had three sections. A priest sat in the center and penitents knelt on either side. Partitions with small curtained gratings separated the three sections. A priest could hear those who confessed, but could not see them.

What an ideal place, I thought, to ask questions about God. I could not be seen, therefore no one would ever know that I was Colored. No—I would never ring a doorbell and face a White clergyman. I was afraid the door would be closed in my face. But the confessional was dark . . . and I was dark. No one could see me.

Since the majority of Colored ministers were Methodist and Baptist I did not think they could be of help in solving my particular problem. The confessional idea seemed the best course to take, but I lacked courage. Only God knows the fears in a Negro's heart.

One day I met two nuns in the library. One of them smiled, and as she stood near me she looked at the author's name on the book in my hand and then asked if I were a Catholic. I told her no. She did not turn away but continued the conversation. Her pleasing smile and sweet personality made me wish to know her better. By the time I left the library I had an invitation to call at the convent and see her.

Obtaining Mother's permission I called.

The moment I crossed the convent threshold I was impressed by the tranquillity of the interior. Religious paintings, exquisitely carved statuary and fragrant flowers adorned the parlor wherein I waited. Sister Mary Mercedes greeted me with true friendliness. We talked of books and school.

I had no knowledge of Religious Orders. She explained that the Community to which she belonged was made up of Sisters who taught school and was known as the Holy Names Order.

When I was ready to go she showed me the chapel. Pausing before a statue she lowered her voice so as not to break the silence rudely: "This is a statue of Our Blessed Mother," she whispered. "She is your heavenly Mother, Elizabeth, and loves you. She will always help you."

I noticed that in the center of the altar there was something shaped like a miniature house—a tiny house with-

129

out windows but two closed doors. This she explained was called a Tabernacle.

"Our Lord is present in the Blessed Sacrament," Sister whispered. "If you are ever in doubt, in trouble, beset by worries, go to a Catholic church, kneel before the Tabernacle and He will hear your prayers."

For days I dreamt of the visit to the convent. But one thought kept revolving in my mind: "Don't be foolish. Remember White Christians told you about God once before. Don't run the risk of being turned out again."

In meeting more young people of my race I discovered that not just a few but many had been subjected to segregation in churches. One young man, boasting of several baptisms in different denominations said:

"There's nothing to religion. Every time I tried to find the Light White Christians threw me right back into the pit of darkness. Now I don't believe in anything."

Another told me: "White people want the whole world and God too. Let them keep God—but get your share of the worldly goods before they beat you to it."

After hearing these things, I withdrew from the young people. I withdrew from the elderly. I withdrew from White people. I withdrew from Colored people. I withdrew from Protestants. I withdrew from Catholics. . . .

I went to the Religious Reading Room of the Santa Monica Public Library. There I secluded myself after school hours. There I sought to find the Christ.

And I came upon a book written by a man named Henry Van Dyke. And in the book were many poems. But one he had written for souls like myself and called it *The Toiling of Felix*. It began:

"Brother-men who look for Jesus, long to see Him close
    and clear,

Hearken to the tale of Felix, how he found the Master
near.

Born in Egypt, 'neath the shadow of the crumbling gods
of night,
He forsook the ancient darkness, turned his young heart
toward the Light.

Seeking Christ, in vain he waited for the vision of the
Lord;
Vainly pondered many volumes where the creeds of men
were stored;

Vainly shut himself in silence, keeping vigil night and
day;
Vainly haunted shrines and churches where the Christians came to pray."

And reading on I learned that Felix sought the Christ
everywhere but not until he had labored among the com-
mon-folk and helped his fellowmen did he find and see
Him as:

"Through the dimness of the temple slowly dawned a
mystic light;
There the Master stood in glory, manifest to mortal
sight."

In preference to wasting time listening to people broadcast scandals about Protestant clergymen or evangelists
or Catholic priests or nuns, I selected the companionship
of good books and walked in the company of the
valiant. . . .

I read the life of Rose Hawthorne Lathrop, younger
daughter of the great writer, Nathaniel Hawthorne, a

131

convert to the Catholic faith who, inspired by Christ, opened an impromptu hospital for cancer patients too ill and destitute to support themselves; who later forsook the world, became a Religious and was known as Mother Alphonsa, foundress of the refuge for the cancer-poor, Rosary Hill Home.

I read the life of the Anglican nurse, Florence Nightingale, who had followed the Son of God "forth to War"; and in thought walked beside her at the Crimea and at Scutari. And a spark from the bright flame burning in her lamp of dauntless courage kindled the smouldering coals of hope struggling within my own soul.

In spirit I sailed on a vessel twice to the dread-isle of Molokai where crippled, mutilated and sore-infected lepers were isolated.

On the first trip I saw a young follower of Christ taking census of eight hundred of the outcasts—he who had exiled himself to work among them as priest, physician and teacher—Father Damien DeVeuster.

And on the second trip in spirit, I saw him, years hence, a weary soul, beginning a sermon to the outcasts with the words: "We lepers"—knowing that he would die in the Service of Christ, a victim of the plague.

And so I found consolation and gained courage as all do who walk in the company of the valiant.

Sister Mary Mercedes' advice did not go unheeded. I found a Catholic church and prayed at the altar when the church was empty. But the scorching brand of race-discrimination had left its mark; and at times I doubted that the prayer would be answered because of my color. Always I could hear a thought-voice reminding: "Remember what happened the last time you sought God."

Hoping to find out how the Negro ranked in the Catholic church I obtained a copy of a Negro magazine that listed

132

all the religious denominations that had exhibited racial prejudice. My heart sank when I read: "The Roman Catholic Church of America owes the American Negro an apology."

That meant that somewhere, at some time, either in schools or churches, some among my people had suffered humiliation because of segregation.

Well, I reasoned, if some members of the Church that claimed to be the One True Church treated Negroes unkindly—why belong to it?

The book, *Wonder Works of Lourdes,* stood out among books in the public library. I read it. Who can read this book and doubt the presence of Christ in the Blessed Sacrament? It described the thousands of pilgrims who prayed annually at this famous shrine. All were not Catholic, all were not White. Here the blind waited for The Light. The crippled and diseased hoped to be cured. Priests chanted prayers: "Hosanna to the Son of David! Blessed is He that cometh in the Name of the Lord!" A procession of the Blessed Sacrament wended its way through the crowds. All were not healed in body—some only in spirit. But faith was a living thing at Lourdes!

There in the public library with the Wonder Works of Lourdes and the Negro Magazine I made the final decision: I would continue the quest.

Saturday afternoon found me at the Catholic church. I went into a confessional and knelt down. I did not know what to say—but at least I had the satisfaction of knowing that I was making a brave effort to find a church home.

The inner shutter slid back. I heard a voice asking: "How long since your last confession?"

As I had never made a confession I merely replied: "Father—I am not a Catholic."

133

Evidently the priest thought his hearing had failed him. He asked me to repeat the statement. I repeated it.

"You *are not* a Catholic?" he questioned.

"No, Father!"

My voice grew a little weaker, but I had one consolation. He did not know that I was Colored. I would not be asked out because my skin was black.

He offered to pray for me, but explained that Absolution could be granted only to a Catholic.

I thanked him and went my way, somewhat disappointed though, as I had anticipated hearing him quote a passage from a spiritual book.

Determined to find a spiritual guide I returned to church on a Christmas eve—one of the busiest times of the year. Long lines of penitents waited. I, too, waited—looking as somber as the rest of them.

In the confessional I announced my presence as before. The priest, a zealous-sounding man, suggested that I join the convert class.

Remembering that I was Colored—I muttered something about being very busy—too busy to study.

"I cannot give you Absolution," he said. "But I can give you a blessing."

I wondered if I dared to state my problem—to say that I was Colored.

When he stepped outside the confessional I asked him to bless a rosary. He did not appear very courteous. After the blessing of the rosary, I journeyed on.

At times I decided to give up the quest. And I know that I would have done so had it not been for one who gave me courage—one to whom I turned in desperation. When I told her my story, revealing how the effects of race-discrimination in the religious world had caused me to doubt God and human beings, she spoke to me in the

134

eloquent language of Silence. Intuitively I knew that she understood my problem—Mary, the Mother of the Crucified Christ.

And I know that it was the "Mother Invisible" who guided my footsteps to a confessional where a very saintly priest told me that though non-Catholics were supposed to study in the convert class, if I had a reason for not wishing to attend one at the present, he would gladly advise me spiritually in the confessional.

Gradually my confidence in God and in human beings was restored.

During my last year in High School studies occupied every moment of my time. The only chance I had to study religion was in Physiology class. This being the one subject in which I had absolutely no interest, I spent the class-period composing religious questionnaires and passing them to the Italian girl (a devout Catholic) with whom I shared a desk.

Julia Campiglia was an ideal Catholic. But she never talked about her religion unless questioned.

Poor girl! She certainly was questioned after meeting me. I wrote:

"Dear Julia—tell me something about the service known as Benediction?"

"Julia—are there as many candles on an altar for a Solemn High Mass as for a Low Mass?"

"Julia—*take your time answering*—the teacher is watching me—has an idea, I think, that I'm not studying."

While Julia wrote the answers I "scribbled" poetry.

When the time came for the final test I knew a great deal about Catholicism but little about the human structure.

135

The hour for the test arrived.

Julia began to write. I began to worry. She felt sorry for me. I felt sorry for myself. She moved her paper toward me. I nodded my thanks.

The next day, the instructor called me to his desk.

"Though your daily grades have been poor, your examination grade is excellent. How do you account for such a marvelous test paper?"

I faced the inevitable. "I cheated, sir."

Mr. Knupp wanted to know why I had never taken an interest in the subject.

Though I knew that this teacher was a deeply religious man of the Protestant faith, I found it impossible to explain that I had been climbing ladders to the heavens.

"Because you've honestly admitted that you cheated, I'll give you another chance to make good," he offered.

I sat up all night studying physiology. Next day I passed the second test without Julia's aid and received what I deserved, a low grade.

Mr. Knupp was understanding. "You'll never find your life's work in the field of science," he smiled. "You are poetic."

No one other than Julia ever knew that the religious world held attraction for me. Teachers thought that I had dramatic and literary talent that should be developed. All through High School I looked forward to a stage career.

I was placed in the special gymnasium class under the capable supervision of Miss Rhea Featherston. As I was numbered among the "heart cases," rest had been prescribed. But I kept the class in something of an uproar. I played harmless pranks on the others and danced jigs behind Miss Featherston's back. But had it not been for

136

her patience and kindness when I suffered serious heart attacks on the campus, I might never have fully recovered.

A week before commencement the girls' vice-principal, Miss Ethel Robinson, called me into her office. My conversation with her is always something that will linger in my memory; it is a precious proof of the faculty's deep concern for a Negro student's future. Indeed, her good wishes and advice, along with those of another vice-principal, Mr. Nathan Shutt, were on the very edge of my mind commencement-night when the diplomas were handed out. In my heart was the desire to go out into the world and make good and thus reward those who had done so much for me.

But at last High School days were over. Mother's graduation gift to me was permission to become a Catholic. I had sought and I had found.

CHAPTER TEN

Torch in My Hand

Mother wanted me to go to college. But as unwise investments had resulted in a financial set-back, disrupting the security of our home, I deemed it necessary to seek employment until we could adjust our affairs.

Mr. Philip Stevens, my Journalism instructor, who seldom wrote letters of recommendation, had given me one hoping that I might secure a job as cub-reporter for a newspaper.

And so—my first adventure out in the world let me to a surburban newspaper office.

The editor, an alert, business-like newspaper man was conscientious but plainly outspoken.

"We use syndicated features so that excludes your chance for feature-writing. And as much as I'd like to hire you as a reporter, it's impossible. Your color's a handicap."

Then he gave me advice. "Give up the idea of a career. Marry while you're young. Raise a family. The average Colored newspaper can't afford to place a large percentage of ambitious young Colored folk like yourself. And a White press can't risk hiring you because of prejudice. So you haven't a chance."

I tried to tell him that I was not a haughty Colored person; that I was willing to write in a cellar and that if he thought the stories good he could publish them under a White reporter's name.

138

When I said that he lowered his eyes to the floor, and when he began talking again the tone of his voice sounded as if he had a cold in his throat.

"I once read about a great leader of your race," he said slowly. "Booker T. Washington was his name. He began his career humbly—by sweeping a floor. But I had no idea that Colored youth of today would consent to start life the lowly way."

He stopped talking for a second or two, then looked at me and shook his head. The next time he spoke his voice sounded as if the cold in his throat was growing worse and that he might not be able to finish saying what he had in mind.

All he said was: "I wonder why God made you Colored and gave you ideals!"

I laughed. "Being Colored isn't so difficult, Sir, if one has the right outlook on life."

The editor argued. "White girls have a hard time making the grade. Colored ones are foolish to try. If you weren't Colored, I could let you start out as a reporter. Mr. Stevens has only sent two other graduates here. They were poor, had to work their way to the top. They've made good. I'd like to help you but ——"

"I don't intend to let *color* stand in my way. Don't you see, if one isn't supersensitive ——"

But the editor was not listening. He suddenly seemed to remember something important that he had almost forgotten and picking up some copy from his desk politely bowed me out of his office.

At the door I hesitated. "If—if ever the prejudiced subscribers move away," I faltered. "Will you let me be a reporter then?"

"Yes, indeed," he said, bowing his head up and down several times in succession.

"Come back a year from now. Maybe conditions will have changed."

Then he closed the door.

Although that door had closed I looked forward to the opening of another as Mr. Stevens had written also to a prominent Colored magazine editor, confident that he would be eager to help one of his own race.

The secretary to the Colored editor sent me a letter: her employer was vacationing; I could expect a prompt reply as soon as he returned.

That was in 1928. This is 1942. The Colored editor must have taken a walking tour to Africa and adjoining jungle territory and finally homesteaded a hut in the wilds as up to date I have not received his communication.

But good fortune favored me. A Santa Monica author, Mrs. Sorensen, employed me part time as a typist. With her, my color was no barrier. She lived in a poet's realm where the dust of race prejudice never drifted. This opportunity made up for my disappointment over being denied the newspaper job.

Between intervals of work I visited Catholic churches and convents. The silent atmosphere never depressed me as I was more accustomed to quietude than gaiety.

One day I met the priest whose voice had guided me— a highly intelligent person, deeply spiritual and eminently kind. On learning that I had sought the confessional as a refuge from race-prejudice his interest in my spiritual progress increased. His inspiring talks helped to shatter the fear of prejudice and instilled assurance. He gave me books—not just prayer books, but books to improve my writing. His implicit faith in me and in my determination to reach a high goal was to me like lamplight on a dark path. He it was who convinced me that God was no respecter of persons—that His graces were not limited to

140

those fair of skin. And in time I came to realize that this priest was worthy of being compared to the grand teachers at school who had befriended me—that he had a white soul and so fine a spirit that his aspirations and ideals soared above the standards of the prejudiced of his race. And I promised him that I would strive to follow the Christ though stoned by persecution; that I would strive also to succeed in the world so that he, as well as my teachers, might never have just cause to regret having placed confidence in one whose skin was dark.

Thus I pay tribute to my first Spiritual Director who once said: "Remember, Child, though the world may segregate you to a hill-top, God can lift you to mountain-heights. When every door is shut in your face go to the Blessed Mother Mary, and She will wrap you within the sheltering folds of Her mantle and shield your soul from harm."

In time friends induced Mother to place her membership in another Protestant church. She did not ask that I join it, but expressed her unhappiness at the thought of going to services without me.

Though I had looked forward to becoming a Catholic, I put aside my own wishes and joined the denomination with her. With a heavy heart I explained this to the Spiritual Director.

"I still believe in you, Child," he said. "No young person would come faithfully to this confessional every Saturday unless sincere. Continue saying your prayers and keep faith."

I did. I ceased grieving. I said a *Hail Mary* when I walked into the other church and believed that the Blessed Mother would provide a way for me to become a Catholic.

A reader may wonder why I followed in my mother's

footsteps as she had not commanded me to. Herewith I explain my reason.

I had been trained by my father always to consider my mother's happiness; to love her devotedly—and to build an invulnerable wall between myself and anyone who dared propose that I ever be less devoted to her—and to look upon such an individual as an enemy.

In a book by a well known Negro author is a passage expressive of the devoted love of African mothers and their offspring for one another:

> "No mother can love more tenderly or be more deeply beloved than the Negro mother. 'Everywhere in Africa,' writes Mungo Park, 'I have noticed that no greater affront can be offered a Negro than insulting his mother.' 'Strike me!' cried a Mandingo to his enemy, 'but revile not my mother!' . . . The Herero swears 'By my mother's tears!' The Angola Negroes have a saying. 'As a mist lingers on the swamps, so lingers the love of father and mother.'"

Though I am not a native of Africa, but American born and surrounded by White civilization, my devotion to my earthly mother is akin to that of the African folk for their parents. My father's mother, having come from Madagascar to this country, had handed down to him certain tribal beliefs and customs of the dark people which she had forsaken to marry his father, a Christian American Negro. And he handed down to me the teaching that my mother's happiness should always be my first consideration.

I respected the priest who directed me because when I explained these things to him he comprehended my love for my parent. Had he not, I might never have returned again to his confessional for advice.

After a while, Mother noticing how bored I was with

142

the services, suggested that I accept the religion of my choice, and I entered the convert class at the Catholic church nearest home.

Father Michael Browne, the director, was well qualified to teach young people. He possessed a cheerful disposition, patience, and willingness to answer questions.

The other converts-to-be were not Colored, but very congenial. Some however were reluctant to believe in saints empowered by God to assist mortals spiritually. The fact that I harbored no doubts was neither remarkable nor mysterious. Had not my father taught me from childhood to see the unseen? Therefore I found no reason to disbelieve in Saint Anthony's miraculous power to find lost articles for people of earth—after all I had once believed that Pan (described in the book of Greek Mythology) found stray sheep and returned them to shepherds; and Purgatory was scarcely unbelievable when I compared it to the Lower World where Pluto reigned and the souls of men were confined after death!

Father Browne baptized the class on a Saturday. Sunday morning we were present in a body at Mass.

The most sacred moment of moments approached. . . . The Consecration . . . and through the stupendous miracle of Transubstantiation the White Host became Christ in the Blessed Sacrament!

The afternoon of the same day we were confirmed. We left church after promising Father Browne to cling to the sacred teachings of our Holy Faith. I especially was grateful to him as he had taken a sincere interest in my religious instruction.

It was not long before I stood in need of the sustaining graces derived from the Sacraments. Mother's health failed completely. Our family physician prescribed rest and cessation from worry as the only hope for her recovery.

"I regret having to tell you this," the doctor told me. "I know how much your Mother means to you. It'll be a long, long time before she can paint or do any active work again. As you're none too strong, you'll have to be careful and not exceed your strength trying to earn a living."

I secured more typing from writers. . . .

Writers! Writers! Writers! Some were temperamental, some erratic, some morbid, some witty, some foolish—the majority just plain crazy.

They disliked any interference with the papers cluttering their desks. All claimed to be writing the "year's best seller." They wrote and re-wrote. Publishers sent frequent letters to remind them that their manuscripts were behind schedule—sometimes they sent telegrams. But the writers contended that it was impossible to rush the completion of masterpieces.

The writers liked me. I catered to their whims: answered when spoken to, typed when ordered to, racked my brains to comply with requests for "a clever idea," and sat as motionless as a mummy while they juggled words into plots. Apparently I never tired hearing a story read and re-read; laughed at whatever was supposed to be humorous; widened my eyes like a dark hoot-owl when the villain crept stealthily through the house and shivered when the ghosts in their mystery plays walked.

As compensation for my appreciation of their genius a few offered to dedicate books in my honor. Others guaranteed to pay me "back salary" on receipt of royalties to be collected *after they had completed their books and found a publisher!* Not many were like Mrs. Sorensen— non-temperamental, systematic, and prompt in payment.

During my last year at High School Mother had put painting aside temporarily and worked as matron at one

144

of the beach theatres. When she resigned because of ill health, the manager let me take her place.

"You're only nineteen," he said. "That's almost too young to know how to be tactful with irritable patrons. But I'll let you take over. Tell everybody you're just substituting."

I can see myself now, that first evening I reported for duty, a frail shadow of a Colored girl wearing a trim black uniform, a dainty apron with strings tied in a perky bow, a frill in my hair.

Night after night I worked at the theatre.

Serving in the capacity of maid I discovered that a large number of women theatre-goers were unable to sit through a picture in which tragedies occurred similar to those encountered in their own lives. Women whose marriages had been thwarted by the death of sweethearts could not bear to witness a handsome movie-idol's screen-demise. Mothers whose babes had died in infancy wept copiously over scenes that brought to mind past bereavement. A picture with a religious theme sometimes had the same effect upon individuals as a sermon. They confessed their sins in my presence and resolved to forsake all evil. Pictures portraying the mental anguish of unhappy wives delighted many of the maiden ladies who expressed thanks to Providence for having endowed them with sense enough to escape being bound by the ties of matrimony.

As women re-lived sad experiences and unburdened their souls to me, I found myself coping with the tremendous task of competing with my mother's reputation as "an understanding soul."

One night a cantankerous old lady shouted at me from the foyer.

"Who're you?"

Stepping forward I explained the matron's absence.

145

"I liked that older Colored woman," she snapped. "She had sense. You're just a young filly."

I envisioned the loss of my job. . . .

With gliding ease I ascended the four steps to where the woman stood defiantly holding on to the iron railing which separated the lounge from the foyer.

I bowed my head slowly, then raised it slowly, saying: "Madame—I am sure you must be the charming lady of whom the manager has spoken."

Before she could catch her breath I placed her right hand on my left arm and guided her down the steps into the lounge.

"Don't let me fall!" she screeched as she relaxed her weight on my arm and I almost lost my balance.

The minute she sank into a leather cushioned chair I grabbed a small hassock and gently placed her feet upon it.

"Dear lady," I began, "the manager desires that every courtesy be shown you. I am at your service!"

Of a sudden the cantankerous old soul grinned. "Well —you're almost as nice as that Colored matron. Poor thing! Hope she doesn't die!"

I removed the ash-tray at her elbow. "I'm sure you disapprove of smoking, Madame."

She beamed. "You recognize a lady when you see one, don't you?"

As no other ladies were in the lounge I, too, grinned, answering: "Yes, Madame!"

She leaned forward. "How'd you happen to know who I am?"

I gulped. Did I dare be truthful? Did I dare say that the manager had warned: "Be on guard. There's a fault-finding old biddy who puffs like a porpoise and complains about everything. I'd like to break her neck!"

No. I did not dare reveal the manager's sentiments.

I tried to be evasive. The weather—what did she think of the weather? Was it too warm—too cold? But the old lady was persistent.

I told her the truth. . . .

"Madame, the manager described a lady who persistently advocates better performances, more efficient service and improvements to be made in this theatre."

This was the truth. Nothing but the truth. I saw, however, no reason to be as brutally frank as the manager.

Then said she: "You're a right nice little Colored maid. Much nicer than those White-upstart-usherettes. You know your place!"

I just bowed and smiled and smiled and bowed. She made an effort to rise and I dashed to her side, assisting her.

"Tell the manager," she puffed, "to see that brighter lights are put in the foyer and to install an elevator. My arthritis is getting worse. I won't be able to climb the stairs much longer."

I looked intelligent. "Bright lights and an elevator," I repeated parrot-fashion.

"That's right!"

As she stepped into the foyer she paused to question further.

"Are you married?"

"No, Madame."

Her head wig-wagged reproachfully. "Young as you are you wouldn't have this job if you weren't supporting a no-good husband and raising a batch of children."

"You're mistaken, Madame. I am not married!" I insisted.

"Don't argue," she snorted. "Serves you right to have to

work so hard after breaking your poor mother's heart by marrying so young!"

She reached into her purse. "Here! Don't waste this. Save it for a rainy day."

She placed money in my hand. I opened my mouth to speak. Silencing me with a gesture she waddled down the foyer.

I looked at the money.

Under the dim lights a brand new penny shed its brilliance in my palm.

A week later she returned.

Before I had a chance to greet her she surveyed the lounge with an approving glance, exclaiming: "Brighter lights at last! That manager's more obliging than I thought."

Knowing the light bulbs had not been changed I disappeared!

I made good at the theatre. . . .

One night the emergency bell rang. Hurriedly I ran downstairs carrying Aromatic Spirits of Ammonia, a glass of water and a damp towel.

A woman had fainted. Her husband, who was a physician, had been seeing the show with her. After she came to he suggested that she rest before going home. While waiting he questioned me.

"Had any hospital training?"

"No, Doctor."

"You'd make a splendid nurse," he said.

I did not reply. Recollections of my physiology grades caused me to feel rather faint myself.

"Maids usually have to make two or three trips to collect emergency paraphernalia," he added. "I think I'll speak to the manager about you."

On receipt of my next pay check I jumped for joy. A

148

raise had been given. There was an enclosed note which read something to the effect that ". . . the manager of this theatre is not unmindful of your efficiency, courtesy and diplomacy in dealing with patrons."

After that I used to just wait for somebody to faint and welcomed the cantankerous!

I enjoyed being a theatre-maid. There was never any dissension between the White usherettes and myself. They were a friendly group of young women. And when they found out that I was not sensitive about my color they bought a large box of candy for me and on the card containing their signatures wrote: *"Little Brown Chocolates for our Little Brown Baby."*

Every day I typed. Every night I worked at the theatre. This I kept up until Mother, against the doctor's orders, returned.

With more time at my disposal, I made application to study drama at a private school as a student of Mr. Luzerene Wescott Crandall. I had heard of Mr. Crandall's excellent system of training but did not know whether he would consider teaching a Colored person. Fortunately, he was not prejudiced. I became one of his students.

Although studying drama I had an insatiable longing to attend a Catholic school. Love of my religion urged me on in this direction. A nun (not of the Holy Names Order) sought to bring this about.

I had visions of living in a Catholic atmosphere, sharing in daily Communion, periods of meditation, prayer and frequent visits to the chapel.

The nun wrote to the faculty explaining that I was Colored. They were willing, they replied, to accept me. However a week previous to the time set for my entrance they informed her that as they had never accepted a

149

Colored applicant they had decided that it was unwise to change their policy.

A second time Christianity had wounded me. But my chief concern was for the kind nun who had tried to help me, as she was heartbroken. The day I went to see her my mother said: "Be sure to comfort Sister—such things hurt kind White people more even than they hurt us, as we grow accustomed to disappointments."

I had great admiration for the nun who had tried to help me, because she was truthful—unlike many Religious who make unreal excuses for racial discrimination. Her honesty strengthened our bond of friendship which has endured.

It was at this time that several priests and nuns, unable to solve my noncombativeness, evinced interest in the Colored race. And I took this opportunity to compile letters with information pertaining to the heroic sufferings of my people and gave them away to those expressing the wish to become better acquainted with the complexities that ravel Negro life. In time, these became known as "Scrap-book letters" because of the newspaper clippings and magazine articles pasted between the messages I wrote. These I sent to all parts of the world even as far as Ireland.

Soon after the disappointment over the Catholic school episode, a Catholic magazine, *The Sentinel of the Blessed Sacrament,* accepted a feature article that I had written.

Father William A. Fox, one of the editors, sent me a very formal letter asking if I would be willing to accept the magazine's "pecuniary reimbursement of only five dollars."

Five dollars? Would I accept it?

My brain turned cartwheels. Dashing to the post office, I sent Father Fox a registered, air mail, special delivery

150

reply and enclosed an air mail, special delivery stamped return envelope for the remittance. A five dollar money order came, but to my surprise, by regular mail, and enclosed, my return self-addressed envelope with its gala array of stamps. The priest-editor suggested that I be more economical or all I earned would be spent obtaining it.

I had not considered the cost—only the magnanimous sum of ten half dollars, twenty quarters, fifty dimes, one hundred nickels, five hundred pennies.

My letter of thanks surprised the editor. A like missive of enthusiasm he admitted never having received before. I had asked him if he remembered selling his first big story? After transacting a sale of five dollars' worth of words why not be in a hurry to receive the "pecuniary reimbursement?" And if he, perchance, did not have too many prayers to offer for others would he, I wanted to know, consider praying for the Colored race?

Father Fox promised daily remembrance of the Colored at Mass. He also wrote that as people seldom reached adult years and retained the happy wholeheartedness of a child, I had something to be thankful for.

Even after Father Fox's term on the editorial staff expired and he went to the Blessed Sacrament Fathers' Community in Australia, he still continued to encourage me by letter. And he still prays fervently for the Colored race.

The occasion of my first retreat is cherished among sacred memories.

Early one morning I went on the street car into Los Angeles knowing that I would be cloistered a whole day in a convent school.

Finally I reached it, a building half-hidden from the street by stately cypress hedges. I rang the bell. A smiling

151

nun responded. I went inside and left the world behind me.

The day was spent in prayer and meditation and listening to spiritual lectures. Retreatants of different nationalities were there. Strict silence was observed most of the time. Brief lectures were given by a Jesuit Retreat-Master, Father James Doyle. At the conclusion of each one, we were at liberty to consult him regarding our individual problems. I spoke to him of mine. I was trying to make a decision.

While I was walking in the company of the valiant—those noble characters that had stepped silently from the pages of books and let me into myriad worlds, Rose Hawthorne Lathrop, Florence Nightingale and Father Damien—one of my own race had looked out at me from the cover of a Negro magazine, *The Crisis*, one whose life had inspired me and whose death was to remain indelibly impressed on my mind—Juliette Aline Derricotte.

This young Colored woman, a Protestant, born and reared in a Georgia town had consecrated her life to the service of Christ. And, "In His Service" had labored to bring about better inter-racial understanding. She had served as student-pastor at Talladega College, her alma mater, and as Dean of Women at Fisk University.

The account of her life which I read was written by a White co-worker, Winifred Wygal, who summarized the Colored woman's pioneering crusade as follows:

"She stood on the high pulpit of the chapel of the Union Medical College of Peking making an address to a large Sunday morning audience. Before her sat the Chinese students and faculty of that great educational and cultural center of China. The few Americans in the audience were Anglo-Saxon and had not

152

before met a fellow country-woman of Miss Derricotte's ability and racial background. Their amazement, naive interest and appreciation paled into unimportance beside the enthusiasm of the Chinese who listened with peculiar gratitude to her intelligent exposition of the religious, racial, and educational forces playing upon students of the modern world. After the service they did for them a most unusual thing. They crowded around her with questions and an urgent invitation to return.

"She sat amid a group of twenty-five students of the University of Madras who had never before met an American Negro. *Do American Negroes dress as other Americans? Do they feel loyalty to their government? Are they prejudiced against white people? Did Miss Derricotte think race prejudice innate or taught?* Although Miss Derricotte was herself the answer to their questions, she made of the situation an opportunity to carry the group deeper in their understanding of the racial issue. For several hours they questioned and came to appreciate more the universality of human dignity and capacity from this young American, their visitor.

"In June, 1929, she stood before 300 white students in the South and opened for them a new world as she told them of the students of the Orient and of what she had come to believe about the solidarity of youth, bound by a desire for mutuality and the method of good will in achieving it."

The character of Juliette Derricotte I set before me as a model. Her martyrdom created a yearning within my heart to carry on in some way a portion of the good work she had begun. She was seriously injured in an automo-

153

bile accident in a state where a hospital, though supported by public taxation, refused to admit her because she was Colored. Medical aid from another source was rendered after she had lain critically ill while the decision was being made as to where she should be taken. Denied the well-equipped surgical apparatus that would have been in time to save her life, Juliette Derricotte died.

The greatest tribute that I have ever read, or ever expect to read written by a White person to honor the memory of the Colored dead and reveal the sincerity of a White person's pure heart, were those I read by Winifred Wygal in lament over the tragedy she witnessed but was powerless to prevent.

"It makes being White about the hardest thing one has to put up with in a very sorry section of the world."

Thus it was—the life and death of Juliette Derricotte was the main incentive for me to work among Catholics as she had among Protestants.

And so, at the retreat, I sought Father Doyle's advice.

"Father," I said. "I'm trying to decide whether to devote my life to a stage career or enter a spiritual channel and work for my race."

After thoughtful deliberation, the priest replied: "God will guide you, child. Depend on Him to make straight the crooked paths . . . and He shall direct your way."

This thought I carried with me as the day of retreat came to a close. And remembering that it had been said of Juliette: "She never missed the psychological moment for action. She did not forsake her deepest purposes"—I left the convent-school determined not to let the blasts of the world extinguish the flame of the dreams that burned like a torch in my hand. . . .

One afternoon I took a short journey to a suburban newspaper office. . . .

154

A blond girl, scintillating with the exuberance of youth, fed paper into a typewriter. "The editor's busy. Have you an appointment?"

"He made the appointment," I replied, and gave her my name.

She left the room.

On her return she indicated the way to the editor's office. "Says he can't place you by name. But go on in."

I went in.

An alert businesslike man looked up from his desk: "Who're you? What do you want? And when did I give you an appointment?"

"You made the appointment a year ago, Sir," I smiled. "Have the prejudiced subscribers moved away yet?"

The editor peered over his glasses. "What? You back?"

He was busy, but he stopped and talked nearly three-quarters of an hour, wanting to know: Had I found a job? Did I still have my ideals? How had the world treated me? Was I discouraged?

I answered each query.

"How about the reporter's job?" I asked.

The editor shook his head. "Not a chance—ever. You knew that a year ago—didn't you?"

"Yes, sir."

"Then why have you come back? I never expected you to after the way I discouraged your efforts."

I looked directly at him.

"To prove that though I'm Colored I can face discouragement and still cling to hope."

And then the White editor extended his hand cordially and said:

"You win. I take back everything I said a year ago. I know now—like Booker T. Washington—you'll reach your goal. The great white world may crush you—but your dreams will survive."

155

CHAPTER ELEVEN

The Great White World

Tenaciously I clung to the opinion that if I were a respectable law-abiding citizen, a devout Christian and not sensitive as to my color, that race-prejudice could easily be shoved out of my pathway.

Although I had made up my mind to enter a convent, I knew that I would have to wait a long, long time as mother's health having failed caused her to be dependent upon me. Even though a non-Catholic, she had no objection to my entering a religious order.

I continued to study drama realizing that my knowledge of it would be of value to young people after I had completed religious studies and college courses at the convent.

The writing of a prose-poem was the portal through which I made my small entry into the White World. I submitted it to a literary club and it won recognition. No one knew anything about the writer except my name and age, which had been required. One of the judges telephoned the good news that my poem had been accepted and the committee marveled at one so young writing with such "mystical depth"—and wished me to meet them personally, which I did upon a given date.

I shall not go into detail as to what took place other than to say that on finding out that the writer was not fair of skin, the judges were all shocked into a state of regret.

I was quizzed: where was my birthplace? Had I been

156

brought up by colored parents or white people? Only a high school education? Surely I must have had more than that!

"You should use Negro themes," someone advised. "Confine your writing to sentiments expressing the simplicity and humility characteristic of your people."

"Write so that readers know you're Colored," said another.

It was hard to keep back the tears as I picked up my poem, thanked them and bade them good-day. One of the judges stepped out into the hall with me, closing the door behind her. She clasped my hand.

"Write," she said, "whatever you're inspired to write. Poetry is the voice of the soul. Don't be discouraged. I can understand your sufferings."

Through a mist of tears I looked at her. I knew she understood—she was a Jewess.

Had it not been for the encouragement of a Catholic priest, Father Leonard M. Henry, an English instructor in the Franciscan Order, I would have torn the prose-poem to shreds. To insure its safety, the priest asked to keep the verse a while lest I, in a moment of despair, throw it away. Then one day he gave it back to me.

Six years later, Mr. Hans Hoffman, editor of *Westward*, a national magazine of verse published in San Leandro, California, published it.

On submitting the poem, I was afraid to tell Mr. Hoffman that my skin was dark. After its publication and that of another, in fear and trembling I wrote him the truth. His written reply was:

". . . I do hope that I have lived and traveled enough to want to judge my fellowman by what he is, and not by what he looks like, that is by his spiritual quali-

157

ties instead of by his complexion. Your work previously published in *Westward* must have impressed me as indicative of the right kind of soul, or it would not have been accepted.

. . . I will say that the surest way to succeed is the hardest, the way of being yourself. It is so much easier to merge in the crowd, to run with the crowd, to speak with the crowd, and to pretend that you feel with the crowd, even if you don't. If you stoutly are what you are intended to be, regardless of obstacles and difficulties, you will at least achieve peace of mind and the experience of balance and harmony in the soul. If you compromise and trim your sails to suit others, your heart and mind will be torn and rent. There is but one road and recipe for success—*Perseverance*—that if *the heavens fall.*"

I have obtained Mr. Hoffman's permission to reprint the poem. It is a blend of my mother's ideal of pre-natal influence as taught to me, and my own imaginary conception of the sublime beauty within the soul of the mother of a priest. It is told in narrative style.

CONSECRATED

. . . A Prose Dream *of* Memories *sacred to the* Mother *of a* Priest . . .

I

I prayed a prayer:
  And from Her shrine
The Virgin-Mother of the God-Man
  Gazed with compassion
158

Through fixéd eyes; and maternal tenderness
    Portrayed with carvéd smile.

I prayed a prayer:
    While the wick-wool
Of a candle gasped.
    And, together, we watched—
She, the Virgin-Mother from Her shrine,
    And I, bowed in dream-travail at Her feet.

And I—I flung wide
    The cagéd doors of my heart,
And let the swift-wingéd Doves of Desire
    Bear my soul's message of prayer:
"Holy Mary! Mother of God!
    Intercede! Intercede!"

Slowly—the candle's dying breath
    Of smoldered scent, writ
"Consecrated—" Mandate Omnipotent—
    'Mid mauve furl of screenéd smoke,
As incense, wafted in air,
    Weaves patterns intricate
Consecrated!—Consecrated!
    I prayed a prayer for you,
    The dream child of my womb.

You—You who are a memory now—
    You—once the dream child of my womb—
The canvas of memory is etched
    By the prayer of my soul,
And your life is the sketch thereon.

II

Mists of varied dawns
    Descended as clouds,
Filling the vastness of eternity.
    And days groveled wearily
Into the hut of night,
    Exhausted with expectancy.

But you—I beheld you
    In maternal reveries of hope;
And the cadence of winds
    Was the prelude of your unheard voice.
To me—you were the bliss of joy first known:
    A covetous gem of stone unhewn.

Yet, Time wrought the commencement
    Of your earthly existence,
As one who approaches with
    Unheard steps. And I—enwrapped in
Childbirth's painéd garment of fringéd love—
    Beheld you—as—My *Son.*

III

Swiftly childhood's undaunted arrow
    Pierced the delicate form of infancy
And revealed you—resplendent in
    Manhood's unstained armor. And, as
Experience counted the decades of your years
    You seemed conscious of a prayer once prayed.

160

For your eyes reflected the Shadow
  Of the Great One Whom you were wont to imitate.
And your voice was attuned to sing the
  Song of Life as He would have you pitch
Its melody to the infinite note of
  His incomparable composition of Divinity.

And then: one evening the sun, a non-human
  Martyr, hovered in the West as a defeated
Warrior; and dripped blood rays, crimsoning the
  Faded, trailing robes of Illumination.
And, having gasped the last breath of day,
  Fainted in expansive arms of the horizon.

And the sky mourned its flaming glory
  Shrouded in twilight pale. And the
Mountains—reclining on the couch of earth—
  Crouched as beasts on desert sands.
And you and I stood enraptured with the
  Beauty of nature's art—God's handiwork.

And you—you told me of your desires,
  And I listened. And, though my eyes held no tears,
The heart within me wept. For the time had come
  For you to go and follow the One who
Called you—the One who bade you deny all
  To match your footprints where He once trod.

As you spoke—your eyes gleamed with the brightness
  Of a silver shield. Your lips quoted the wisdom
Of psalms. Your heart was a censer consuming the incense
  Of His Love. And your soul—your soul a sacrificial
Victim to be placed on the Sacred Paten of Service
  And consecrated by the Sacrament of Holy Orders.

161

Thus it was—you went from me.
And I hearkened unto your retreating footsteps
Until all was still. And there was a loneliness
Akin to the echo of deserted halls, the emptiness
Of submerged ruins. And you—you were gone:
And I remained in the silence—alone.

"Jesu! Maria!" I cried. And I raised my eyes—
Sunken worlds concealed in darkness—to the blackboard
Of the firmament, where the chalk rays of the moon,
As though guided by a phantom hand, proclaimed your
Destiny 'mid the blaze of dazzling starlight—
"Consecrated! Consecrated!"

IV

And, when I saw you again, though you were aware of
    my presence,
You knew me not. For you were no longer of this world.
Shafts of sunlight filtered through stained glass windows,
    And gilded the altar before you. White jasmine perfumed
The atmosphere. The flames of ivory tapers towered high:
Moments Triumphant! Your First Mass!

And I—enthralled as though by celestial vision, waited:
    Breath abated—while the Sanctus chimed. And when I
Raised my eyes—I beheld you—your features beatified—
    And knew you were overpowered by the Omnipotent
    Majesty
Of the God-Man in your hands; as Christopher, Pilot
    Sanctified,
    Staggered under the weight of the Unknown Child.

For, as the Virgin-Mother looked upon the Christ Child
  At the moment of His Divine Birth—so you—you—
    my son—
A priest—touched His Sacred Body at the sublime moment
  Of His incarnation. And the Consecration ending—
I heard no more. For, though joyful
  My heart was pierced by a prayer once prayed.

You—you who are a memory now, I saw you
  No more until long after years; not knowing
That you were soon to walk through dim, silent
  Vales of oblivion.
A Vesper-Eve—and you stood brown-robed—
  Silhouetted against the autumn sky.

Ere I took leave—you blessed me. And the golden
  Rays of the sun were as a glittering monstrance
Held in your hands. Slowly you wended your way toward
  The Mission gardens. And because you were kind to the
Children of the village they, too, loved you, and walked
  With you, the Padre, until you reached the cloister gates.

And, closing the gates, you went into the monastery.
  But betwixt the passing of night hours—
You went forth again—silently (accompanied by Death),
  No one knew when—
But you went—a holy traveler—
  On the last journey.

And now—in memory of a prayer once prayed, at eventide
  I stretch forth my hands in supplication: *"Jesu! Maria!"*
And the winds—scurrying from the depths of caverns—
  Re-echoing weird cries from spacious valleys—

163

The winds—only the winds, resound in plaintive murmuring:
"*Consecrated! Consecrated!*"

Strange, indeed, were the happenings in the interim of
six long years before the poem found its place.

CHAPTER TWELVE

Depression

Financial disaster—*The Depression*—engulfed the enormous melting pot of races in America. Scarcity of employment prevailed and I, like millions of others, resorted to domestic service. Regretfully, I gave up my dramatic lessons, having no time to spare for them.

Catering took me into homes where some among the wealthy had managed somehow to preserve themselves from bankruptcy.

My home-training stood me in hand. I was courteous, obedient. I anticipated people's wishes. But I was not accustomed to the obscene talk I heard at some parties nor the wild life. I used to cringe when uproarious guests came near me.

I had never realized that the conduct of white people could be so revolting.

Once while I was serving a party, a white woman began ridiculing me.

"Where'd you find this shy little dark cloud?" she called across the table to her hostess, gesturing in my direction.

Everybody laughed. I went right on serving as though I had not heard.

Then a young white man tried to attract my attention by whistling; but I never raised my eyes. He grew provoked and hurled an oath at me, followed by an insulting remark.

165

"Come here," he ordered. "You're a simple looking Dinah-doll."

I walked over to where he sat and silently stood there. He leaned back in his chair and began laughing—so did everybody else, and they kept on laughing until he suddenly stopped and they heard him say: "Somebody, do something—she's crying."

Nobody said anything. And I just stood there trying to wipe the tears from my face and keep them from splashing down the front of my black uniform.

Then a woman with thickly rouged lips and red painted fingernails swore at the man who had laughed at me, and rising came over and placed an arm about my shoulder and led me out of the room.

In the kitchen I put my head on her shoulder and cried.

"Don't pay any attention to folks like us, Baby," she said. "The world's turned our hearts to stone and we think everybody else is like we are."

She held her handkerchief for me to blow my nose. "I'll make them pay for this," she said. "The heels."

I did not have long to wonder what she meant to do, as soon all the guests came tramping out to the kitchen each carrying his or her own plate—all except the young man who had made the remark.

"We need exercise," the hostess giggled, "so we're bringing out the plates."

Then they all began supplementing their own words to the hymn "Bringing In the Sheaves" singing irreverently:

> "Bringing out the plates
> Bringing out the plates
> Here we come rejoicing
> Bringing out the plates."

166

After I had washed the dishes, I put them away, tidied the kitchen and was ready to go when the man who had made the remark came out to the kitchen.

"I—I'm sorry," he blundered. "I didn't really mean to hurt your feelings. I didn't think a Colored girl would care ——"

Incidents like the above were the motives for Dr. Moton writing:

> "The beauty of Negro womanhood is not often exposed to the public gaze. School girls may be seen at certain hours of the day; but except as sheer necessity requires an occasional excursion for shopping or business, Negro women of refinement and culture are not often seen in public places, except among their own people. They prefer the protection and shelter of their own homes. . . ." [*What the Negro Thinks,* pages 34-35]

At this point, I wish to touch upon a delicate subject—yet one that is of vital importance in this book—"The Shadow" over Negro womanhood.

Elise Johnson McDougald, a Negro woman, speaks of it in her essay, *The Task of Negro Womanhood:*

> ". . . the general attitude of mind causes the Negro woman serious difficulty. She is conscious that what is left of chivalry is not directed toward her. She realizes that the ideals of beauty, built up in the fine arts, have excluded her almost entirely. Instead, the grotesque Aunt Jemimas of the street-car advertisements, proclaim only an ability to serve, without grace or loveliness. Nor does the drama catch her finest spirit. She is often used to provoke the mirthless

167

laugh of ridicule; or to portray feminine viciousness or vulgarity not peculiar to Negroes. *This is the shadow over her.* To a race naturally sunny comes the twilight of self-doubt and a sense of personal inferiority. It cannot be denied that these are potent and detrimental influences, though not generally recognized because they are in the realm of the mental and spiritual. More apparent are the economic handicaps which follow her recent entrance into industry. It is not surprising that only the most determined women forge ahead to results other than mere survival. To the gifted, the zest of meeting a challenge is a compensating factor which often brings success. The few who do prove their mettle, stimulate one to a closer study of how this achievement is won under contemporary conditions. . . .

We find the Negro woman, figuratively struck in the face daily by contempt from the world about her. *Within her soul she knows little of peace and happiness.* But through it all, she is courageously standing erect, developing within herself the moral strength to rise above and conquer false attitudes. She is maintaining her natural beauty and charm and improving her mind and opportunity. She is measuring up to the needs of her family, community and race, and radiating hopes throughout the land.

The wind of the race's destiny stirs more briskly because of her striving." [*The New Negro*, edited by Alain Locke, pages 369, 370, 382]

Since slavery, a Colored woman has had to tread the earth with "The Shadow" of false attitudes obscuring the light on her path.

Many white people, including Religious are of the opinion that Colored women are morally impure—owing to miscegenation during days of slavery. This is untrue.

I, as a Negro woman can attest to the fact that the greatest battles to retain purity of body, mind, and soul arise not from any inherent tendency to sexual sin in the Colored woman but from the occasions of evil so prevalent among the Whites.

It must be remembered that a Colored domestic servant is not always blessed to be in the employ of white aristocrats. Were it possible for Colored domestics to live in the homes of the finer type of white men and women, the Negro problem of detrimental environment and low wages would be no more.

As I do not intend mentioning "blood admixture" anywhere else in this book, I quote from Mr. Edwin R. Embree's *Brown America* so that readers may understand the "New Negro." Mr. Embree states:

"A new race is growing up in America. Its skin is brown. In its veins is the blood of the three principal branches of man—black, white, yellow-brown. The new race numbers twelve million in the United States, and other millions in the West Indies and Central America. The group is new in its biological make-up, in its culture; it is almost entirely cut off from the African home.

The slaves were by no means of uniform lineage. They represented tribes as divergent as the several peoples of Europe. They were captured from provinces covering large parts of Central and Western Africa: Guinea, the Ivory, Slave, and Gold Coasts, a great part of what is now French West Africa, the vast stretches of the Niger Valley, the Cameroons, the Congo, and Benguela. Among them were Arabs and

169

Moors from the northerly coasts, the small yellow Hottentots from the south, and Bantu tribes from the equatorial regions, although most of them were large-bodied blacks from the huge area called Guinea. For four centuries the great commerce in slaves ranged over four thousand miles of African coast, from the Senegal River on the north to the southern limits of Angola, and reached up a thousand miles or more inland.

The early manuscripts record the greatest diversity in the African peoples dealt with. Many were Mohammedans; the religion of others consisted of primitive voodoo rites. In some kingdoms, government and social order were well-established; other groups existed in primitive savagery. Up the great stretches of the Gambia River slave ships found peoples of every kind of culture, of greatly varying physiques, and of color ranging from tawny to deep black. Along the banks of the Senegal were found kingdoms with highly developed arts and with 'vast meadows which feed large herds of great and small cattle, and poultry numerous.' Wars constantly waged between the tribes and often fomented by the Europeans, furnished thousands of captives; others were enslaved by their own chiefs, and all were poured down to the factories on the coast.

Members of these diverse tribes, captured over an area as large as the whole continent of Europe, were completely mixed in their distribution in the New World. They were first mingled in the African slave ports. Shipped to the transfer stations of the West Indies, they were further mixed and transhipped to the United States. Finally, on reaching the mainland, they were distributed through American slave marts and sold to all parts of the country, with little regard for family, let alone tribe. Members of tribes which in Africa would not have met for centuries were thrown together on the large plantations or as fellow slaves in the smaller households. *Even if there had been no admixture of white or Indian blood, the generations which grew up in America would have been different from any single tribe in Africa and would have represented a mingling of all of them into a new race.* . . .

Contrary to the custom of most blood groupings, anyone having the slightest trace of African blood is classed, regardless of other races involved as a Negro. Other mixed breeds are usually given the name of the dominant blood. Persons born of white and Indian parents are classed as half-breeds, catalogued under one of the ancestral races, or spoken of as part Indians. Vice-President Curtis and the cowboy comedian, Will Rogers, are classed as white, though both take public pride in the fact that they are in part descended from Indians. With Negroes alone, classification follows a single drop of the blood of one of the ancestral races—the African. This custom grew up during slavery in order to increase the number of slaves, who constituted valuable property. . . .

While there are probably only three or four million persons in this country of purely African ancestry, nearly twelve million are reported to have some African blood and are thus enumerated as members of the new race: 'American Negroes.' [*Brown America,* pages 3, 4, 5, 31]

I was misunderstood because I represented the New Negro—the thinking Negro. Was life, I asked myself, a

171

procession in which ambitious young people of my race had no place?

I carried my ideals into White homes and in most cases the occupants ridiculed and tried to crush them.

I recall the first time a woman ordered me to pack her husband's traveling bags, preparatory to a trip. She laid out a handkerchief to put in his coat pocket. I packed the bags, but carried the coat and kerchief to his wife.

"What's the idea?" she asked.

I tried to explain: though I had arranged her husband's clothes, I was sure she wanted to put the kerchief in his coat pocket.

She regarded me strangely. "What difference should it make who does it?"

I was nonplussed. Had not my mother often said: "If you ever marry remember this: it is a wife's sacred privilege to wait upon her husband—to do the little things that please him such as putting a handkerchief in his coat pocket or brushing his hat. The highest paid servant can never do these things satisfactorily because they are deeds of love."

Floundering for words I attempted to give the reason why I hesitated to take such a liberty.

The White woman laughed saying, "Nonsense! You have old-time Colored sentimentality. I don't care who puts my husband's handkerchief in his pocket. That's why I hired you, to help wait on him."

That was that.

Then, there was the incident of the Expectant Mother.

She was to be present at a luncheon. On learning of this, I placed a cushion in the chair in which she was to be seated, went out into the garden, selected a flower and placed it beside her plate. Why not? Was she not numbered among the chosen of earth whom I had been

172

taught to reverence? I tiptoed about the living room lest my heels make too much noise and disturb her.

As she entered the dining room I stepped back of her chair to seat her. Then my heart sank.

She flung the cushion from the chair and brushed the flower aside.

All the while my employer kept clearing her throat and trying to smile at me at the same time. I remember hearing her say something to the effect that her little Colored maid had "quaint ideas."

Two years later the "little Colored maid with the quaint ideas" had adjusted herself to the ways of the Great White World. Instead of offering the average Expectant Mother a cushion for comfort and a flower that she might gaze upon beauty, she offered a small glass of liquor and a choice of cigarettes.

But the two years of adjustment were hard to endure; always my mind was in an unsettled state.

A Hungarian Sister—Sister Frederica Horvarth, Superior of the Sisters of Social Service in Los Angeles whom I had known long before I became a Catholic—understood a working girl's problems better than teaching or cloistered nuns, as her Community was engaged in serving humanity in the manifold needs arising from social, religious, economic, hygienic, cultural and civic conditions. The Community was an unusual one as the Sisters worked out in the world; wearing simple gray uniforms, not unlike secular attire, and hats with gray veils. Their emblem, a silver medal bearing a Dove (symbolic of the Holy Ghost) was worn around the neck, suspended by a chain. Sister Frederica, realizing how discouraged youth can become, regretted seeing me lose my dreams as the result of the chaotic conditions produced by racial prejudice. And it was through her intercession that I had the

173

privilege of corresponding with the Foundress of her Community, Sister Margaret Slachta of Budapest, Hungary, the first woman member of the Hungarian Parliament in 1924.

From then on letters from Sister Margaret roused me from the lethargy caused by rebuffs and discrimination. Her cosmopolitan spirit—her liberal praise of Communities other than the one she had founded—impressed me in these lines she once penned:

> "Every Order represents an idea of the Being of God and of His love; for instance the merciful love of the nursing Orders, the Carmelites who pray for all the sins against the justice of God, and the Missionary Orders filled with apostolic zeal."

Sister Margaret's letters reflected her dynamic personality and vision. No one could read the message and remain in materialistic darkness.

My heaviest trouble lay in adapting myself to the ever-changing routines and tragedies of White households; to learn to steel myself against the horror of fights between husbands and wives which sometimes resulted in a wife being struck by brutal blows; to live day after day with a gloomy, quarrelsome family where each constantly found fault with the others; to live where decency and self-respect did not prevail.

With reference to Negro housemaids and other servants, Dr. Moton has written:

> "A Negro housemaid, for instance, becomes familiar in a very short time with practically all phases of the life of her mistress. Not only is she familiar as a matter of fact, with the contents and uses of every room

174

in the house, and the disposition of her mistress's most valued possessions, but she also comes in time to learn the habits of every member of the household, the topics of their conversations, the peculiarities, faults and virtues of their friends and acquaintances; and, what is more to the point, in many and many a case these servants become the confidants of their employers, to whom many secrets are divulged and many confessions made—all in the strictest confidence. . . .

Now White people generally feel that they have nothing to fear from their Negro servants who may learn the details of their lives, inasmuch as they are not in a position to use their information to their employer's disadvantage. Indeed, they often feel a deal of comfort in opening their minds to such of their servants who show themselves capable of understanding and sympathy; and frequently they seek and accept their advice, particularly in matters of personal relationships. And one seldom, if ever, hears a White man or woman complain that their confidence so placed has been betrayed." [*What the Negro Thinks,* pages 2-4]

As a maid, I learned so much about the lives of people that I preferred not knowing. I saw so many sins committed that I wished I had never seen. My soul cried out for a way of escape. Many a time I cried myself to sleep because I had no means of fleeing the foulness that permeated the atmosphere of some of these homes.

And then I chanced upon a passage from Coleridge's *Life of St. Francis Xavier,* one of the most beautiful I had ever read on sanctity:

175

"A far more consummate sanctity, must be that which can mix freely and easily with the crowd and condescend thoroughly to its ways, and not only remain pure as the sunbeam that pierces the foulest dungeon, but be also a source of light and moral health and renovation to all around it."

I copied the passage and discussed it with The Director of the Church Sodality, Father Michael C. Healy. One special tribute I pay to Father Healy. He is one among the priests I met soon after leaving High School. Since then he has met many White laymen who were prejudiced against the Colored race. But he has never let their influence turn him against my people. He it was who told me that out of the conflicts of my life I could compose a symphony, a symphony to be played in the unseen music-chamber of my soul.

"Sometimes people ignore a musician," he said, "but never forget the music."

Four years went by.

One day I looked at myself in a mirror. It was as if another stared at me from the reflection—an older woman, overburdened, weary.

I had managed other women's households. I had laid out bridal trousseaux for their daughters. I had seen their sons leave to make homes of their own. I had watched over infants and helped to raise children. . . . Children —they had annoyed me at first; fidgety, noisy and sometimes ill-mannered. Then, they won their way into my heart until the incident occurred that caused me to shun a White child's love for me. I could not bear to tell it in detail. The child (Little Girl I called her) was one not wanted in the home wherein she had been born. No one had time to spend with her until I went there.

176

Her parents were social figures. The husband spent most of his time at the club. The wife was seldom at home except to change her attire. My presence gave the parents the freedom they longed for.

Little Girl was three. Her hair and eyes brown. Always she stretched out her arms to greet me. And every day I told her stories of the wonders of the child's kingdom wherein I had dwelt in former years.

I noticed though that she was listless, and I called her mother's attention to the fact. I suggested a tonic. If that brought no result, an examination by a physician. The mother informed me that I was there just to take care of the child, not to diagnose its physical condition.

The night the mother and father dressed to go to a masquerade party, Little Girl had been sick for two days. I begged them to leave the telephone number where they could be reached if the child grew worse.

But the parents, dressed in costumes, were in a hurry, they had no time to spare.

I sat beside the child's bed and watched her labored breathing. The house was cold. It was always cold. The husband complained of high gas bills. He wanted a new roadster. The wife usually went about shivering. She was saving to buy a fur coat.

But that night I lit the stove.

Little Girl kept whining and calling my name in between spasms of coughing.

Along about one o'clock in the morning the cough sounded as if a hundred strings were crossed in the child's throat. When she gasped for breath I jumped up and braced her with my arms. Tears rolled down her cheeks and when the coughing subsided, she clung to me.

After a while, I could not stand it any longer. I telephoned a physician.

177

Then, I kept walking back and forth to the window, watching for him. A wind had risen. It whimpered and rattled the window panes like a half-crazed creature trying to raise it from the sill. The street was covered with white moonlight. I do not know why it made me think of a winding sheet.

The doctor came. So did the parents. There was a terrible scene. They condemned me for calling him. He commended me and was furious at them.

The next day I was dismissed. I did not tell Little Girl that I was leaving never to return. I just slipped into her room. She was weak, but put out a frail hand to touch my cheek. I kissed her gently on the forehead and promised to buy her a new doll.

She tried to smile, "Buy it tomorrow E'Buff," she pleaded.

I resolved to buy her one and send it by special messenger. I knew I could never return again to the house. Her parents would never hire another meddlesome Colored servant. Doctor's bills had to be paid. The husband would have to keep the old car longer; the wife do without her fur coat.

That was on a Monday. Wednesday someone telephoned home. The father and mother were frantic. They had been so stupid. They had not realized how serious the child's illness was. The funeral would be at a mortician's chapel on Saturday.

Friday evening, a White mortician ushered a young Colored woman to the main parlor.

"Do you wish to view the remains?" he asked.

She handed him a box. "No thank you. Just please give this to the Little Girl."

As she walked out of the chapel, a White woman followed her to the door. Her voice was strained. "Elizabeth *darling*—please come back and work for us. You're the only Colored girl we'll ever want to hire."

On Monday, in a local newspaper, there was a write-up about a Little Girl who was buried with a doll in her arms. It had been left at the mortuary, the paper stated, by a faithful Colored servant.

CHAPTER THIRTEEN

Illness

IT WAS June. The day was warm. I sat in an employment bureau. I was getting used to it now: the smeared windows, the floor littered with pieces of wadded paper, gum wrappers, cigarette ends and ashes.

An electric fan droned like a swarm of bees buzzing in a hive.

There were many people. Some of them argued religion; disputed over politics; others sat pensive, musing perhaps on the departed grandeur of estates; the prematurely aged and enfeebled sat as if in a stupor.

The telephone rang. The thin wiry woman at the desk answered.

A job!

I rushed forward.

She motioned me to be seated. "I've told you over and over again there's no work coming in for Colored!"

I was insistent.

"I must get work. I can't help it because I was born Colored!"

"Sorry, dearie. Don't take it out on me. I'm not to blame. Depression's terrible. White people have to help their own first these days."

A White man cursed. I did not flinch. I had grown accustomed to hearing men curse, and women too. And I had learned to listen to the under-tone of prayer in a

180

curse, something only God and a poet would recognize. The man had a sick wife at home, he said, and hungry children.

An old Colored woman probably seventy years old, probably seventy-five, groaned: "Have mercy, Lord, have mercy!"

A Colored youth in his early thirties snickered. He flipped a match across the room. "I used to believe in that holy stuff. But not any more. You've got to fight in this world."

Nobody answered. He had not addressed anyone in particular.

The old Colored woman spoke to him.

"Son, you've got a lot to learn."

He flipped another match. It landed at her feet. He walked over and picked it up. "Excuse me, Ma'am!" he said, then sat down again.

She closed her eyes and began to sing:

> "Guide me O Thou great Jehovah,
> Pilgrim through this barren land.
> I am weak but Thou art mighty
> Hold me with Thy Powerful Hand."

The thin wiry woman at the desk interrupted. "I'm trying to get you a cooking job, Honey. But your age is against you an' ——"

The dark singer acknowledged this with a nod, and without opening her eyes, continued mournfully:

> "When I tread the verge of Jordan,
> Bid my anxious fears subside;
> Death of death, and hell's destruction,
> Land me safe on Canaan's side."

181

A scrawny White boy of about nineteen shook his head. "Colored folks sure got faith."

The Colored youth in his early thirties answered back. "It's never fed me."

An unshaven White man folded a newspaper. "You've said something. Your race has been oppressed long enough. Colored people got a right to eat too ——"

The old Colored woman's body swayed slightly, but her voice was steady:

> "Lord multiply the salt-sea fishes
> Bless and break more loaves a-bread."

The Woman with the Painted Face dabbed her eyes. "Bless her heart!"

Closing time.

Everybody filed out.

I stood on the steps not knowing which way to go. Everybody had trouble. Nobody had much money.

The Woman with the Painted Face paused beside me. One of her penciled eyebrows was crooked. Rouge-roses bloomed against the weather-beaten trellis of her cheeks. The rings on her fingers sparkled with ten-cent lustre.

"Catholic—aren't you?" she asked scrutinizing the Miraculous Medal I wore on a chain around my neck. "I used to be—a long, long time ago."

"I have special devotion to the Blessed Mother," I said.

She pressed a dime into my hand. "Keep this for luck. Be a good girl. And say a prayer for me sometime."

Opening a small bottle of cheap perfume she emptied the last drop on her handkerchief, tilted her broad brimmed hat, straightened her shoulders and turned away.

I borrowed money to take a bus in to Los Angeles. At

182

the end of the line I started walking. I walked. Walked. Walked. Walked.

Housewives shook their heads when they saw me approach their houses. Sometimes doors were slammed in my face.

No work for Colored. No work for Colored. No work for Colored. Street-car bells clanged it. Automobile horns honked it. Stop-signals shrieked it. No work for Colored. No work for Colored. No work for Colored. No work for Colored.

Charity?

No. I was determined to keep struggling . . . to keep begging for work.

Then the street-car bells began a-clanging louder. The automobile horns a-honking louder. The stop-signals a-shrieking louder. Rhythm . . . Rhythm . . . Rhythm.

Above the din I heard the Negro poets chanting.

Paul Laurence Dunbar, beloved pioneer poet led the chant:

> "To have come near to sing the perfect song
> And only by a half-tone lost the key,
> There is the potent sorrow, there the grief,
> The pale, sad staring of life's tragedy."

Countee Cullen, contemporary, raised his voice: *Yet Do I Marvel*

> "I doubt not God is good, well-meaning kind,
> . . . Yet do I marvel at this curious thing:
> To make a poet black and bid him sing!"

Chant . . . Chant . . . Chant! Hush . . . Hush . . . Hush!

A Negro soprano voice in solo. . . .
George Douglas Johnson, singing: *My Little Dreams*

"I'm folding up my little dreams
    Within my heart tonight,
And praying that I may soon forget
    The torture of their sight."

A Negro tenor solo, Arna Bontemps beseeching: *God Give To Men.*

"God give the yellow man
    An easy breeze at blossom time. . . .

Give blue-eyed men their swivel chairs
To whirl in tall buildings. . . .

For black man, God,
No need to bother more
But only fill afresh his mead
Of laughter,
His cup of tears."
                    . . . Silence . . .

The gasping breath of Joseph S. Cotter, a dying Negro poet in *Supplication*:

"I am so tired and weary,
    So tired of the endless fight,
So weary of waiting the dawn
    And finding endless night."

Langston Hughes (the misunderstood) a-crying out at the *Feet O' Jesus.*

184

"At de feet o' Jesus,
Sorrow like a sea.
Lordy let yo' mercy
Come driftin' down on me.

At de feet o' Jesus
At yo' feet I stand.
O, ma little Jesus,
Please reach out yo' hand."

The din of the traffic ebbed. The chant was heard no more. I turned down a side street. The doors of a Catholic church were open. I went in. I knelt down.

The whispering echo of one of the Negro poets followed me there. A fragment of the spiritual admonition Frank Horne wrote for the despondent in his poem: *On Seeing Two Brown Boys In A Catholic Church:*

". . . Look you on yon crucifix
Where He hangs nailed and pierced
With head hung low
And eyes a'blind with blood that drips
From a thorny crown . . .
Look you well,
You shall know this thing."

In the dim light of the church I lit a candle before the life-size crucifix. I bowed my head and wept.

My mother lay sick at home. . . .

I earned our living—such as it was. I brushed window-screens. I washed windows. I wiped ceilings. I beat rugs. I dusted furniture. I scrubbed floors.

Once I mowed a lawn for fifteen cents. Then a woman

185

offered me a shining silver quarter to move an ice box. The box was heavy. It took me half an hour to shove it from the kitchen to the back porch. But I moved it. Right afterwards, though, a queer little pain shot through my heart like an arrow piercing a target.

Some days I had something to eat. Some days I had nothing.

Hunger drove me to a breadline.

After a while I secured steady employment in Los Angeles. One morning I awoke, helpless. I lay in bed all day. I tried to say my rosary. But my lips seemed numb. Hours passed. Somebody sent for a doctor. He came, Dr. Leonard Stovall, one of my own race.

A few moments later, from afar I heard it, a siren in the night, drawing nearer, nearer.

Two men carried me out on a stretcher. The ambulance glided off smoothly, like a white bird flying.

The interne was inquisitive. "You're the only patient I know of that ever brought along a statue."

My statue of the Blessed Mother stood on the seat beside him. What he did not know was that I also had my crucifix in the pocket of my robe.

For a few days after being admitted to the hospital, I was too ill and weary even to think. I felt, almost, as though I did not want to live. Yet one tie bound me to earth, my mother.

A nurse sent for the hospital chaplain. I received the Last Sacraments of the Church.

When the chaplain, Father Bernard Gannon, discovered that I was not putting forth much effort to live he tried to revive my hopes. But it was hard for me to believe that the future held anything; the hardships of Negro life had almost bested me. One day, Father Gannon brought another priest—one whose spirit was so Christlike that in

186

his presence others became conscious of divine healing power radiating through the soul of a disciple, Father Raymond Tepe. I remember, well, how by the prayers of these two priests I began to realize that all my efforts in life might not be fruitless. I recall Father Gannon telling me that somewhere he had read: "Disappointments are only candles blown out by the winds of adversity, and the Good God who created the winds has the power to re-light them all again."

Doctors, nurses and attendants provided thoughtful kindnesses that I never dreamed they would find time to administer, a cheerful talk from one, a magazine, a smile, a friendly greeting. I shall always think of the hospital as heaven-on-earth as it was there that my tired body found rest, and mortal angels-of-mercy surrounded me.

As my life had been made up mostly of solitude, and as I had been obliged to take over the greater part of the responsibility of earning the living, I had had no time for recreation such as most young people have. Social life was practically unknown to me. Therefore my friends were among older folk. Three Colored friends came to my rescue. Two—a husband and wife—a Mr. and Mrs. John Brown who proved faithful friends and whose tender regard for my mother's welfare helped to give me peace of mind. The other, was a very dear soul who lived a quiet, Christian life—a woman who did many kind things for others but never boasted of it—"Mother Beall" everyone called her. These three of my own race, and my physician, Dr. Leonard Stovall, were without exception, untiring in their efforts to help me get a foothold on life.

Though not a Catholic, Dr. Stovall was sufficiently liberal-minded to encourage me to try to accomplish something for Negro youth through my own Church. He never once discouraged my hopes of someday becoming a

187

nun. Like the famous Negro scientist, Dr. Carver, Dr. Stovall believed in prayer—a Negro intellectual who advocated it and encouraged youth to combine spirituality with everyday living.

Determined to battle discouragement I started out again, a little less fearful of the obstacles that might be ahead of me—knowing that, though the lessons of life were difficult, the Divine Teacher would instruct me. Experience had given me more confidence to believe as Henry Van Dyke had believed when he wrote:

"The Lord is my teacher,
I shall not lose the way.

He leadeth me in the lowly path of learning,
He prepareth a lesson for me every day;
He bringeth me to the clear fountains of instruction,
Little by little He showeth me the beauty of truth.

The world is a great book that He hath written,
He turneth the leaves for me slowly;
They are inscribed with images and letters,
He poureth light on the pictures and the words.

He taketh me by the hand to the hill-top of vision,
And my soul is glad when I perceive His meaning;
In the valley also He walketh beside me,
In the dark places He whispereth to my heart.

Even though my lesson be hard it is not hopeless,
For the Lord is patient with His slow scholar;
He will wait awhile for my weakness,
And help me to read the truth through tears."

188

CHAPTER FOURTEEN

Symphony of Life

I HAD cause to rejoice when my health was restored and I could definitely plan my entrance to the convent. Mother's second marriage had given me the right to go.

At this time I met a staunch Catholic of the white race, Miss Edythe Tierney, who was interested in the progress of Negro youth in the Church; a woman of fine sensibilities who believed in Catholic Catholicism—nothing less. As a daily communicant and an active member of the Third Order of Saint Francis, her growth in grace manifested itself in her daily life.

Before our meeting I had met many slip-shod Catholics who professed to be devout but who had disgusted me by their ostentation.

Miss Tierney shared my dream of helping to eradicate racial prejudice by means of interracial study. We had many interests in common. She it was who consoled me when, a week prior to the date of departure for the convent, I learned of mother's unhappy existence with my step-father. Mother had tried to conceal her sorrow from me. On learning the truth I gave up work in Los Angeles and returned home.

Mother did not ask that I postpone entering the convent, but as she was no longer able to stand the strain and suffered a collapse, I knew she needed me. New debts sprung up seemingly out of nowhere and I was right back

189

where I started from. A few months later she and my step-father separated. Three years later he died.

I gave up the idea of following a religious vocation and turned my attention to a literary and theatrical career.

New channels of opportunity opened for me when Dr. Louis Knott Koontz, a historian at the University of California at Los Angeles, spoke to others of his race in my behalf. He is a Virginian—a gentleman born and bred of Southern aristocracy. He is also a Protestant. Dr. and Mrs. Koontz fought my battles as no other white people have fought them.

Having been born in the North, I was under the impression that all Southerners were against the Negro. But this I have learned: when cultured Southerners fight the Negro's cause there is no trace of cowardice on their part —no cringing. There is no bemoaning: "This is a terrible problem—such a cross!" But by the tenacity of purpose they obtain justice.

Then Mr. Ralph Freud, Director of Dramatics at the University, gave me a voice test which I successfully passed and he accepted me as a private student. He also encouraged me to continue writing plays of Negro life— adventures of the New Negro. His faith in the Negro race gave me courage.

The transition from a religious vocation to that of a literary and dramatic career was not attained without spiritual combat. It was as though I had been walking through a quiet woodland sweet with the scent of purple violets and came unexpectedly upon a grove of tangled undergrowth, where the air was dank with wet moss and no sunlight shone.

I sought solace at the Plaza-Mission, Our Lady Queen of Angels, in the heart of old Los Angeles. Here I met the Very Reverend Father Estaban Emaldia, Provincial of the Claretian Missionaries, whose experience in guiding souls

190

is well-known. Many young men and women of various nationalities owe their success in life to him; for of this disciple it can be truthfully said that no one oppressed by sorrow or affliction can hear him speak of the blessings of God without their wavering faith being strengthened. His words and prayers gave me courage—new courage and new strength.

It was Father Benjamin F. Bowling, chaplain of the University Newman Club, who made it possible for me to obtain books from the Paulist Fathers' library that I might have access to the best in Catholic literature, and whose never-failing counsel brightened dark days.

I wish it were possible to continue relating, in chronological order, the series of events and experiences through which I have lived. Many are comical and would temporarily eliminate from one's mind the cruelty of the environments into which a Negro is plunged by racial animosities. But as *Dark Symphony* is supposed to deal primarily with my quest for Christ Our Lord, the incidents in lighter-vein would defeat the purpose of this book.

Thousands of Negro boys and girls throughout the world could tell a story similar to mine, but few are given the chance.

Negroes change from one religious denomination to another many times because they are looking for justice.

Some Catholics are quick to deny that race prejudice exists within the church. Yet, *The Interracial Review*, a Catholic publication, informs its readers that even in the Catholic church there have been priests who have passed by Negroes seeing them waiting by a confessional, or ordered them to come last to the altar to receive Communion.

Noble priests with understanding hearts, true disciples of Christ, are trying to eradicate such offences. No greater work has been done for the Negro cause in religion than

191

that by Father John LaFarge, S. J. and Father Vincent S. Warren.

Many Negroes are turning to radical groups because both the Protestant churches and the Catholic have failed in many respects to show a truly brotherly attitude toward them.

Ofttimes Catholics seek to appease the Negro with such words as: "Of course, do not confuse the attitude of the Church with the actions of certain Catholics." But this does not add to the Negro's happiness, nor open doors of opportunity. It does not make up for the fact that certain Catholic schools refuse to enroll colored children—that certain colleges have no room for Negro youth.

Sometimes White Catholics ask me: "Why can't other Negroes believe as you believe?"

My answer is thus. . . .

I consider my past experiences of great value. The injustices I have seen have taught me religious tolerance. I am a Catholic, and with the grace of God I hope always to remain one. But I worked out a system of my own—a prayer system. I learned that *knowledge* must accompany faith. I never enter a church without asking God to give me more faith in the Blessed Sacrament. I never kneel at an altar for Holy Communion without being fearful lest I be passed by. This will never change. . . . I am Colored. I have learned what it means to be Colored. The Negro who tries to be spiritual learns more about being detached from earthly things than many people who are in Religious Orders. Always at the altar I pray: "And, if dear Lord, anyone should pass me by . . . help me to have faith in Your Presence in the Blessed Sacrament just the same."

I never pray for suffering because my skin is black. Many White Christians have almost a mania for begging

God to let them suffer. But when the prayer is answered in a different manner from the way they expect, they do not want suffering.

Think of the number of Religious who pray daily to suffer—to share humiliations like those endured by the Christ; yet, if accepting a Colored child in a school or boarding home would mean financial loss to their institution, they would deny that child admittance.

Before you criticize Negroes for being emotional, remember that if you were forced to live through some of their experiences your cool, calm fortitude would be broken into bits.

Dr. Robert Russa Moton, in his book, *What The Negro Thinks* has said:

"The Negro minister has far wider contacts among whites of all classes than the white minister has among Negroes. As a class, white ministers appear to have fewer contacts with Negroes than any groups of their race. But they, too, are breaking across the barrier, and the young white minister today rather seeks to cultivate an acquaintance with Negro life and to find some avenue of helpful service in the tasks of racial adjustment. All such people are discovering that they have nothing to lose and much to gain by making Negroes comfortable and happy, as well as secure in their person and property and hopeful in their outlook for the future well-being of their homes and families. It is from these individual contacts that one gets the impression that the vast majority of the white people in all sections of this country stand ready to give the Negro fair and just consideration and equal opportunity when once the shield of tradition is broken and the power of an aggressive minority can be counteracted."

Religious teachers should remember the words of the writer who said: "What had the life of Jesus been to us, if we had only the words of His sermons, without record of His going about doing good?"

The road is often beset with stumbling blocks for the Negro. But I keep in mind the lines written by one of my people, James David Corrothers, who wrote *The Negro Singer*, for he has said:

> "But I shall dig me deeper to the gold,
>   Fetch water, dripping, over desert miles,
>   From clear Nyansas and mysterious Niles
> Of love; and sing, nor one kind act withhold.
> So shall men know me, and remember long,
> Nor my dark face dishonor any song."

I found the Nazarene Whom I sought . . . how long and winding the road is before me I do not know. Of this one thing I am sure: I have more valleys to walk through, hills and mountains to climb.

I would have no one say that I had or have unusual faith. I have learned that Christ lives and works through mankind on earth.

I have told my story.

May no lasting bitterness engulf my soul, or take from my sight the beauty of this earth nor glory yet unseen.

The music of this world is sorrowful, yet triumphant. May those who have known me with my imperfections, zeal and few virtues remember my life as a Dark Symphony.

I voice my plea to Mary, the Mother of God:

"Ave Maria . . . let earth's last sunrise break on me
  Still reaching arms and heart to thee."

194

OTHER WORKS

THE FINDING OF A SOUL

E. L. ADAMS

"He that is a searcher of My Majesty shall be overpowered by Its glory: God is able to work more than man can understand."
—FROM "THE IMITATION OF CHRIST," BY THOMAS À KEMPIS.

IT WAS DURING my travels that I met him . . . a kindly man . . . and a very holy monk. And though we were not of the same faith . . . we became friends.

It must have been the light within his eyes that created an interest in my Desire World of Thoughts . . . and made me wish to converse with him. I know it was not because of his religious belief . . . for I had no interest in that. I deemed myself a man of science . . . and not one to be impressed with idol fancies. He also . . . was a man of science . . . but as I have said . . . a monk.

Thus it was . . . I met him. And often I would seek to converse with him between the holy hours of None and Vespers. His knowledge of science astounded me . . . and I was glad to speak with him.

Sometimes . . . we would walk in the spacious gardens surrounding the humble abode where he and his Brothers dwelt. And he would touch the petals of the flowers with the tenderness of a woman. And once . . . when a stray tendril invested itself apart from the bush to which it belonged . . . and clung to the brown habit in which he was garbed . . . he dislodged it with such extreme gentleness . . . that the thorn was not broken away from the stem. And when he removed his hand from its clasp . . . I noticed it was bleeding. But he murmured not.

Yet . . . when he spoke of the Universe and its cosmic ele-

[197]

ments . . . his words were Thought Manifestations of Strength and Courage.

The tone of his voice was as soft and low as the wind whispering to the clouds of the heavens as it hovers o'er the silver peak of a mountain.

And when his voice was stilled . . . the silence revealed more than I could comprehend.

Thus . . . the links of our Rosary of Acquaintance became indulgenced with the blessings of Friendship.

And then . . . one day he extended to [m]e an invitation to go with him to the little chapel . . . the little chapel within the humble abode where he and his Brothers dwelt. And I accepted it . . . because of my curiosity.

When I saw him genuflect . . . bowed deeply in adoration . . . before the High Altar . . . within my heart I chided him for so doing . . . for I did not understand. And later . . . as we walked out of the chapel . . . I asked him why he humbled himself so . . . and he said he did so because of the . . . Real Presence.

But I . . . I could not understand how such a learned man could believe in something that appeared to be so vague. So . . . as I did not respect his religious convictions . . . I laughed at him for believing as he did. And afterward . . . I was sorry . . . for the light . . . the tender light within his eyes that had first attracted me . . . seemed dimmed by a shadow of disappointment in me for my irreverence. And because I respected and admired that light of Understanding . . . and because he only smiled at my abruptness . . . I asked that he give me proof concerning the reality of what he held so sacred . . . known as . . . the Real Presence.

How can it be . . . I asked the holy monk and pondered to myself . . . material substance . . . mere bread . . . transformed . . . and in its stead . . . Christ incarnate.

I listened to the doctrines explained for my enlightenment . . . but would accept none of the theories.

And so it was . . . the holy monk brought forth a book from which he read . . . and admonished me to do as was written. And I listened to the words which were thus:

"Go forward therefore with simple and undoubting faith, and

with the reverence of a supplicant draw thou near to the Holy Sacrament; and whatsoever thou art not able to understand, commit with confidence to Almighty God. God deceiveth thee not; he is deceived that trusteth too much to himself."

And when he finished reading . . . I promised to do as told . . . to "Go forward therefore with simple and undoubting faith" . . . and "as a supplicant draw near to the Holy Sacrament" . . . though in my heart . . . I knew I believed naught concerning the Sacrament.

But I said I would return . . . if convinced . . . and tell him of my convictions.

Thus it was . . . we parted.

Many months passed . . . and I did not seek the companionship of the holy monk . . . for I had not obtained sufficient courage to proceed with my quest.

But my heart yearned for the hours we spent together. And often in my dreams I beheld him . . . the holy monk . . . his Rosary and Crucifix suspended at his left side. My ears were alert as though to note the steady tread of his measured step . . . the soft tap of sandaled feet. The memory of his voice was as a musical reverie.

And yet . . . all these pleasant memories did naught to hasten my visit to the . . . Holy of Holies.

We are the beads of God's Rosary of Life. Sometimes we are numbered among the Joyful Mysteries . . . another time the Sorrowful Mysteries acclaim us . . . but only the grace of God can link us to the eternal Glorious ones.

Thus it was . . . in my wanderings I found it . . . a little chapel beside the sea. The waves lashed the shore with intense fervor. The weird mourn of a distant buoy echoed . . . "Mockery . . . Mockery."

But I would not be daunted . . . and with an indifferent shrug of my shoulders . . . I entered. It was past the hour of evening . . . and twilight graced the sky in a flimsy veil of pale . . . mystic . . . moonbeam shades.

The interior of the chapel was silenced by a cool . . . mysterious calm.

Crude wooden statues . . . antique . . . cast solemn reflections. A brass sanctuary lamp burned steadily before the High Altar.

A smoky odor pervaded the atmosphere . . . for one of the two candles lighted on a candelabrum before the shrine of the Madonna and Child . . . smouldered away its brief existence.

Red vigil lights glowed faintly casting flickering shadows.

As soon as my eyes became accustomed to the dimness . . . I walked slowly down the center aisle . . . and knelt before the High Altar.

Moments passed . . . and I continued to kneel enveloped in the coolness of the atmosphere. And then . . . I laughed to myself . . . and jeered aloud . . . uttering these words:

"The Real Presence . . . The Real Presence . . . 'Tis naught but folly to think of such a myth."

And so saying . . . I would have arisen to my feet had I not felt my entire being overpowered by an unseen force . . . a force that descended upon me with the rapidity in which the denseness of fog forms a screened equator between the realms of earth and sky. And with it . . . came the echo of the distant buoy without . . . resounding the strains of:

"Mockery . . . Mockery."

Terrified . . . I clung to the altar rail.

The red flame of the sanctuary lamp leaped as sparks from a gleaming coal of fire from the pit of Hell.

Rays of twilight diffused streaks of light over the tongue of the wooden serpent coiled at the base of the statue of the Madonna and Child . . . and appeared as breath vaporizing in the air. The glare of its bulging eyes pierced my glance as a stiletto pierces flesh. And I trembled . . . my body quaking with fear of evil possession.

I cried aloud . . . and as I did so . . . I felt the gentle pressure of a hand upon my shoulder . . . a tender pressure . . . gentle as a woman's touch. I looked up . . . but the sedate features of the wooden Madonna and Child revealed no significance of a miracle . . . but at that touch . . . the atmosphere changed. The sanctuary lamp flickered slowly. The figure of the serpent became less prominent . . . and the globe dotted with stars at the feet of the

Madonna . . . portrayed a symbol of victory . . . the conquering of evil.

And then I knew . . . sheltered beyond the golden doors of the Tabernacle . . . within the Holy of Holies . . . veiled within the Sacred Host . . . was the Living . . . and Real Presence of Jesus Christ.

And contrite and penitent . . . I beseeched Him . . . the "Prisoner of Love" to grant unto me His peace. And I was reluctant to leave as I desired to carry with me the ecstasy of the moment.

And I heard a voice say unto me:

"Let not therefore thy heart be troubled, neither let it be afraid. Trust in Me, and put thy confidence in My mercy. When thou thinkest thyself farthest off from Me, oftentimes I am nearest unto thee."

"My child, I have been with you always, but you have not hearkened unto My pleadings. I created you in My own Image and Likeness, and gave you a soul . . . the truest symbol of My love for you."

And these words marked the finding of a soul . . . my soul.

And forthwith . . . I set my footsteps in the path that led to the monastery where the holy monk abided . . . and when in his presence . . . I fell at his feet crying . . . and kissed the Crucifix that hung by his side.

And as he blessed me . . . the tender light within his eyes beamed as one who beholds the answer of a prayer confirmed by the benediction of Faith.

And he stretched forth his hands to me as though I were a little child . . . and led me to the chapel where a few months before . . . in my ignorance I had mocked him . . . where I had scorned the reality of the Real Presence.

And together we knelt and prayed:

"BLESSED BE JESUS IN THE MOST HOLY SACRAMENT OF THE ALTAR."

Until I Find You

A PROSE DREAM

UNTIL I FIND YOU

> I shall go on
> Gathering the lengthening shadows
> Of weary days and weaving them in the loom
> Of a hopeful *tomorrow*.

UNTIL I FIND YOU

> I shall go on
> Wrapping my heart-pained body in the multi-colored serape
> Of Indian summers, and the silken tapestries of mulberry
>   sunsets.
> And, thus robed, I shall climb—ascend the lacquered moun-
>   tainside
> Where lavender mists drape over the deep set valleys like wis-
>   taria sprays,
> Entwined with ivy about a marble fountain.

UNTIL I FIND YOU

> I shall go on
> Burning the gold of memory's incense
> In the glittering, spangled censer of the sun;
> And in the heat of day—linger beneath the coolness
> Of an idling palm;
> Waiting there—a solitary figure—
> Until the day (a gray dryad seeking the wooded foliage in the
>   forest of forgotten yesterdays) fades from sight.

Until I Find You

And then—looking up—I know I shall behold the magnificent
Pageant of the stars as they creep through the night's sable
        groves
Like vestal virgins bearing flaming torches as they file
Unto a graven sepulchre.

UNTIL I FIND YOU

I shall go on
Losing myself in triumphant meditation—
Though time (like a mysterious hand closing in the painted
        scenes of a delicate, sandal-wood perfumed bamboo
        fan) enfolds the years;
And erase from the scroll of thought—inscriptions tarnished
By the print of foul minds that seek to harm you.

UNTIL I FIND YOU

I shall go on—
Forever on—holding to the belief that some day, when the
        sun dies
Like a red-lit lantern blown out by a harsh wind's tempestu-
        ous blast,
And the pavilion of earth is divested of all, save my love for
        you—
You will return; and let me clasp you in my arms again.
For you will have grown wise; and learned the secret I tried
        so long
To teach you. You will believe it then; and believe in me.
There is no doubt.
You will not know that the power of the world's breath will
        always be as
The wind—
The wind sometimes returns stray leaves to the foot of trees—
And leaves them there—alone.

UNTIL I FIND YOU

I shall go on
Billowing the soft, fluffy clouds into a pillow for your aching
head;
Letting the sweat from my brow fall to earth as I lift the heavy
weight
Of rocks and stones from the roadside which leads to the
abode
That you and I once shared—so that your wounded feet may
have less pain.

UNTIL I FIND YOU—UNTIL I FIND YOU!

I shall wait—
Keeping the larkspur in my heart abloom.

CONSECRATED

A PROSE DREAM of MEMORIES sacred to the
MOTHER of a PRIEST

(*For: Rev. MICHAEL C. HEALY*)

I

I prayed a prayer:
   And from Her shrine
The Virgin-Mother of the God-Man
   Gazed with compassion
Through fixed eyes; and maternal tenderness
   Portrayed with carved smile.

I prayed a prayer:
   While the wick-wool
Of a candle gasped.
   And, together, we watched—
She, The Virgin-Mother from Her shrine,
   And I, bowed in dream-travail at Her feet.

And I—I flung wide
   The caged doors of my heart,
And let the swift-winged Doves of Desire
   Bear my soul's message of prayer:
"*Holy Mary! Mother of God!*
   Intercede! Intercede!"

Slowly—the candle's dying breath
   Of smoldered scent, writ

[205]

"*Consecrated*—" mandate Omnipotent—
  'Mid mauve furl of screened smoke,
As incense, wafted in air,
  Weaves patterns intricate.
Consecrated!—Consecrated!
  I prayed a prayer for you,
  The dream child of my womb.

You—You who are a memory now—
  You—once the dream child of my womb—
The canvas of memory is etched
  By the prayer of my soul,
And your life is the sketch thereon.

II

Mists of varied dawns
  Descended as clouds,
Filling the vastness of eternity.
  And days groveled wearily
Into the hut of night,
  Exhaused with expectancy.

But you—I beheld you
  In maternal reveries of hope;
And the cadence of winds
  Was the prelude of your unheard voice.
To me—you were the bliss of joy first known:
  A covetous gem of stone unhewn.

Yet, time wrought the commencement
  Of your earthly existence,
As one who approaches with
  Unheard steps. And I—enwrapped in
Childbirth's pained garment of fringed love—
  Beheld you—as—*My Son.*

III

Swiftly childhood's undaunted arrow
    Pierced the delicate form of infancy
And revealed you—resplendent in
    Manhood's untainted armor. And, as
Experience counted the decades of your years
    You seemed conscious of a prayer once prayed.

For, your eyes reflected the shadow
    Of the Great One Whom you were wont to imitate.
And your voice was attuned to sing the
    Song of life as He would have you pitch
Its melody to the infinite notes of
    His incomparable composition of Divinity.

And then: one evening the sun, a non-human
    Martyr, hovered in the West as a defeated
Warrior; and ripped blood rays, crimsoning the
    Faded, trailing robes of Illumination.
And, having gasped the last breath of day,
    Fainted in the expansive arms of the horizon.

And the sky mourned its flaming glory
    Shrouded in twilight pale. And the
Mountains—reclining on the couch of earth—
    Crouched as beasts on desert sands.
And you and I stood enraptured with the
    Beauty of nature's art—God's handiwork.

And you—you told me of your desires,
    And I listened. And, though my eyes held no tears,
The heart within me wept. For the time had come
    For you to go and follow the One who
Called you—the One who bade you deny all
    To match your footprints where He once trod.

CONSECRATED

As you spoke—Your eyes gleamed with the brightness
    Of a silver shield. Your lips quoted the wisdom
Of psalms. Your heart was a censer consuming the incense
    Of His love. And your soul—Your soul a sacrificial
Victim to be placed on the sacred Paten of Service
    And consecrated by the Sacrament of Holy Orders.

Thus it was—You went from me.
    And I hearkened unto your retreating footsteps
Until all was still. And there was a loneliness
    Akin to the echo of deserted halls, the emptiness
Of submerged ruins. And you—you were gone:
    And I remained in the silence—alone.

"*Jesu! Maria!*" I cried. And I raised my eyes—
    Sunken worlds concealed in darkness—to the blackboard
Of the firmament, where the chalk rays of the moon,
    As though guided by a phantom hand, proclaimed your
Destiny 'mid the blaze of dazzling starlight—
    "*Consecrated! Consecrated!*"

IV

And, when I saw you again, though you were aware of my
    presence,
    You knew me not. For you were no longer of this world.
Shafts of sunlight filtered through stained glass windows,
    And gilded the altar before you. White jasmine perfumed
The atmosphere. And flames of ivory tapers towered high:
    Moments Triumphant! Your First Mass!

And I—enthralled as though by celestial vision, waited:
    Breath abated—while the Sanctus chimed. And when I
Raised my eyes—I beheld you—Your features beatified—
    And knew you were overpowered by the Omnipotent
    Majesty
Of the God-Man in your hands; as Christopher, Pilot Sanctified
    Staggered under the weight of the Unknown Child.

[208]

CONSECRATED

For, as the Virgin-Mother looked upon the Christ Child
   At the moment of His Divine Birth—so you—You—my
     son—
A priest—touched His sacred body at the sublime moment
   Of His Incarnation. And the Consecration ending—
I heard no more. For, though joyful,
   My heart was pierced by a prayer once prayed.

You—You who are a memory now, I saw you
   No more until long after years; not knowing
That you were soon to walk through dim, silent
   Vales of oblivion.
A Vesper Eve—and you stood—brown robed—
   Silhouetted against the autumn sky.

Ere I took leave—you blessed me. And the golden
   Rays of the sun were as a glittering monstrance
Held in your hands. Slowly you wended your way toward
   The Mission gardens. And, because you were kind to the
Children of the village they, too, loved you, and walked
   With you, the Padre, until you reached the cloister gates.

And, closing the gates, you went into the monastery.
   But betwixt the passing of night hours—
You went forth again—silently (accompanied by death).
   No one knew, when—
But you went—a holy traveler—
   On the last journey.

And now—in memory of a prayer once prayed, at eventide
   I stretch forth my hands in supplication *"Jesu! Maria!"*
And the winds—scurrying from the depths of caverns—
   Re-echoing weird cries from spacious valleys—
The winds—only the winds, resound in plaintive murmuring:
   "Consecrated! Consecrated!"

YES, I'M COLORED

SPACE

Though mechanical birds fly
high in
mid air
Man, in cloud challenge,
oft loses
the dare.
Though buildings and mountains
toward heaven
loom high,
Neither domes nor towers
can reach
the sky.
We surmise there are

spheres beyond
the sky,
But only a soul

can soar
that high.

HIS FAITH

He has faith
to believe
Heaven's gate unlocks

For those
placing checks
In the church money-box.

DEATH OF THE COLORED DANCER

The church

    Brothers and Sisters watched Death tie

The silver

    Cord that can reach the sky.

They called

    Her brazen to go to meet

The Great

    Lord Jesus with her dancin' feet.

They prayed

    The psalms King David meant

When over

    Sins he did repent.

But while

    They moaned an' began to shout

A-hollerin'

    Aloud to keep Satan out,

Two of

    God's angels brought a lyre

A-playin'

    His message to *"Come up higher!"*

A cloud

    Sailed down from the heavens above

An' carried

    Up the dancer to *Eternal Love.*

"THERE MUST BE A GOD . . . SOMEWHERE"

A True Story of a Convert's Search for God

BY ELIZABETH LAURA ADAMS

I am a young colored woman. Frequently kind Caucasian friends and associates question me concerning the spiritual and temporal welfare of my people. They ask: "Is it true that the majority of Negroes are emotional?" "Is the spirituality of the average Negro superficial?" "Why do Negroes change from one religious denomination to another?" "Is it easy to convert Negroes to the Catholic faith?" "Why is the Negro youth of today turning to Communism?"

THE MAJORITY of newspaper and magazine articles about my people are written by authors of other races. Now and then a broadminded Caucasian editor permits a Negro to sketch the lives of our people, but most of these writers are men. The Colored woman's attitude toward life, her reactions to its problems, her struggles, ambitions and hopes seldom reach print in magazines published by White editors. True—the Colored woman has a voice, but it may be likened to a singer's whose vocal chords cease to function properly—the melodious tones cannot be heard because the delicate strings of the human-lyre, the throat, a[r]e mute. So, to the editors of THE TORCH. I am grateful for the opportunity granted me to present a Colored woman's viewpoint pertaining to religious and racial conflicts in a series of articles.

Although my skin is dark and I belong to a somewhat misunderstood and despised race, I am not antagonistic toward those who are fair of skin. I have found beauty in the world even though being unjustly persecuted; and it is this beauty—these scenes of rare spiritual loveliness that I wish to portray to readers by means of word-pictures. I have no "verbal-arrows" to throw—only a story to tell in absolute simplicity, with a prayer in my heart that in sharing it with others they may seek to know and understand—the Negro.

✠MANY PEOPLE cling to pre-conceived false ideas about the Colored race. There is a popular consensus of opinion that immorality and indolence are supposedly "Negro character traits." Therefore, any Negro possessing refinement and ability to achieve a commendable goal seems apart from the public's idea of being "typically Negro," and is usually described as "different." On the other hand, many people believe we possess innate spirituality. It is, indeed, very flattering to be told by fair friends that dark folk are "born spiritual" and "born with forgiving hearts," but being Colored I know that we, too, must strive to attain these graces bestowed by the Omnipotent. So even though numerous readers may be amazed at learning that *Negroes seek God*, I assure you that I speak the truth when stating that sometimes we spend years searching for the "peace that surpasseth all understanding."

This article is not meant to be an entire autobiography—at least not the sort of autobiography that begins from the cradle and ends as the narrator glimpses the grave. It is the story of my conversion. In relating it, however, certain incidents of my life in connection with material activities must be included.

PART I

Early Religious Training

"To look backward for a while is to refresh the eye, to restore it, and to render it the more fit for its prime function of looking forward."
—Selected.

FIRST I want to say that I do not consider myself a convert in the true meaning of the word because I never wanted to join any religious denomination other than the Roman Catholic. But circumstances over which I had no control wrought serious religious conflict in my life and I waited years to become a Catholic. I tell my story without exaggeration or any attempt to hide my doubts and fears under a cloak of pretense in order that readers may consider me a person of great faith. I have been a Catholic for eleven years and I am still desirous of deeper faith, for I am convinced that one of the most precious of all divine gifts is *faith*. I compare it to a stream of crystal-clear water where the thirsty may kneel, cup their hands and drink, and always return for more of the refreshing draught regardless of the seasons. Aye, for the winter ice cannot conceal it, nor the red-yellow, wind blown leaves of autumn ever cover its mirror-like surface. Neither dust nor sand storms can pollute the strengthening purity of its water—for of such is the enduring quality of faith—true faith.

✠UNLIKE MOST CONVERTS I give credit to my parents (both non-Catholic) for the religious training of my childhood. They were sincere in their endeavors to give me the proper outlook on life and their efforts should not be discredited. On the subject of church-going, however, our home was divided. My mother was a devout Methodist—a beautiful, Christian character—kind, charitable and conservative in manner. My father went to church only to please mother. He had his own philosophy of life. Often he would say to her, "My dear—you understand God better than I. Go to service every Sunday if you wish. But I cannot comprehend the meaning of Christianity as practiced by most of the so-called Christians." Then he would smile and add, "I see some of the White Christians turning hungry Black men from their doors, and Black Christians so filled with hatred that they will refuse White men bread. You go to church, my dear, and pray for baby and for me."

When Sunday came Mother took "baby" to church. She firmly believed in weekly church attendance. Her parents had been devout Methodists. But it seemed that I inherited my father's dislike for regular religious service. Mother spent Saturday giving me religious instruction which invariably slipped my memory by Sunday morning. I was the chief dunce in Sunday school. The only two outstanding memories I have retained of this period are—firstly, the joy of receiving holy pictures (especially the ones whereon Jesus was pictured blessing little children and healing the sick. Secondly, my admiration for my first Sunday school teacher. Bitter were the tears I wept the day promotion elevated me to the ranks of first grade religious class. First grade demanded learning more bible verses. In my childish opinion this was more punishment than honor.

✠"EVERY little girl and boy must learn a new bible verse for each coming Sunday," our teacher announced one morning in the song-song tone so many religious teachers use—why, I do not know. I knew four verses: (1) "The Lord is my Shepherd, I shall not want." (2) "Suffer little children to come unto Me and forbid them not, for of such is the kingdom of heaven." (3) "Jesus wept." (4) "God is love." Generally a race took place between boys and girls to inform the teacher that "Jesus wept" and "God is love." The instructor objected to repetition. I discovered that the child seated nearest the teacher had the advantage over others. So I cleverly arranged to greet "Teacher" at the classroom door. Poor "Teacher"—a gentle, God-fearing woman never realized that I spoke sweetly to her, placed my hand in hers, carried her bible so that I might obtain the "first seat." Such loving devotion was prompted solely that I could have first selection of the four best known bible verses. Yes, I am ashamed of myself, but she should have heeded the words: "Watch as well as pray."

✠AS I grew older I came to the conclusion that the quickest way to cultivate patience was to attend a Colored Methodist church. After spending an hour or more in Sunday school, service began at eleven o'clock. It lasted until about one thirty or two o'clock. Children grew weary—some drew pictures in hymnals, but alert parents or a very particular parent (such as my mother was) would not permit this. There was nothing for a child to do except sit throughout the hours listening to a clergyman spiritually froth at the mouth while he preached a "mighty and powerful sermon."

Why is it most clergymen like to preach from the Book of Revelations? Until this very day I can fall asleep whenever a minister of the gospel announces "My text is taken from such and such a chapter of Revelations." As a child I heard such wildly descriptive scenes of the destruction of the world, and watched so many ministers hold up imaginary blue-prints upon which hell was supposedly outlined, that I failed to develop a pietistic-fearful view of religion. In fact I grew to detest church attendance—except for the music.

✠MUSIC always aroused me from lethargy to spiritual alertness.

When the deep organ tones resounded and a robed choir sang I sat up and took notice of what was happening. Now and then bass voices would proclaim the Unseen Creator *"King of Kings"* and the sopranos add *"Lord of Lords."* Then, suddenly, the trend of service would change. Choir members seated themselves. The minister stood silently before his congregation. His eyes were closed. The congregation became motionless. The silence filled one with awe and reverence. The hush that fell over the vast number of Negroes was almost indescribable. Now as I recall its effect I know it was like the pause following a prelude—those moments of profound quietude during which a music master sits with upraised hands over a piano keyboard before continuing to play a great composition—the silence of evening awaiting the approach of night—the silence of the desert awaiting the sunrise. Then someone in the congregation (usually an elderly white haired and wrinkled person) began to hum the first notes of an old-fashioned hymn or spiritual. Slowly, other voices joined in.

✠NEGRO VOICES! Oh my readers! If you have never heard hundreds of Negro voices singing you have missed a great concert. As I traverse the familiar corridors of memory I can hear the sweetly mellow voices of my people. Sometimes the tones were almost inaudible—seemingly afar off like the distant murmuring of the sea pounding against a rock-piled shore. The soft tapping of their shoes made accompaniments not unlike the beating of drums. Dark bodies swayed slightly to the rhythm. Sometimes the sacred song depicted the saints marching up the "stairs of glory" or Daniel walking about the lions' den unharmed because God's protecting Power overshadowed him. I admired Daniel's faith, but continued to be afraid of lions and other wild animals when present at a circus. It took me a long time to realize the symbolical significance of God's protecting love in the midst of temptations.

Shouting frightened me. It became the principle orgy of church-going. One dear old lady used to proclaim her devotion by screaming aloud, walking up and down the aisles, embracing people and knocking their hats off. I lived in constant fear lest some day she knock my hat to the floor.

A Sunday school teacher informed me that the Holy Ghost "came down" upon Sister Hartie (as she was known to all) at such times. I was informed also that every individual should look forward to the descent of the Holy Ghost.

"It will happen to you, my dear child," the teacher explained, "if you are a good girl and pray." From that moment I *feared conversion*.

I thought of God as the Divine Creator. His home, I believed, was somewhere "way up" in the sky. His home was known as heaven. He made the earth, set out the brown hills and green valleys, streams and rivers—erected the purple mountains and placed the sun, moon and stars in the blue sky. He had a great golden throne, glittering with jewels and beautiful angels with golden trumpets surrounded it always faithfully carrying out his commands. God was far, far away. How impossible it was to imagine Him interested in a little girl! My mother was shocked when I told her that I loved her much more than I did God. Horrified, she hastened to explain that parents were supposed to watch over their children, but they should always love God FIRST and ADORE HIM.

I REMAINED unconvinced. Yes, it was proper to love God, but when a door closed on my finger it was "Mamma dear" who kissed the pain away and made the finger "all well again." My own dear "Mamma dear" tucked me into bed and told me stories. God had other things to do. He had to light up the moon and the silver stars. He had to keep the waves of the ocean rolling. The sun had to be reminded to shine the following day. Millions, billions and trillions of sick people had to be healed. Why, then, should God be concerned about me?

"Don't question God!" religious people exclaimed. They spoke seriously. It seemed as though a person had to be afraid of God for Him to be happy. You couldn't tell Him the things you liked or didn't like without Him becoming offended. Yet, they said He knew your thoughts.

Brought up in a home where courtesy was considered essential to proper home training, I had no desire to be converted if it meant the descent of the Holy Ghost making me fling my hat to one side, or causing me to run up and down church aisles shouting not very politely of the Holy Ghost to impose Itself upon people—to make them do unsightly things.

"Don't contradict the Almighty!" teachers warned if you said you didn't believe something they stated to be a fact. God was a God of wrath. It seemed to me He grew offended very quickly to be so wise. I reflected that I never had a chance to ask God about being a Methodist. It did not seem fair to send a person to earth, permit parents to christen the child Methodist and then not let the child have its "say so" about conversion.

"Repent and believe!" was the church-cry.

✠WHEN I did wrong I admitted it to my parents. They said that if I disobeyed them and concealed the fact I harmed no one but myself. They raised me according to the honor system. When I did wrong they punished me. I reasoned that God being all-wise knew about it; He gave me parents to punish me when I did wrong. There, I disliked the idea that conversion meant I had to wail repentance. I was only a child. Why should God want to see children cry?

Secretly I decided that perhaps if I did not think about the Holy Ghost, the Holy Ghost would not think about me. We could avoid one another. The multiplying religious perplexities caused me to develop an inferiority complex. I thought everybody in the world knew more about God than I could ever attempt to learn even in little ways.

During service I saw children of my own age testifying: "Jesus walks and talks with me." I had an analytical mind. I knew that these same youngsters played many pranks and told me confidentially they never intended telling their parents of their misdeeds. I did not consider myself a perfect child; but I did try to obey my parents. So I concluded that Jesus evidently selected certain people to "walk and talk" with. Why had He slighted me? I decided it must have been because I feared to be converted.

Teachers explained the mystery of the Holy Trinity to the best of their ability. I never understood what they were talking about except that God the Father, God the Son, and God the Holy Ghost were One. I respected God the Father, "way up in the heaven as Manager of the world. God the Son was Jesus. I cannot help but smile now when I reflect and realize that within my own childish heart I thought Jesus "very pretty" as He was pictured blessing little children. God the Holy Ghost was to be shunned. My biggest problem was to always evade the Holy Ghost. I told no one of my plans.

(TO BE CONTINUED)

"THERE MUST BE A GOD . . . SOMEWHERE"

(A Colored Convert's Spiritual Autobiography)

By ELIZABETH LAURA ADAMS

(Continued from October.)

A T THIS JUNCTURE I WISH to exonerate my teachers from the blame for my stupidity. Teachers should never be held responsible for a student's inability to mentally grasp explanations. In later years when I expressed these fears to my mother she told me she would have enlightened me about these things if I had only asked her. But I had failed to ask.

Mother never shouted. She was never fanatical. Sometimes, during service, her eyes filled with tears. As I grew older I discovered this sign of emotion was manifested when she saw other women with their husbands beside them in church, and usually my father's place in our pew was vacant.

Mother taught me my first lesson in learning how to forgive. Born in California, I attended mixed-schools. The only Colored teachers I have ever known were Sunday school instructors. I have never lived in the South. My father had a very good position and our home was like any other well-regulated modern home. I have discovered that many White people have strange ideas about Negro home life. They imagine we live in shacks without rules or regulations. Some think we "hail from the South" as they call migration to the North. Hundreds of Negroes have never seen what lies beyond the Mason Dixon line and never will. I have never even visited the South.

✠CHILDREN of all races played together at school. One day a stranger arrived on the campus. When asked to join a game she shook her head and refused. Pointing in my direction she declared: "I won't play with her because she's a nigger."

It may seem almost unbelievable when I tell you that I had never heard the word "nigger" before. My parents did not use it. I was a very small child when this happened, but I can remember the queer expression that passed over the countenances of the children who were fair.

I think every Negro in the world can remember the first time he or she was called by this uncomplimentary title.

Countee Cullen. Negro poet, wrote a poem about it. The title of the poem is INCIDENT. The poet says:

> *"Once riding in old Baltimore,*
> *Heart-filled, head-filled with glee,*
> *I saw a Baltimorean*
> *Keep looking straight at me.*

> *"Now I was eight and very small,*
> *And he was no whit bigger,*
> *And so I smiled, but he poked out*
> *His tongue, and called me, 'Nigger.'*

> *"I saw the whole of Baltimore*
> *From May until December;*
> *Of all the things that happened there*
> *That's all that I remember."*

In my case I wondered what had happened to change me so suddenly that my playmates would stare so wild-eyed. One little White child patted my hand and said, "Never mind, Elizabeth, I love you." Our house was next door to the school. After school hours I marched home, ran into the house and asked: "Mamma what am I?"

✠MOTHER was busy and replied nonchalantly, "You're Mamma's little girl." I shook my head. This was the wrong answer. She then informed me that I was Mamma and Papa's little girl if it would make me any happier to have both parents included. I shook my head again. I asked: "Mamma—what's a 'nigger'?"

To a reader this may appear to be humorous. I can laugh about it now myself. But to Negro parents it is serious, for the dark child has reached a new roadway in life that leads out into the wide, wide highway of experiences.

Mother was tactful (bless her heart). She inquired first where I had heard the word. I told her. She realized life was extending, but I still dwelt in a small world. It is not easy to explain these cruel things of life to a child. This is an ordeal White parents do not have to go through.

She told me that the word "nigger" was not a "nice" word. It was not complimentary, but hastened to add that perhaps the little White girl who called me that did not know any better. Next I was admonished to love the little girl just the same, even though she refused to join in a game in which I was playing. Yes, mother wanted me to think kindly of her. No matter how many times she called me "nigger" I was not to strike her. "I do not want you to strike her," mother said, "It is not that she is better than you, but you must not strike at people. A lady never strikes back." Then I was told that if any difficulties came up that I was to tell mother and she would see my school teacher. Mother wanted to know the little girl's name. It was Lillian. (How could I forget it!)

✠THAT night when I said my prayers before retiring my mother saw to it that I asked God to "bless Lillian." I did so because I had to obey. I did not hate the child—I was rather dazed about it all. But oh the days to follow! Lillian addressed a few of the other Colored children by the "naughty word" and they made plans for her to be torn from limb to limb.

"We're goin' to beat her up!" they informed me. But I was helpless.

"I can't fight" I told the ring-leader.

"Why not?"

"Because my mother says I can't. My father says I can't," I replied.

"Beat her up and don't tell them" the ring leader suggested.

"I can't" I retor[t]ed. "If I don't tell them they will know anyway because God will see me."

It was not because I was religious that I added this last statement, but my parents had told me that all things done in secret would be witnessed by God. Yes—I was in agony of spirit. God was always peering down through the fleecy white clouds to tattle on you when you were tempted. I presumed there was some invisible method of communication between God and my parents so that He could let them know if I disobeyed.

✠THE ring-leader then threatened to beat me "up" if I failed to comply with her wishes. That night I decided I would not ask God to bless Lillian. This White child was a burden on my soul. So I avoided asking God to give her toys and make her a good girl. Mother made me repeat my prayers. I avoided the subject of Lillian

Mother reminded me to mention the name of my schoolmate. Reluctantly I asked God to bless her.

Every night my mother went through this ceremony. I fought a battle. If being called "nigger" was supposed to make a person fight, then I wanted to fight. But my hands were tied by the invisible cords of obedience. Once or twice I wondered how God would like it if someone called Him "nigger". But I remembered that I was not supposed to wonder. Finally, owing to the blessed patience of my dear mother, I ceased battling. Of my own volition I beseeched the Great Unseen Giver of Gifts to give my little adversary bountiful treasures from His storehouse of supplies.

I am grown now . . . but only God knows how grateful I am to Him for such a wonderful mother. That one word—a word of few letters, "nigger" has started street brawls. Men have killed their fellow men at the sound of it. Women have forgotten their dignity to make vulgar retorts when it has fallen on their ears. Children have grown up with resentment in their hearts which has turned into hatred because of it. Those who have mothers and fathers who believe in teaching the beauty of practicing divine love should be grateful—eternally grateful to their parents.

✠SOMETIMES White friends ask, "Isn't it true that Negroes often use this particular word when angry with each other?" The answer is "Yes"—but it is *never used by the better class of Negroes*.

I learned many lessons. Many of the ordinary religious practices people adhere to were foreign to me. My father's influence prohibited me from becoming involved in what he termed "stereotype-forms of religion." The practice of offering up acts of charity or suffering to God was unknown to me. I was taught that God made a law and that law demanded that people be kind to one another. For example, I shall illustrate how I was taught to be thoughtful of others.

Sometimes when I went walking with my father we would see a crippled person walking down the street. My father would turn to me and say, "Run along now and offer to assist that poor soul across the street. Don't be afraid of the automobiles; I am going to follow you." I would step up to the individual and offer assistance. When the person smiled and said, "You are a kind little girl," I was very happy. But one day an old lady frowned and muttered, "Go away! I don't need your help." Children are easily hurt. I turned to my father and said, "I don't want to help any more old ladies. She was mean." He looked at me and replied: "Now you have a lesson to learn. No matter how many people are ungrateful, *you* must continue doing *your part*."

✠I WAS dumfounded when I became a Catholic to discover that Christians were of the opinion that they were doing something "extra" for God by performing acts of charity. I was amazed to hear even priests and nuns (a few of them) remark that God had a special reward for Colored people because they suffer so much—that He loves them better than White people. Such remarks I do not understand. I am very glad that I was brought up not to believe that God love[s] me better because I belong to an oppressed race. Yes, I believe there are rewards for us in the Eternal City, but I do not believe that because I hand a cup of cold water to one who is fair that I will receive a larger reward because the person belongs to the group that often oppresses mine. In many instances our White brothers and sisters have peculiar ideas about Christianity.

I cannot recall ever hearing my father pray except to say

grace at meals. He never attended prayer-meeting. The only religious article ever given to me from him was a small book of daily meditations. But some years after his death I met a man who spent months in the hospital and he told me this: "Child, you have a rich heritage. For years I have worked in my church. But when sickness came and I looked for my Christian friends, they were all too busy to take time to come and see me. I was one who used to try and convert your father. But the time came when I realized he knew more about God than I thought. He was the one who came to see me. He was the one who left me money when I had none. He was the one who read to me and encouraged me during dark hours."

Yes, he was like that. My admiration for my father is great. He was not a hypocrite. he admitted his faults and failings. His religion was following the Golden Rule. I am sure that secretly he must have picked up the Book of Books, opened it and read these words:

"Though I speak with the tongues of men and of angels and have not Charity, I am become as sounding brass, or a tinkling cymbal. And though I have the gift of prophecy, and understand all mysteries, and all knowledge; and though I have all faith, so that I could remove mountains, and have not Charity. I am nothing. And though I bestow all my goods to feed the poor, and though I give my body to be burned, and have not Charity, it profiteth me nothing."

And so I started out in the world with a Christian mother who attended church and prayed daily and had great faith; a father who said little about church or bible reading, but who found time to help his fellow man regardless of race or creed.

(TO BE CONTINUED)

"THERE MUST BE A GOD . . . SOMEWHERE"

BY ELIZABETH LAURA ADAMS

PART II

CONVERSION

"Conversion, that phenomenon of light to the intellect and persuasion to the heart, is not ordinarily produced in the way of sudden illumination, like a flash of lightning in a dark night, but rather under the form of growing daylight, like that which precedes the sunrise."—

—CHOCARNE.

AT THE AGE of eleven (almost twelve) I still disliked church service. I prefered to remain at home and read the funny papers instead of going to Sunday school. My mother's health was very poor, and we had returned to Santa Barbara—my birthplace.

Father continued working in Los Angeles. Circumstances compelled me to be a serious-minded child. With illness in the home I had to learn how to amuse myself. Most of my recreation period was spent reading. I loved good books and loved music. My parents seldom joked. Father was jolly, yet when he spoke to me he expected me to obey instantly. I spent many, many lonely days as a child. The shades in the house would be drawn; everything was neat and clean, but I had to be quiet. Of course when school was in session I was not lonely, but during vacation I was. I dreaded Sunday. I would grow weary reading, and then I would stand for hours at a time, watching the cars go by our house.

Santa Barbara is a beautiful town and I was happy there. Some friends invited us to go with them to the old Mission. It was Good Friday. The thought that anyone would think up "church-going" as a "pleasant time" was more than I could figure out. I dreaded going.

✠WE ARRIVED at the old mission. We entered. We were seated.

Members of the congregation paid no heed—they were kneeling. I saw prayer-books for the first time. I noticed the strings of beads they fingered. I did not know the "beads" were called Rosaries. I heard the voices of the priests. I beheld the altar. This was a new world. And while I sat there something said to me: "If this is church—why have I disliked it so!" I concluded I could be very happy visiting the mission.

Surely the Great God knew that a little Colored girl feared the descent of the Holy Ghost. Surely the Great God knew that deep down within the soul of the Colored child was a wish that Jesus might "walk and talk" with her as other children testified that He spoke and made journeys with them.

I heard the words *Ave Maria*, not knowing they meant "Hail Mary." But I never forgot the rhythmic beauty of *Ave Maria*. I knew I wanted to remain at the old mission until the end of service—and I wished to return thereafter.

✠WEBSTER'S dictionary defines conversion as a "change from one state, or from one religion, to another." Conversion came to me quietly like the slumber that gently closes an infant's eyes— like pearl-white twilight hovering over a lilac and rose garden. I experienced no other emotion—just the desire to attend service for the rest of my life at the old Santa Barbara Mission.

That night, at home, I wrote father a letter telling him I planned to "join church at the old Mission." On receiving it he telephoned mother long distance. He wanted to know if I had lost my mind.

"Why did you write your father such a letter without telling me!" exclaimed mother.

I was frightened. I had no idea I had done something wrong. Mother offered an explanation. She looked worried.

Then I realized (after listening to her explanation) that the world was divided into groups of people. Some called themselves Protestant, others were Catholic, and there was a certain group of men who called themselves members of the Masonic lodge.

"Your father is a Mason, Elizabeth," poor mother concluded. Really, dear readers, I was a dumb child. It took a long, long time for the "electric light bulb in my head" to work. I did not see what this had to do with me. Mother explained some more. It seemed that for thousands of years all these groups had been throwing stones at each other. Some of the Protestants did not like the Catholics, and some of the Catholics were not too friendly with the Protestants, and the Masons . . . well, it was a long story. But at the end of it I still did not see what all this had to do with me. All I wanted to do was visit a church—a place called the Santa Barbara Mission.

✠WHEN my father came home to visit he reminded me that I was very young and did not know what I wanted. He also told me very emphatically: "You cannot become a Catholic!"

For the first time in my life I wanted to do something that I knew to be contrary to the will of my father. However, although permission to enter the church was denied me, I want to make it clear to my readers that NO UNKIND STATEMENT WAS EVER MADE AGAINST PRIESTS OR NUNS IN OUR HOME. My parents never permitted people to tell immoral stories about clergymen of any denomination while under their roof.

"What is so bad about being a Catholic?" I asked my father.

"There is nothing bad about it," he replied. "I just will not permit you to become one."

Again my brain went on a strike. I could not figure it out. Both mother and father had always told me: "We will not prohibit you from accepting anything *good* in life." Father said there was nothing "bad" about being a Catholic; then to join the church "must be something good" I reasoned.

"Never discuss the subject again," my father said. I was silenced. But I did not forget the words *Ave Maria* . . . the reflection of the Old Mission was mirrored within my soul.

PART III

CRUCIFIXION

"They crucified my Lord, and He never said a mumbalin' word;
They nailed Him to a Tree, an' He never said a mumbalin' word."
—NEGRO SPIRITUAL.

✠I WAS fifteen years old when my father died. He went to sleep one evening, and while he slept the phantom known as *Death* anchored its boat for a few seconds, and then lifted anchor and sailed away to the Land Beyond the Horizon. Dreary days followed. As I was growing older, mother did not exact that I go to church unless I wished to go. Even though my father had gone from this earth I would not have mentioned becoming a Catholic to mother. Her heart was grief stricken; I would not burden her with any thought that had been displeasing to my father. Though he was not with us—his verdict should be respected.

But one day I found a church "almost like the Catholic church." I shall not name the denomination for reasons which I shall give later. It was quiet—there was an altar and candles. You can imagine mother's surprise to find me up early Sunday morning in order to be ready for seven o'clock service.

✠CIRCUMSTANCES had not yet forced me to meet many White people of the prejudiced class. So I thought nothing of the fact that it was a "White church." I said nothing to the people I met. But the clergyman noticed that every Sunday at seven o'clock there was a dark lamb in the midst of the fleecy white lambs. Thus—one morning as I left church he stopped me.

"You come to church every Sunday, child," he asked. "You are always by yourself. Have you no parents?"

I had never talked much to ministers—not even those of my own race.

In a few words I explained that I came there simply because it was quiet. He smiled kindly and offered to give me a little book to read. He gave me a couple of books. One was about: "The Holy Eucharist."

✠FOR the first time in my life I became interested in reading something religious. To read about the "Holy Eucharist" was to take up a new phase of thought. I felt that I was (to use ordinary vernacular) between the devil and the deep blue sea. I did not want to join any church but the Roman Catholic, and I couldn't join that—I had to respect the wishes of my dead father; and I was not interested in going to the Methodist or any other church—except the church I had "found."

I asked mother's permission to join the "church I had found." Dogmas meant nothing to me. I never stopped to think who founded the church or why. I only wanted a quiet place in which to pray. Mother gave me permission to select a church and I joined the one I had "found." Mother became interested in the books I had and joined also.

A few weeks later we moved to another town. Everyone knows it is not easy to interest young people fifteen or sixteen years old in religion. I decided that since I could not be a Catholic I would do my best in the "new religion." And I did. I went to church every Sunday. I read everything I could read that pertained to this particular faith. I listened to the minister as he declared: "If you belong to this church you should not visit other churches."

On Sunday morning the clergyman pictured Jesus Christ hanging on the cross. "Jesus died to save all men," he instructed the congregation. He spoke of the terrible sin of missing church on Sunday. His sermons convinced me that I had done a great wrong by not wishing to attend church as a small child. I even decided I had something to repent over . . . and when I closed my eyes and prayed I told God I was sorry I hadn't loved Him sufficient to go to church instead of reading the funny papers.

✠NO HUMAN BEING ever tried to be more sincere. At school most of the Colored children were Methodist or Baptist. Sometimes, though, they told strange stories—stories I refused to believe. One girl said she joined a church and the White people didn't want Colored. Another girl said she knew some people who had had the same experience. They laughed about it. But my parents had taught me that if one was a good American citizen, cultured and peace-loving, that being Colored would not make any difference among the right class of people. I recall how quickly I told one of the girls: "You are mis-judging White people. They do not do such things." She laughed in my face saying, "Go on taking up for White people. Some day they will show you what's really in their hearts."

When I heard the clergyman tell the congregation it was wrong to visit another church I decided he was right. You had to believe what you believed! I decided there was something in learning about dogmas.

(TO BE CONTINUED)

"THERE MUST BE A GOD. . . SOMEWHERE"

(A Colored Convert's Spiritual Autobiography)

BY **ELIZABETH LAURA ADAMS**

(Continued from December)

PART III

CRUCIFIXION *(Continued)*

MOTHER DECIDED that we should visit the Colored Methodist church in the evening so that we might have social contact with those of our own race. Of course, we never attended any social gathering at the church, or wished to do so, because the group was a White group. But I had heard the clergyman speak. I was willing to attend social gatherings in the homes of our own people, but it did not seem right to visit another church. It couldn't be right—the clergyman said so. Even if it demanded sacrifice on our part—we should ma[k]e it. The clergyman said it was what God demanded. It seemed as though God disapproved of a person of one denomination visiting another.

One Sunday morning . . . I shall never forget it . . . the sun's rays blazed through the stained glass windows . . . the organ played soft music . . . white candles burned on the altar, and we knelt at the altar rail to receive Holy Communion. My lips had just touched the Chalice, and I looked up to gaze at the cross and thank God for the gift of Communion when I beheld a strange sight. The clergyman stood before me—with a cloth he wiped the Chalice where my lips had touched it. He took time to wipe the Chalice—it was almost as though he had to polish it. A White person was beside me. After he wiped the Chalice he continued giving Communion.

✠THOUGHTS are like birds . . . they can wing their way speedily.

The thought came to my mind: RACE PREJUDICE AT THE ALTAR! Then I became terrified. How could I think such a thought at such a *holy time* and in such a *holy place*? I begged God to forgive me. In fact, I spent all the following week asking forgiveness.

Next Sunday . . . the same thing happened. This time the clergyman took much longer to wipe the Chalice. When giving Communion to Colored (after passing the Chalice to a White communicant) HE DID NOT WIPE THE CHALICE. BUT *FROM COLORED TO WHITE*—THE CHALICE WAS WIPED.

I said nothing to mother. She said nothing to me. But during the week the White clergyman called to see us. He stated his mission while tears filled his eyes and streamed down his cheeks. We were informed that White communicants did not wish to kneel at the altar with Negroes . . . he hoped we would not hate him . . . but he had to make a living. . . . White people contributed so much to the church . . . he had more White than Colored. . . .

Mother told him she was sorry and assured him we would never attend church again. She promised him we would not hate him.

We had contributed to the church, for at that time we were in a position to do so. Colored members were present ONLY ONE MORNING A WEEK—yet White Christians objected.

After delivering his message, the clergyman went his way. There was a lump in my throat. I had tried to be such a good Christian! But—ah—I had discovered the trouble at last . . . my soul was encased in a dark body. I wondered about God . . . about dogmas and creeds. What about this theory that God was displeased if a member of one denomination visited another church? What about this theory of regular church attendance? There were no Colored churches in the town of that denomination. What then—was a Colored person supposed to do? What sort of a God was it that laid down a lot of rules, and then did not make a way for them to be carried out?"

The only words my mother said were: "We must not think unkindly of the minister . . . or the congregation." She added that after the incident I was absolutely free to do what I wished in the spiritual world so far as joining church was concerned. We agreed to go separate paths . . . each her own way.

I was sixteen years old—and when you are sixteen you do not take much time to reason things out that seem to have no solution. I remembered shrugging my shoulders and saying to myself: "Oh well—I never liked church as a child. Guess I made a mistake bothering at all." But the hurt was there . . . in my soul. I doubted God's justice . . . I doubted His love for Colored people. I never set foot in that church again. . . . I passed it a couple of Sunday mornings and heard the congregation singing . . . singing hymns of praise to the Almighty.

The minister? Yes . . . I saw him again. The faculty of the High School I attended selected him to appear on an Armistice day program to pray the opening prayer. I stood, surrounded by students of various nationalities, and heard him beseech the God of Peace to grant peace to the hearts of men . . . to bless all nations . . . and grant true brotherhood on earth.

Hate him? No . . . I did not hate him. I had been brought up to avoid hatred. But I wondered what "religion was all about."

At sixteen years of age I decided to give up the idea of belonging to any church. I had been tremendously interested and had been turned out of the House of God. I had discovered that the other Colored people were truthful when they told of their experiences.

I was discouraged. . . .

PART IV

THE LONG ROAD HOME

✠SCHOOL work kept me occupied. Now and then someone would inquire as to what church I belonged. I replied: "I do not belong to any church."

[234]

On Monday morning some of the White girls used to talk about the sermons they heard on Sunday. One afternoon, one of the girls (a beautiful character) looked at me and said: "You are the first Colored girl I ever met that frankly admits she has no religious affiliation."

Colored students invited me to visit their church-homes. I went once in a while in order to be sociable.

I am, however, a very determined person. I never like to leave a task unfinished . . . a mystery unsolved. Within my soul I was not satisfied with the opinion I had formed of God. I considered Him "a God of the White race." If God was for the White race there was no need of me saying my prayers—this time could be put to better use. But suppose He was just . . . suppose He did love Colored people . . . then I realized I would be missing the benefits of His help.

While looking up some school work at the public library I found some books written by a priest named Father Finn. They were children's books but attracted my attention—one in particular bore the title: BY THY LOVE AND THY GRACE. Reading this book reminded me of the fact that "long, long ago" I had wanted to become a Catholic. The story gave me information I knew nothing about . . . the confessional. It was little closet somewhere in a Catholic church . . . the priest could not see the person who entered to confess sins. I began to think . . . suppose I started out once more to learn about God . . . suppose I went back to the church I wanted to join. . . . No—I would never ring a rectory doorbell and face a White clergyman. I did not trust my own courage to this extent. I was afraid the door would be closed in my face. But the confessional was dark . . . and I was dark. No one could see me. I could ask a lot of questions about the spiritual life.

But fear possessed me. Only God knows the fears in a Negro's heart.

To make a long story short, when I returned to the library to find more religious books I saw two nuns. One of the nuns smiled, and as she stood nearby looked at the books I had in hand. She noticed the author's name and inquired if I was a Catholic. When I said "No, Sister" she did not turn away but continued the conversation. Her personality and pleasing smile made me wish to know her better. When I left the library I had an invitation to visit the convent and call to see her.

I obtained mother's permission and went to call. After the portress admitted me I nearly broke my neck looking around. Priests and sisters have since asked me how I chanced to be so willing to go since there are so many evil-minded people in this world who tell untruthful statements about convents. Well—you see my father and mother had brought me up to turn a deaf ear to scandals . . . to look for the beautiful in life.

✠I NEARLY broke my neck looking around because I saw so many lovely paintings. My own mother being an artist taught me how to appreciate beauty. It may be interesting to readers to know that in the meantime (during the period of reading Father Finn's books) I had asked my mother for a rosary. She made me a present of one, and also gave me a rosary case. The rosary case had the picture of St. Therese, The Little Flower. But alas—I did not know one saint from another and thought it the Blessed Virgin. Each night I had kissed St. Therese and said "Ave Maria." No . . . I needed no huge books written by Doctors of the Church to prove that Mary was the Mother of Jesus, and to believe in the Immaculate Conception. Even the Protestants believed Jesus had a Mother. I loved my mother and I wanted others to love her. I was a mere mortal—why shouldn't Jesus want people to love His mother. It was all very simple!

I had no knowledge of the names of the various religious orders. At the convent the nun told me her name was Sister Mary Mercedes and that she belonged to the Holy Names Order. She asked me if I had a rosary, and I proudly showed her mine. When she saw the rosary case she exclaimed: "Oh—do you know the story of the Little Flower?"

I smile now when I think how tactful I managed to be. I never let her know I did not know of whom she was speaking. But oh, in my heart I was so disappointed. Think of the prayers I had been saying, "Ave Maria" over and over again . . . and the Beautiful Lady of the picture was someone called "Little Flower" and not the Blessed Virgin Mary.

It was Sister Mary Mercedes who took me up to the chapel.

This dear nun—a woman whose skin was fair and whose soul radiated the white purity of kindness—opened the chapel door.

"Here is our Blessed Mother" she said pointing to one of the statues. "She is your heavenly mother, Elizabeth, and loves you. She will always help you."

She explained why she genuflected before the Tabernacle.

"Our Lord is present in the Blessed Sacrament" Sister whispered. "If you are ever in doubt, in trouble, beset by worries . . . go to a Catholic church, kneel before the Tabernacle and He will hear your prayers."

I left the convent with an extra rosary and a lovely box of candy. Christmas had just passed . . . and Sister Mercedes said she knew most girls liked candy.

For days I thought about the visit to the convent. But this thought presented itself: "Don't be foolish. Remember White Christians told you about God once before. Don't run the risk of being turned away again."

I became intellectually pious. After all, you know, Negroes are supposed to be easily converted. In fact, many people state that "Negroes and Indians and Mexicans and Italians" are so "spiritually emotional" that you can lead them to an altar by giving them pretty prayer-books and beads. I read books—not story books but books giving church history. I found out that the Roman Catholic Church claimed to be the only True Church. This was a new angle.

The only remark my mother made when she discovered I had regained interest in the spiritual things of life was: *Remember, dear, you are Colored.*

✠NEVER once did I tell the nuns of my former experience. I remembered what my father had said about Christian people as a whole: "Never tell one Christian the faults of another. Christians gloat over the weakness of another sect."

In the physiology class at High School I met a young Italian girl—a devout Catholic. Poor girl! I wrote question after question inquiring about the Catholic Church.

"Dear Julia—what is benediction?"

"Dear Julia—don't answer right away because old man K is

watching." (Old man K was our instructor). But how often do you go to confession? Does the priest speak to you in Latin or in English?"

I spent most of the time I should have been studying obtaining information from Julia. Had she been older I would not have done this, but we were the same age. She did not think it ridiculous to be young and love the spiritual things of life.

Then . . . I made my decision. I would go to church, find a confessional and talk to a priest. Again the reminding thought: "Remember what happened the last time you tried to find God." I listened to the thought-voice. It was right . . . I would never make another attempt until I found out where the Negro stood. Back to the public library I went. I found a Colored magazine. In this publication the names of all religious denominations were given that had throughout the year exhibited racial prejudice and kept the Negro back. You can imagine how my heart sank when I read "The Roman Catholic Church of America owes the American Negro an apology."

I knew . . . somewhere, at sometime, either in a school or church, some of my people had suffered humiliation.

Well, I argued, if some members of the True Church treated the Negro unkindly by being prejudiced, why belong to it?

Sister Mercedes' advice had not gone unheeded. I found a Catholic Church and made visits to the Blessed Sacrament. I was not going to be fooled. IF GOD WAS THERE HE WAS GOING TO HAVE TO PROVE HIS PRESENCE. But even before the Tabernacle I thought about the article in the Negro publication. I did not want to be a spiritual vagabond. I could not be happy roving from one church to another.

When I knelt before the Blessed Sacrament I spoke to our Lord in simple terms. Many, many times I prayed this prayer: "Dear Lord—I don't know whether You are present or not. After what's happened I'm afraid to believe in You. But I want to love You. Amen."

✠SCRIPTURE states that Jesus Christ has said: "Him that cometh to Me I will in no wise cast out."

Before the Tabernacle I found that peace filled my soul. I

found that if I went to church today, I wanted to go tomorrow. No clergyman was preaching . . . I was not being influenced.

The book, WONDER WORKS OF LOURDES, stood out among books on one of the public library shelves. I read it. Who can read this book and doubt the presence of Christ in the Blessed Sacrament?

Lourdes! Here thousands and thousands of pilgrims prayed for healing. All were not Catholic . . . all were not White. The blind wait anxiously for The Light . . . the crippled sat in wheel chairs . . . the afflicted of various diseases lay stretched upon stretchers. Priests chanted prayers: "Hosanna to the Son of David! Blessed is He who cometh in the name of the Lord!"

A procession formed—the procession of the Blessed Sacrament . . . and the same Saviour of the World—this same Jesus of Nazareth Whom Sister Mary Mercedes told me about, ever present in the Most Blessed Sacrament healed those who cried. "Jesus Thou Son of David have mercy!" No—not all were healed, but those not healed in body were healed in spirit.

I reflected . . . my spirit was broken. Spiritually I longed for the healing power of the Great Physician. And so, there in the public library with the book, WONDER WORKS OF LOURDES, before me—and the Negro magazine—I made the final decision.

Saturday afternoon found me at church. I knew not where to find a confessional. I watched people going in and out from somewhere to the side of the side aisles. A few moments later found me on my knees in a confessional. I did not know exactly what to say—but I was making a brave attempt to find a church home.

(TO BE CONTINUED)

"THERE MUST BE A GOD . . . SOMEWHERE"

By ELIZABETH LAURA ADAMS

(Continued from January.)

PART IV (CON'T.)

The Long Road Home

SATURDAY AFTERNOON found me at church. I knew not where to find a confessional. I watched people going in and out from somewhere to the side of the side aisles. A few moments later found me on my knees in a confessional. I did not know exactly what to say—but I was making a brave attempt to find a church home.

The inner shutter slid away . . . I heard a voice. I said: "Father . . . I am not a Catholic."

Evidently the priest thought his hearing was failing him. He asked me to repeat the statement. I began: "Father . . . I am not a Catholic. Will you please pray for me."

"You are not a Catholic?" he questioned.

"No, Father"—by this time my voice was getting weaker. But I had one consolation . . . he did not know I was Colored. I couldn't be thrown out for the simple reason that my skin was black.

I was disappointed in a way because I thought he would begin to give me advice . . . quote some passage from a religious book. I thought my announcement would be like putting a nickel in one of the old time player-pianos the movies used to have. The coin made the piano play. I thought my words would be the signal for him to preach.

✠HE informed me that he could not give me absolution. He would pray for me. (I learned later that he was a visiting priest). I thanked him . . . he said nothing more.

Time had been passing . . . it was almost Christmas again. I selected Christmas eve as time for my next "confession." I was looking for someone to help me spiritually, but never dared to go to a rectory for fear of being turned away.

I stood in line with the other penitents, looking for all the world as though I had been a Catholic for years. I had a little more courage.

I announced my presence as I had done before. The priest asked the same question: "You say you are *not* a Catholic?" He appeared to be very zealous. Indeed, why not join the convert class? I muttered something about being very busy. I was ready to leave.

"I cannot give you absolution, but I shall give you my blessing." I discovered that the Catholic Church gave away blessings. You could get one *absolutely free!*

There shone in the priest's side of the confessional a little light. His features were outlined. I wondered if I dared trust him to the extent of stating my problem. Afraid to take a chance I waited until I saw him outside the confessional. I asked him to bless a rosary. He did not appear very friendly . . . I went on my way.

✠RULES were rules—but I wondered if I could find a priest who would let me tell him some of my problems and spiritual failings and give me a blessing instead of absolution each week?

My last attempt proved successful. There came a Saturday when I knelt in the confessional and told the priest I was a non-Catholic. He asked me if I knew any prayers. His questions were not fired at me . . . he had had much experience guiding souls. How happy and delighted I became when I recited the "Hail Mary" right straight through without one mistake. And there where souls are supposed to lose their pride, my little soul *beamed* with pride because I knew this prayer "backwards and forwards" as I used to say when a little girl.

He believed in me. As you may imagine, this meant a great deal to one seeking refuge from the storms of life. Best of all he granted permission for me to return to his confessional as often as I wished. Yes—I could return each week and confess my sins. He could not give me absolution, but he would give his blessing instead. When he discovered I faltered at the suggestion of attending a convert class he dismissed the subject.

Every Saturday found me at his confessional. He taught me the little prayer: "O Sacred Heart of Jesus I place my trust in Thee." He said this prayer and one Hail Mary every day would make me a Catholic.

Gradually I confided in him . . . but I kept my race a secret.

✠PHYSIOLOGY class gave me ample time to continue worrying my Italian friend concerning religious questions, but when time came for the final test I knew a great deal about Catholicism and little about the human structure. My daily grades were poor. I made a frantic effort to cram my head with knowledge the night before the test. But you cannot spend days asking "How often do you go to Mass?" "Do you say the Rosary every night?" and win out in a physiology test.

The hour for the test arrived. Julia began to write—I began to worry. She felt sorry for me and I felt sorry for myself. She moved the paper toward me . . . I nodded my thanks. The next day the instructor called me to his desk.

"Your test paper is excellent," he said. "Your daily grades poor. I can't understand what's happened to you. You don't take any interest in this class. How do you account for such a marvelous test paper?"

I faced the inevitable. "I cheated, sir."

"What's on your mind that you can't settle down in this class? Your other teachers have good reports for your daily lessons."

Good old teacher! Of course I made good grades in my other classes. Julia was not in them. I could think about Catholicism but had no one to write notes to about it. He gave me a second chance to make good. But he never knew the real reason for my neglect of study.

✠EVERYTHING seemed to be going well. Then, some friends interested mother in joining a Protestant church. She felt that since I was so dear to her it would be glorious if we both joined it. She did not ask it . . . but I knew if my father had been living he would have expected me to do whatever would make her happy. With a heart heavy as lead I joined it because I knew it would please her. When Saturday came I wept bitterly in the confessional. I told the priest what had happened.

"I still believe in you, child. No young person your age would come faithfully to this confessional every Saturday and not be sincere. Keep saying your prayers and have faith."

I did. I ceased to grieve. I said a Hail Mary when I walked into the other church and believed that the Blessed Mother would let me become a Catholic. I continued to go every Saturday to confess my sins and learn a new prayer. The priest would always take time to tell me something about the love of Christ. My soul, like a wilted flower, came back to life at the sound of his words.

In a book by a well known Negro author on the subject of the Negro in Africa can be found this excerpt:

"No mother can love more tenderly or be more deeply beloved than the Negro mother. 'Everywhere in Africa' writes Mungo Park, 'I have noticed that no greater affront can be offered a Negro than insulting his mother.' 'Strike me,' cried a Mandingo to his enemy, 'but revile not my mother!' . . . The Herero swears 'By my mother's tears!' The Angola Negroes have a saying. 'As a mist lingers on the swamps, so lingers the love of father and mother'."

✠I WAS not born in Africa, but America. From birth I have been surrounded by the American White civilization, but my devotion to my earthly mother goes back to the devotion that black folk cling to. All the clergymen in the world could have quoted Bible verses telling me that Jesus would give me the entire kingdom of heaven had I not joined that church to please my mother . . . and I would have remained unmoved. I admired this priest because he did not quote these Bible verses. He comprehended my love for my mother. Had he not . . . I would never have returned to his confessional. My father taught me that mother is always queen of the home. She is ruler. She is not exacting . . . nor makes rules difficult to keep.

I am not "tied to her apron strings" as one might imagine. She always gives me liberty to go where I please; she trusts me to go always to the right places. But if I live to be one hundred years old I would never think of leaving the house without asking her permission. It is not that I am such an ideal daughter; it is that I have such an ideal mother.

I did not "steal off" to the confessional. I asked her permission.

@ WHEN I was nineteen years old I went to her and asked for her consent to become a Catholic. She gave me permission.

In time, of course, the priest discovered that I was Colored. I had a great trial to bear, and he said he would like to speak to me outside the confessional. I had learned to confide in him . . . I forgot about being Colored. When I met him he extended his hand and shook hands cordially.

The morning I made my First Communion . . . only Mary, the Mother of God, and Her Divine Son knew the joy within my heart. I had walked through the valley of despair . . . briars and thorns wounded my feet. But I had heard a Voice saying:

"Fear thou not; for I am with thee; be not dismayed; for I am thy God: I will strengthen thee; yea, I will help thee."

(TO BE CONCLUDED IN THE NEXT ISSUE.)

"THERE MUST BE A GOD. . . SOMEWHERE"

BY ELIZABETH LAURA ADAMS

PART V

CONCLUSION

"What had the life of Jesus been to us, if we had only the words of His sermons, without the record of His going about doing good?"

—Selected.

I HAVE TOLD MY STORY. Do not say. "Oh, she had great faith." Do not take this article and hand it to the Colored people you know with the hope of converting them. Listen . . . I have something to say to you.

If YOU ARE WHITE I call your attention to the poem written by a poet of my race: "IS IT BECAUSE I AM BLACK?" The poet, Joseph Seamon Cotter, cries out:

> *"Why do men smile when I speak*
> *And call my speech*
> *The whimperings of a babe*
> *That cries but knows not what it wants?*
> *Is it because I am Black?*
>
> *"Why do men sneer when I arise*
> *And stand in their councils.*
> *And look them eye to eye,*
> *And speak their tongue?*
> *Is it because I am black?"*

Before you criticize the Negro for being emotional, remember that if you were forced to live through some of their experiences your cool, calm fortitude would be broken into bits.

✠NEGROES change from one religious denomination to another many times because they are looking for justice. Thousands of Colored boys and girls throughout the world could tell you a story similar to mine, but no one gives them a chance.

Catholics are quick to deny race prejudice having any claim within the Church. I suggest that these Catholics read THE INTERRACIAL REVIEW, a Catholic publication. There are copies that inform readers that even in the Catholic church there have been priests who have passed Negroes by; seeing them waiting by a confessional they have not bothered. Do not "Oh" and "Ah." These conditions exist. Noble priests with white hearts and souls are trying to eradicate such offences. Read about the work done for the Negro by Father John LaFarge, S.J., and Father Vincent S. Warren. Negroes today are turning to Communism because both the Protestant churches and the Catholic have failed in many respects to show a true attitude toward the Negro. It is little consolation to a Negro to hear these words: "Of course, do not confuse the attitude of the Church with the actions of certain Catholics." This does not add to the black person's happiness—it does not make up for the fact that certain Catholic schools refuse to take Colored children. That certain colleges have no room for Negro youth.

✠SOMETIMES Catholics inquire: "Why can't other Negroes believe as you believed?"

My answer is thus . . . I consider my past experiences of great value. I also inform them that I had not been in the Catholic church six months before I was refused entrance to a Catholic institution. "But you are still a Catholic," some people argue.

Yes . . . I am a Catholic. And with the grace of God I hope to always remain one. But I worked out a system of my own. A prayer system. I learned that *knowledge* must accompany faith. I never enter a church without asking God to give me more faith in the Blessed Sacrament. I never kneel at an altar for Holy Communion without being fearful lest I be passed by. This will never change . . . I am Colored. I have learned what it means to be Colored. The Negro who tries to be spiritual learns more about being detached from earthly things than many people who are in Religious Orders. At the altar I pray: "And, if dear Lord, anyone should pass me by . . . help me to have faith in Your presence in the Blessed Sacrament just the same."

I never pray for suffering . . . because my skin is black. White christians have a mania for begging God to let them suffer BUT WHEN THE PRAYER IS ANSWERED IN A DIFFERENT MANNER THAN THE WAY THEY EXPECT . . . *they do not want suffering.* Think of the number of Religious who pray daily to suffer . . . yet if accepting a Colored child in a school or boarding home would take money from the institution THEY WOULD HAVE TO SUFFER. So they do not accept the child. O my friends . . . is there none among you willing to forsake talking about Christianity and live it?

✠IF YOU ARE WHITE and read this article and have remained away from church because of some petty dislike for the parish priest . . . or some difficulty of another nature . . . I ask you to put aside these things and return to your Father's House.

White Catholics who have fallen away from the church sometimes tell me. "We met a priest who didn't understand our problem. We left the church"

What a shame: White folk with every advantage—every opportunity will remain away from the sacraments because of such misunderstandings. For your benefit I offer these beautiful thoughts from LIGHT AND PEACE by R. P. Quadrupant. After suggesting that you find a spiritual director, he says:

"When choosing a director, be careful to select one who has the necessary qualifications. He should be not only virtuous, but prudent, charitable and learned. St. Francis de Sales gives the following opinion on the subject: 'Go,' said Tobias to his son, when about to send him into a strange country 'Go seek some wise man to conduct you.' I say the same to you. Philothea. If you sincerely desire to enter upon the way of devotion, seek a good guide to direct you therein. This advice is of the utmost importance and necessity. And the Scriptures tell us: 'A faithful friend is a strong defence: and he that hath found him, hath found a treasure . . . a faithful friend is the medicine of life and immortality: and they that fear the Lord shall find one. (Ecclesiastes. c. VL. vv. 1–16.) 'But who can find such a friend? They that fear God, the Wise Man answers—that is to say, those humble souls who ardently desire their spiritual progress. Since it is so essential, then, Philothea, to have a skilful guide in the devout life, ask God fervently to give you one according to His Heart, and rest assured that when an angel is necessary to you as to the young Tobias, He will give you a wise and faithful director.

"In fact, the selection once made, you should look upon your spiritual guide more as a guardian angel than as a mere man. You place your confidence not in him but in God, for it is God who will lead and instruct you through his instrumentality by inspiring him with the sentiments and words necessary for your guidance. Thus you may safely listen to him as to an angel sent from heaven to lead you there. To this confidence, add perfect candor. Speak quite frankly and tell him unreservedly all that is good, all that is evil in you, for the good will thus be strengthened, the evil weakened, and your soul shall thereby become firmer in its sufferings and more moderate in its consolations. Great respect should also be united with confidence and in such nice proportion that the one shall not lessen the other: let your confidence in him be such as a respectful daughter reposes in her father, your respect for him such as that with which a son confides in his mother. In a word, this friendship, though strong and tender, should be altogether sacred and spiritual in its nature"

✠THE average White Catholic argues: 'But where can one find such a person. In the days of the saints . . . when they walked the earth . . . it might have been possible."

It is possible today . . . but you will have to put forth the effort to find such a guide. From the same book we are told:

" 'Choose one among a thousand,' says Avila: among ten thousand, rather. I should say, for there are fewer than we would suppose fitted for this office of spiritual director. Charity, learning and prudence are indispensable to it, and if any one of these qualities be absent, your choice will not be unattended with danger. I repeat. ASK GOD TO INSPIRE YOUR SELECTION AND WHEN YOU HAVE MADE IT THANK HIM SINCERELY AND THEN REMAIN CONSTANT TO YOUR DECISION. IF YOU GO TO GOD IN ALL SIMPLICITY AND WITH HUMILITY AND CONFIDENCE, YOU WILL UNDOUBTEDLY OBTAIN A FAVORABLE ANSWER TO YOUR PETITION."

". . . It may be well to remind you that the director and the confessor have not necessarily to be the same priest. St. Francis de Sales was the spiritual director of many persons to whom he was not the ordinary confessor. 'To a director,' he says, 'we should reveal our entire soul, whereas to a confessor we simply accuse ourselves of our sin in order to receive absolution'."

Most White Catholics pride themselves on "intellectual piety." I have a marked distinction between intellectual piety and soul piety. One may sit under the soft glow of lamp light at home and read the lives of the saints, the masterpieces by the doctors of the Church, but it takes love of God to bear the daily crosses.

✠IF YOU ARE COLORED and re[a]d this article, know that I, too, have suffered. These words were not written according to "theory"—they are result of suffering. If you doubt God . . . if you have ceased to believe in Him . . . I suggest that you find a statue of the PIETA in some church. Behold the compassionate countenance of the Mother of Sorrows bending over the crucified body of Her Son and hear Her whisper in the words of Jeremias: "all ye that pass by the way, attend,—and see if there b[e] any sorrow like to my sorrow." As Negroes our problem is to forgive . . . our White brothers and sisters['] problem to learn religious tolerance and practice more true christian living.

The road is beset with stumbling blocks for the Negro. But let us keep in mind the lines written by one of our people, James David Corrothers, who wrote THE NEGRO SINGER, for he has said:

"But I shall dig me deeper to the gold. Fetch water, dripping, over desert miles. From clear Nyansas and mysterious Niles Of love; and sing, NOR ONE KIND ACT WITHHOLD.

[249]

SO SHALL MEN KNOW ME, AND REMEMBER LONG,
NOR MY DARK FACE DISHONOR ANY SONG."

From all who read this article I beg a prayer. I found the Nazarene Whom I sought . . . how long and winding the road is before me I do not know. Of this one thing I am sure: I have more valleys to walk through, hills and mountains to climb. With trembling hands I pick up the delicate petals of my blighted dreams . . . dreams taken away from me that can never be realized because my soul is in a dark body. Aye, some dreams will come true, but others cannot in this world. I voice my plea to Mary, the Mother of God:

> "Ave Maria . . . let earth's last sunrise break on me
> Still reaching arms and heart to thee."

(THE END.)

———————

OUR COLORED SERVANTS

By ELIZABETH LAURA ADAMS

MISS ADAMS is, to our mind, one of the most talented writers in America. Very shortly one of our leading Catholic publishers is to release her autobiography which, we believe, is "going to be something." When Miss Adams sent us these poems she assured us that they were satire. "Every colored servant, she wrote, "lives through the ordeal of hearing Madam speak about the former 'dear departed servants.' Madam usually sniffs and wipes her eyes with her lacy handkerchief as she says. . . . "

I
AMANDA

AMANDA wanted a purple plush casket
In which to rest—

Poor tired soul!

AND thought it best
To be attired
In her "Third Order dress"—

Poor tired soul!

SHE wanted "Reveren' Father O'Riley"
To "preach De Word,"
And a soprano to sing

Our Colored Servants

"Like a mockin' bird!"

Poor tired soul!

OH, I dearly loved Amanda!
Though she proved to be too slow,
           I used to joke and say her feet
           Were numb from heel to toe.

SHE always worked on Monday
From six to eve of day,
           And washed the clothes for five of us
           To earn her dollar-pay.

SOMETIMES she *took the liberty*
To ask for car-fare too,
           They say a Negro's bound to beg
           No matter what you do!

ON summer days I used to sit
Beside a whirling fan,
           I had a cushioned wicker chair
           'Twas painted green and tan.

AND while I'd rest Amanda'd sing
Of angels "up in glory,"
           But paid no heed when I foretold
           The pains of purgatory.

SHE said someday her spirit
Would dance through wooded-dell,
           Good land! She weighed two hundred,
           Sometimes I'd almost yell!

But she'd continue talking,
And believed her funeral knell,
           Would be the tinkling music
           Of a canterbury bell!

Our Colored Servants

AND AMANDA said "King Jesus"
>   (Would walk with her "way back")

TO SEE the house where she was born,
>   (A broken-windowed shack)—

WHERE NODDING morning-glories,
>   (Elf-painted purple-blue)

SLIPPED NATURE'S honey nectar
>   (From drops of crystal dew)—

A PLACE where weeds grew very tall
>   (And stood with wind-bowed heads)

LIKE GRACEFUL, slender white cranes poised
>   (In sage-green tulley-beds).

AND THEN she said she'd sing and shout, "An' praise Holy
Holy Name"—

POOR SOUL, she had the wildest dream; and then, alas,
death came.

THEY SAY she suffered terribly—she lingered for a year.

I INTENDED *to go, see her—but we kept so busy here.*

SHE LEFT three little children—she was a widow too;

I WONDER *how on earth they'll live and what they'll ever
do!*

I DIDN'T send a floral wreath—they're far too high this year,

BUT AMANDA KNEW I LOVED HER—SHE WAS SUCH A
PRECIOUS DEAR!

II
DAN

DAN was really the BEST we ever hired:
> *he never complained,*
> *seldom grew tired.*

HE cleaned, repaired and drove our car:
> *pleased our guests*
> *when he tended bar.*

HE walked erect with a stately pace:
> *never once forgetting*
> *to keep his place.*

HE toiled for years—good service gave:
> *we buried this servant*
> IN A FAMILY GRAVE.

THE SUMMONS

By ELIZABETH LAURA ADAMS

ONE night . . . down in Barbadoes . . .
In a Pan-American cafe, A Negro trombone player . . . played a
strange tune,
Sang a strange song:—

A hot night . . . that night . . . in Barbadoes . . .
Sultry and foreboding;
And the cafe . . . crowded with half-drunken, boisterous
people;
And loud laughter . . . care-free and riotous;
And the air . . . heavy with smoke . . . smell of liquor and cheap
perfume:—

A frenzied swing-band whittled rhythmic notes.

SUDDENLY . . . the lights went out!

Women shrieked . . . and their sharp, shrill voices cut the darkness
Like white spears of lightning darting into storm-clouded
space.
Then a beam of light shot forth.
And a spotlight's milky-white glare was focused on the Negro
trombone player;

A jet black Negro with narrow, cat-like eyes;
A huge, powerful Negro, heavy-jowled and hare-lipped.

A LOUD BLAST SOUNDED!
So loud that the bamboo shutters (caught in the net of vibra-
tions)
Quivered like a pongee-coloured moth when foiled in the drag-
net of a spider's web.

CAFE patrons looked up . . . aghast.
Women shivered,
And men left foul curses suspended in the air like skeletons
dangling from ghostly scaffolds.
THAT BLAST COMMANDED! IT SPOKE TO THEM!
And when the Negro . . . threw back his head . . . and played,
Hundreds of tiny notes scrambled into a heap and fell from the
trombone
Like luscious fruit from a Horn-Of-Plenty.

And someone whispered, "He's playing a Spiritual" . . .
And the South American proprietor heard and said, "I'll throw
him out!"
But when the proprietor tried to move . . . his feet seemed
clamped to the floor,
And loops of music formed a lasso around his neck.

OH yes . . . that tune spoke to listeners:—
It was a book that the blind could read;
A stile that the crippled could walk,
Because . . . when the Negro player put aside his trombone
And began to sing *"TIME TO GET READY"* (one of the spiri-
tuals his foreparents had sung),
Although the people thought it odd,
Strange things happened: . . . .

THE dark-eyed Mexican dancer
Remembered her childhood days spent in Mexico City,
And a pilgrimage made to a shrine in Guadalupe
Where a jeweled-crowned, olive-tinted Virgin stood with
clasped hands,

[256]

And remembering . . . drew the lace shawl over her bare shoulders:—
A young sailor . . . in from Singapore . . .
Tried to picture his soul,
And saw slimy-black water in a stagnant pool:—

A grey-haired, immaculately dressed American banker,
Admiring the platinum bracelet he was clasping about the slen-
        der wrist of a foreign woman,
Remembered, against his will, that he had a wife in the States;
And the three white flowers arranged like a crescent in the
        woman's hair,
Reminded him of the pure souls of his children.—

THEN . . . just as suddenly as he had begun . . . the Negro
        musician stopped singing.
And he began to talk,
Telling them that while he played and while he sang
Almighty God had talked to him:
And he said God said a *ghost-wind* was coming. . . .
      —(A-comin' . . . a-hummin' . . . a-strummin');
He said that the *ghost-wind* had sea-tousled hair,
Wore a scarf of bridges . . . and a girdle of fences;
And because, woman-like, the *ghosts-wind* was vain
She fluffed houses into minute powder puffs,
And carried a bouquet of trees in her arms.

HEARING the words . . . the listening, crowd laughed
Because they thought his prophecy an act.
But when the Negro began to shout . . . and then ran up and
        down between the lamp-lighted tables,
They grew frightened;
And the proprietor gave a signal . . .
And two strong men rushed forward and grabbed the Negro.

BUT the *ghost-wind* was no fable,
For a second later
A hurricane swept the coast and wrecked the cafe:—

THE SUMMONS

BUT . . . in that second
The jewel-crowned . . . olive-tinted Virgin of Guadalupe
Spread her mantle, as a winding-sheet, over the dead-body of
      the Mexican dancer:—

AND the Great Captain,
Who piloted Peter's barque when a fierce gale whipped the
      waves of Lake Genesareth,
Called to the sailor and said, "Come Unto Me!":—

AND the American banker . . . sinking low . . .
Saw a Shepherd handing him
A Rod and Staff:—

AND the Negro trombone player,
Gulping and strangling on chunks of sea-weed and salt-water,
Heard a blast of music
And saw standing before him
The Angel-Gabriel who handed him a brand new silver
      trumpet.

✠ ✠ ✠

SEVERAL hours later . . . when grim-faced rescue workers
Cleared up the wreckage where the cafe had stood,
The only living creature was a scarlet-cadmium-yellow parrot,
      minus many feathers,
Clawing and screeching in a battered green cage.

AND all the while the grim-faced rescue workers
Sorted out the tattered garments of human flesh,
The scarlet-cadmium-yellow parrot, minus many feathers,
Clawed and screeched in the battered cage,
Shrieking the words "TIME TO GET READY .. TIME TO GET
      READY".

BUT nobody knew what the poll-parrot meant.

THE COUNTRY DOCTOR

A dark country lane
(And cold winter rain)
The stormy winds wheeze
Through low willow trees.

The horse quickly leads
(The old carriage speeds)
Flashing out of the drear
Signal-lanterns appear.

Then into the shack
(Coat thrown on a sack)
A life waits to bloom
In the dingy sick room.

Late stars of new morn
(A boy the first born)
With gift-peck of grain
He starts homeward again.

"She Talks Like We Do!"

By Elizabeth Laura Adams

Dear Sister Aloysius and Sisters:

No doubt by this time you have received my brief message telling you that the lovely statue of Blessed Martin de Porres has been received, and that this letter is to be mailed to you.

Although I am grown, people still continue to tell me that I will never grow up, because when I am happy over anything I'm so elated that I yell for joy. So, not having attained the degree of sophistication that it seems the world demands for most of its "grown ups," I am telling you the truth when I admit that when I beheld the statue of Blessed Martin I was as happy as a little child.

I see now what dear Sister Aloysius meant in her letter when she wrote:

> ". . . Well now, Brother Martin should certainly pay a visit to any-
> one who is so anxious to have him as a guest and I don't doubt that
> he will someday!"

I thought that this meant that Blessed Martin would come spiritually.

For days, my dear Sisters, I have admired the tiny statue in the window up town in one of the Catholic stores where religious articles are sold. I always told myself that there was no harm in *wishing* Blessed Martin could be a guest in our home. This stat-ue—the one you, my dear Sisters, sent is so much larger than the one I dreamed of having. It is impossible to find words to express my gratitude.

One day while looking at a picture of Our Little Brother Martin which I had long ago cut from a booklet and placed in a frame, I said to him: "If you really want to help me . . . and if you are really going to stand me in the future, then I wish you'd prove it by letting me have a statue of you."

Having no funds to purchase a statue, I decided my little prayer and my dream would be as one, and continue to drift somewhere out in the Universe. So . . . when Blessed Martin arrived, I knew not only joy, but also experienced the realization of knowing that prayers do not always "drift somewhere out in the Universe"—in fact, they do not "drift" at all; but words have little wings as the poet says, and reach Our Divine Lord, His Holy Mother and the saints, and the Blessed Ones in Heaven.

I wish, my dear Sisters, that I could tell you what this gift means to me. Because my skin is dark kindness means so much. Sometimes kind white friends ask: "Don't you think that Colored people are born with sympathetic hearts?" I reply that I do not think we are born with sympathetic hearts, but experiences in life either make a Negro soulful or antagonistic. The Negro either becomes spiritual and decides to keep his or her vision upon the Compassionate Face of the Saviour and try not to mind the stumbling blocks . . . the suffering and pain that living in this world brings . . . or the Negro loses faith.

Of all the sad sights that earth has to offer . . . the most pathetic is a Negro who has lost faith in God. I have met some—and I know.

White or black—we have our battles, but there are a few things I want to say in this letter that will enable you to see what you have done for me . . . and what you do for others of my race when you say one kind word . . . or give a friendly smile . . . or write an encouraging letter.

You realize, of course, that one of the major problems of the present time concerns youth. Owing to the economic situation people all over the world are trying to give youth encouragement . . . trying to find places for suitable recreation . . . trying to keep youth occupied.

Negro youth is to most communities an additional "problem."

I have found that being colored is intensely interesting. Now don't laugh . . . 'cause it's true. Some people say that I should write up my experiences as they believe they will help others. It is interesting because you never know what is going to happen next. You get all set and believe that a dream is going to come true—then it vanishes. So—one learns to persevere. You must keep believing and keep struggling.

Youth finds it difficult to struggle without encouragement. I have been fortunate during the critical periods of my life when so much gloom has overshadowed to have a sympathetic and tender-hearted Mother—who, though not a Catholic, is very, very spiritual and has great faith. In fact, I wish I had the never-faltering faith that she possesses.

I discovered that between the ages of nineteen and twenty-five many Negro youths give up. During this period of one's life one is ambitious. We build up dream-structures only to see them fall. There is a great work to be done. Someday when I am successful . . . I hope to accomplish something worthwhile by helping my people.

Do you know that many times when I've been on the verge of growing careless about prayers, when I've just about decided that perhaps it won't make much difference whether I get to Mass on Sunday or not . . . a letter from a convent from a nun who is close to Our Lord has been like a gentle hand leading me back to Christ in the Blessed Sacrament?

Yes . . . I know what you are thinking. You say, this is merely "a mood" and that one should be constant in loving God. That this is being temperamental . . . and that a person doesn't have much courage who gives up so easily. Thus far, Our Lord has helped me to explain to many priests and nuns things that the Negro endures that cause one to be thus tempted. And now . . . these priests and nuns pray daily for the colored race.

When a school teacher notices that a child is shy she tries to help the little one overcome this handicap, lest the child have what we call "an inferiority complex." One should not be boastful . . . but to feel inferior keeps one from making proper progress.

During my own lifetime I found that it is difficult to keep courage when the world whispers: "Well, if the Negro is ambitious, one must assume there is white blood in the family somewhere."

Or—hear this: "If the Negro is not ambitious . . . well, Negroes are usually lazy."

I used to cry because these things hurt so badly. I was born right here in California so I do not speak with any trace of Southern dialect. And I can recall how hurt I was one day while working in the home of one who was fair to hear her say to her guest (and nodding in my direction): "She talks like we do."

As one grows older—one learns not to be hurt. You learn to laugh. A Negro must learn to laugh. Most writers say we are happy, care-free. We are not care-free . . . we are not always happy. But we learn how to cover the wounds of our hearts by the smile on our lips.

Sister Aloysius—I have something that may be of good use to you if you ever contact a member of my race who seeks your advice. It is something that has helped me. I find out that sometimes the older you grow the more tempted you are to say to yourself (if you are colored): "This religious idea of trying to strive to be spiritual is all right when you don't have so many problems. It's fine for a dreamer. But I have to be more practical."

Life sent me so many "slaps and knocks" until I found myself slipping into this state. Something had to be done about it. So I made out an outline. Then a friend made up the mimeograph copies. I never show the copies after they are filled in to anyone; Except the "failures"—these I take to my Spiritual Director or send to him if he happens to be away. But the "virtues" (which are few) I destroy.

Now please don't get the idea that I am spiritual. Don't think that I fill these out every day. They should be filled out daily, but—I am such a "bad child of Mary" at times that the day goes by with hurried prayers, and sometimes no prayers at all.

So, my dear Sisters, you can see what your kindness has meant to me.

I am grateful to God for your friendship. May Little Brother

Martin shower upon your Community many, many blessings for helping one of the "least of His little ones."

My dear Mother is quite happy, for she too, loves Brother Martin.

You should see him now . . . he is standing on my little altar. He is smiling . . . and is very, very happy. He is a beautiful "chawklite brown" and I am glad. Because he is colored and I am glad they painted him "Culid."

I want each nun in the Community to know that I wish I could thank you individually . . . I hope that Our Lady will grant you your heartfelt wishes . . . and that Little Brother Martin will help me to grow spiritually and also be successful so that you may be proud of the "colored girl" (although I'm supposed to be "growed up" like Topsy) in the future.

Your gift brought sunlight where shadows had fallen . . . hope where discouragement had entered the heart.

I have a little petition box which stands near Blessed Martin. In it is a slip of paper which reads: "Dear Blessed Martin, please bless all the Sisters who sent you here."

Again thanking you . . . and sending you loving thoughts . . . please pray for us.

With love and deepest spiritual affection. . . .

Gratefully,

"A Child of Mary,"

HYPOCRISY

She stepped from her car,
Quickly gathering aside her skirts
Lest the grimy, outstretched hand
Of a stray tenement child
Pollute the purity
Of its silken folds.

A lame dog
Limped across her path;
With brocaded tip
Of a Parisian slipper
She brushed it aside.

Then—gently lifting her prayer-beads
From an ivory-clasp purse,
She raised her eyes heavenward,
Crossed herself
And walked into Church

THE LAST SUPPER

By ELIZABETH LAURA ADAMS

(A story as related to me by a Caucasian priest and retold in a prose-poem)

CHAPTER I

When the old Prison chaplain died
The warden sent for me,
The newly appointed priest,
To take his place.

I was a young disciple at the time,
And eager to hold aloft
The flaming Torch of Faith
Burning within my soul,
That worldly pilgrims might see
And be guided by—*THE LIGHT*.

My apprenticeship, as a Servant of Souls,
Had been spent fulfilling the duties of chaplain in
    jails
And occasionally substituting for the priest
In charge of religious work at the state penitentiary;
But none of my experiences in this field had ever led
    me
To the Execution Chamber to witness—*condemned
    death*.

That was why, as I sat on the train
Journeying toward my destination.

THE LAST SUPPER

The warden's letter to me trembled in my hands—
For his well-chosen, typewritten words
Foretold the execution of a convict
Scheduled to take place
Three days after my arrival. . . .

CHAPTER II

My Arrival—Monday Night

It was a long ride from the station
To the House-of-Cells-and-Dungeons
The warden's chauffeur (a carefully trained
    automaton)
Proved to be a man of few words,
So there was little conversation.

On leaving the city
The car passed through scarcely populated suburbs,
Gaining speed as it glided on to a wide, smoothly
    paved highway;
But farther on the scenery changed—
And I was awed by the sight of bare stretches of
    tableland
Broken by deep gorges over which hung jagged rocks
That seemed to make hideous faces in the moonlight.

Slowly the car climbed over the dirt-dusty roads
Of huddled hills and circled mountain summits
Until we reached the crest of the highest peak
Where before us a tree-trimmed driveway narrowed
    to a lane,
And fantastic shadows of leafy Eucalypti branches
Were interwoven like the welded iron links
Of a mammoth slave-chain.
We sped along for a mile or more.

[267]

Suddenly our path was barricaded by huge steel
      gates.
Flanked on either side by armed guards.
From a look-out-tower high powered revolving flood-
      lights
Dry-drenched us in a downpour of artifical ray-rain.
Then—the proper signals given and our identity
      made known—
The gates rolled back—the car turned in,
And I was within the prison confines,
On the Territory-of-Tears—the Acres-of-Atonement.

Although the hour was late
The warden and his wife had waited dinner for me.
Their hospitable welcome seemed, somehow, to lift
The pall of somberness that settled everywhere
Like dusk falling from sky to earth.
And so, when the meal was over, I accepted their
      invitation
To sit in the living room and chat for a few minutes
Before retiring. . . .

I well remember the occasion:

The warden filling his pipe as he began to talk;
His wife seated in a comfortable chair.
The soft glow from a table-lamp throwing a single
      beam
On the half-finished sweater she was knitting:
A copper-coloured kitten frolicking about the room,
Gleefully tangling itself in the skeins of blue yarn. . . .

All these things I well remember
Because it was while observing the homelike atmos-
      phere
That my attention was distracted by the warden
      asking me
A strange question.

[268]

The Last Supper

Of a sudden he faced me and spoke quickly—
An unaccountable note of anxiety in his voice:
"What do you know about Negro people?" he asked

His words surprised and startled me
As the inquiry bore no relationship
To previously discussed topics.
Therefore I questioned before answering:
"Why do you ask?" I wanted to know.

Through a thin grey haze of tobacco smoke
The warden looked at me and said:
"Because the man condemned to die
Thursday night—is a Negro. . . ."

A moment's silence invaded the room
While I mentally turned the pages of my Album-of-
        Memories,
Searching for familiar pictures of dark folk.

I recalled my childhood days:
And remembered the Colored cook
Who had cut bears, elephants and kangaroos
Out of dough and baked them for me—
So I said that Negroes were kind and generous.

I recalled the day that my father died:
And remembered the old Negro gardener
(Whose friendship my father cherished)
Wending his way up to our house with a floral trib-
        ute
Of home-grown flowers—
Therefore I said that Negroes were sympathetic.

And then I recalled an evening
When cares and responsibilities preyed upon my
        mind,
And, in an attempt to forget them

And assuage the pangs of sorrow wrought by death,
I went for a walk which led to the outskirts of town;
And so wandering found myself in the poor district
Housing many nationalities . . .
Dense fog was drifting in from the sea
And the damp air cold—thick—and clammy. . . .

Unexpectedly, I chanced upon a clearing
Where the mists had not yet descended,
And stumbled on to a small shack
With a crooked cross leaning on the roof,
And heard the mellow voices of Negro church folk
      singing:
*"Take yo' burdens to de Lawd an' leave them
      there."*

And then, as I drew closer to the one broken window
(Midway of which was drawn a ragged green shade)
I saw them . . . happy Negroes . . . their dark bodies
      swaying . . .
Feet marking time . . . uplifted hands . . .
Open Bibles . . . and white handkerchiefs waving
Like unfurled banners in the air
Tears streamed down the wrinkled cheeks of some;
Others shouted praises and screamed incoherent
      words.
Remembering this scene, I told the warden and his
      wife
That Negroes were religious but extremely emotional.

Then I said that that was all I knew about Negroes
Except that I had heard of a great leader named
Booker T. Washington, who had done much good
For those he called his people:
And a poet, Paul Laurence Dunbar,
Singer of songs—dreamer of dreams,
One whose work I had read and shared
With others of my race until I discovered

The Last Supper

That many could not understand how a black man
Could be so versatile;
For I noticed that most white people
Praised only his verses lyrically lovely
With the soft, sweet dialect of the South,
For that, they declared, was a part of him.

Only a few, like myself, seemed to find
The mystic-depth and beauty in his masterpieces
Of non-dialect—
For circumscribed by biased opinions
The majority could not perceive the mind of a Negro
     unlimited,
And free in the heritage of God-given liberty
Capable of drifting away from banjo strumming,
Loud laughter, jungle rhythms, beat of drums and
     voodoo rites,
To soar above this world to the enchanted realms
Of celestial heights.

When I had finished telling all these things
To my listeners, the warden laid aside his pipe.
Thoughtfully he remarked:
"Father—Joseph is the type of Colored youth
Known today as *The New Negro* . . .
To no man has he confided the secrets of his soul."

And then the warden went on to say
That though Joseph had accepted
The friendship of the former priest,
He had refused the Divine help and consolation
Of the Sacraments.

"Were it not for the circumstances
That brought Joseph here," the warden continued,
"The young Negro would be a prophet for his people.
It's unfortunate that he must die a voice unheard—
A song unsung . . ."

[271]

I marveled at the warden's confidence
In one convicted of murder—
And I was eager to meet the Negro
Described by him as the *Prince of Prisoners*,
And a Catholic strayed from his faith . . .

CHAPTER III

Joseph

Tuesday morning I met—Joseph.

In all the years that have followed
Since first I saw him
Always I have found my speech inadequate
When attempting to describe this youth:
Aye, for is it not difficult
To visualize the sun without it's brilliance?
The sea void of endless eternities of perpetual
        motion?

Of Joseph I can but say that his skin was brown—
Dark brown, like the newly ploughed soil of a fertile
        valley;
And his body erect and tall of stature.
And in his eyes there gleamed an unforgettable light
That made one think it possible for a candle to burn
In the path of the North wind and never be extin-
        guished.

His greeting was cordial . . .
His conversation of current topics
And world-wide interest amazed me.
His lack of religious fervor perplexed me.
I wondered how a man
(With only two days in which to live)

Could give no thought as to the welfare of his soul,
And so—I spoke to him of religion.

He made no comment.
And thinking that I glimpsed a smile upon his lips
(Which I mistook for a sneer)
I spoke of the futility of human beings
Using false pride as a defence-mechanism
To steel themselves against the approach of the
     inevitable.
But apparently my words were as seeds sown in
     barren ground,
For Joseph only stared at me—blankly.

My next approach led me to speak
Of the mercy of God.
I compared it to a giant drawbridge
Over which the repentant could cross
Safe from the deluge of their sins
Raging beneath like a mighty torrent.
For three hours I talked, sermonized, implored,
But to no avail.
The condemned man neither argued, questioned
Or discussed the subject.
Finally I took from my pocket
A book of short prayers and ejaculations:
"Joseph—will you read these?" I asked.
Without a word he nodded his assent.
And then promising to return later in the day,
I went forth from his cell—discouraged.

When I returned that afternoon
My heart was none the lighter,
For the librarian had informed me
That Joseph read only newspapers,
Having no inclination to peruse books.
Therefore I knew that one of the main avenues

Leading to the kingdom of his inner-self
Was a closed thoroughfare to me.

Realizing that there was no time for procrastination,
I bluntly asked the young Negro if he feared death.
And then he smiled again
(The same bewildering smile which I mistook for a
    sneer)
And he laughed—laughed aloud,
And the deep resonance of his voice filled the cell
Like the sonorous tones of violincellos in a concert
    hall.
Then his voice quieted to a monotone,
And looking directly at me he said:
To a poet, Father—Death comes as a patient listener
Who grows not weary of hearing sonnets;
To an artist, Death is the return of a master-painter
To lead the student-of-palette and brush
To Elysian fields of never-fading colours.
And to me—Death will be a guide
To show me a world from whence no man would
    wish to return."

Never before in my ministry had I met such a
    character:
Not discourteous, nor gruff—nor unsociable,
But apparently self-sufficient in his time of trouble.

Scrutinizing the cell I noticed the prayer-book
I had given him, and seized the chance to ask
If he were not conscious of spiritual loss
While absent from the Sacraments.

At my words he sprang to his feet,
Faced me and spoke hesitatingly
As if awakening from a stupor:

THE LAST SUPPER

"I believe the words of Raoul Plus,
A learned Jesuit," he commented, "who has
      written—
Those who have drunk at fountains
Find the water of cisterns insipid. . . ."
Shocked by this unexpected outburst
I could not immediately summon strength
To utter a sound.

And then—seemingly oblivious of my presence,
Joseph began pacing his cell—
Talking—gesturing—
At times almost whispering
As if afraid of being overheard.

"If you would know what I think of Christ,
Then I shall tell you," he began:
"He is as the Book of Books describes Him,
'All things to all men'—
A Light for those groping in a land of shadows,
A promised spring for the aged who wait resignedly
In the winter-twilight of their latter years;
His life on earth was a symphony of immortal
      dreams,
His words a cooling draught to quench the thirst
Of parched and aching throats. . . ."

"Joseph!" I breathed. "Joseph—"
For at his words my spirit became imbued
With new courage and new hope
As I visualized the return of a prodigal son
Unto His Father's house. . . .

But he heeded not the interruption.
Lost in thought he went on talking
As if delivering an oration.

THE LAST SUPPER

To my astonishment he quoted verbatim
Several passages from the Confessions of Saint
      Augustine;
And spoke of the Abbot Sinibald at the Monastery of
      Monte Cassino
Whose teachings influenced the life of the child
Destined to become the greatest theologian of the
      Middle Ages,
The Sicilian Dominican—Thomas Aquinas. . . .

The while he talked—I found myself speechless.
Then as suddenly as he had begun, he ceased speaking
Of the Doctors of the Church and their writings,
And clenching the bars in the door of his cell, cried
      out:

"O, to be free—free again!
To witness the age-old ceremony of green-vested
      hills
Donning the gold chasuble of California poppies;
To walk quietly down the long aisles of country
      paths
Hedged in with cottonwoods and alders;
To trudge a valley road bordered with cactus,
Sage of silver-grey and blue lupine;
To watch the ivory-blossom-spires
Of wild Yucca swaying in a summer breeze;
To see once more an old adobe Mission,
And standing in the shelter of it's cloister,
Behold pepper boughs drooping with heavily laden
Clusters of bright red berries
Genuflecting in the sunset;
To hide myself in a mountain cave
During a cloud-burst of April showers,
And listen to the roar of rumbling thunder
Echoing like the hollow-thud of spirited horses hoofs
Clattering down the sand-strewn speedway of a
      Roman arena;

[276]

To swim once again in the cool, foam-crested waves
    of the sea
At the break of dawn—
While birds carol the approach of day
And the silent majesty of God. . . ."

And listening to these words,
I knew that the young Negro
Had at one time walked with the Son of God.

That night I prayed fervently;
I could not sleep
Suspecting that between Joseph and his God
A secret barrier stood of which he might not speak.

CHAPTER IV

The Parting

Wednesday afternoon
(Under the supervision of a keeper)
Joseph conversed for the last time with his fiance.

Elsa—he called her:
A young woman of rare dignity
And conservative manner.
Her eyes were soulful,
But in them I detected a frightened look,
Like that in a timid faun's
When persued by hunters.

They mentioned naught of their own dreams,
These two—
But discussed commonplace things
Such as the sun-flowers growing in Elsa's garden,
Jars of quince preserved by her elderly grandmother;
And programs heard over the radio
That Joseph had made for her. . . .

[277]

THE LAST SUPPER

Then the moment of their parting came,
And the woman's courage failing
She bowed her head and wept.

But Joseph, calm and stalwart,
Without a quiver in his voice,
Was heard reminding her
That true love could know no parting.
And rising from his seat, murmured:
"God be with you. . . ."
And then he turned and departed from her presence
With never a backward glance.

Only once did he speak of her to me,
Saying:
"She with a woman's tender heart,
Thinks that the evening star will never twinkle again
Because the shadow of a cloud passes over it. . . ."

And then he sighed,
And in that sigh could be heard
The wailing of a night-wind
Crying for an infant-zephyr
Lost in the labyrinth of a forest.

All my pleadings with Joseph
Seemed in vain.
And so, in desperation, I sought
Another Colored convict known as Sleepy Slim,
Thinking that perhaps he might suggest
Some means of comfort for Joseph's last hours
Since he refused that which I offered him.

But Sleepy Slim,
(A sleepy-eyed, sloven Negro)
Was not interested.
He merely blinked
And said that Joseph was crazy,

And that all he needed was a good supper
To enjoy before he left the place.

Dismayed, I went my way.
I had expected him to offer a solution,
Confident that he would understand one of his own
      race. . . .

CHAPTER V

The Last Supper

The next morning (according to law)
Joseph was removed to the pre-execution chamber.
And it was then that I learned from the warden
That he was fasting
And requested that all meals be omitted.
We were discussing his case
When word came that he wished to see me.

I hurried to his cell,
And to my amazement
Joseph asked if I would hear his confession. . . .

He showed no signs of religious hysteria,
Or emotion of any description.

And when I questioned as to why
He had hesitated for so long a while
Before availing himself of the privileges
Bestowed through the Sacrament of Penance,
He smiled faintly—murmuring:
"Do seeds of the earth burst forth
Into plant or vegetable life
Before the time appointed?
Do buds herald the silent birth
Of their mysterious bloom?"

[279]

THE LAST SUPPER

And then he said that he had
Had to forgive an enemy. . . .

Taking from my pocket
The stole which I carried at all times,
I pressed the purple side (signifying penance) to my
     lips;
And then blessing Joseph,
Spiritually knelt with him at the Feet of Christ. . . .

Of his confession I cannot speak,
For a penitent's words
Are guarded more securely than the Pharaoh's tombs
Within the Pyramids of ancient Egypt,
For the seal remains forever—unbroken.
And after a brief interval
Joseph received the Holy Eucharist
As—his last supper.

That night—I saw him walk to the chair
Fortified, sustained—and unafraid.

I shall never forget the sight:
Joseph wearing the customary black shirt
That looked like a symbol of mourning—
His hair clipped close to his head,
And his hands swinging at his sides
(For the warden had granted his request
To walk unhandcuffed to his doom).

And he was like a soldier confident of victory,
A conqueror invading a city,
King Solomon ascending his throne.

Hastily the executioner applied an electrode
To the calf of his right leg,
To the top of his head;

THE LAST SUPPER

And then his arms, legs and torso
Were fastened by strong leather straps.

I saw the warden wipe his forehead with a handkerchief,
And some among the other witnesses coughed ner-
  vously.
And I who had never before witnessed an execution
Felt as though my legs were made of straw.

And then as the electrician threw the switch into it's
  socket
The drone of sputtering current
Became like the whirring sound of hordes of locusts
Swarming across the sky.
And the condemned man's body leaped forward
As if he would be free:
The cords of his neck bulged—
And from under the helmet holding the head elec-
  trode
A spiral of smoke wafted out and circled up to the
  ceiling.
Then the odour of scorched flesh reached my nos-
  trils.
The body relaxed—and I knew that Joseph was dead.

Drops of sweat fell from my forehead
On to the crucifix in my hands
And dripped like tears from the eyes of the Christ. . . .

For days afterward
I dwelt as though in another world—
A world wherein Joseph walked and talked with me.

A year later a *man of another race*
Pleaded guilty to the murder charge
For which Joseph had paid
The penalty with his life.

And so it was that I wrote the Bishop
Asking for a parish in which to work among the
    Colored.
And in due time it was granted me.

And ever since—
In the countenance of every Colored girl
I have seen the reflected image of Elsa;
And in every Negro youth
The sterling qualities of the one she loved;
And in all the sorrow-songs of the race
The voice of the martyr—Joseph.

ABOUT THE EDITORS

Henry Louis Gates, Jr., is the W. E. B. Du Bois Professor of the Humanities, Chair of the Afro-American Studies Department, and Director of the W. E. B. Du Bois Institute for Afro-American Research at Harvard University. One of the leading scholars of African-American literature and culture, he is the author of *Figures in Black: Words, Signs, and the Racial Self* (1987), *The Signifying Monkey: A Theory of Afro-American Literary Criticism* (1988), *Loose Canons: Notes on the Culture Wars* (1992), and the memoir *Colored People* (1994).

Jennifer Burton is in the Ph.D. program in English Language and Literature at Harvard University. She is the volume editor of *The Prize Plays and Other One-Acts* in this series. She is a contributor to *The Oxford Companion to African-American Literature* and to *Great Lives from History: American Women*. With her mother and sister she coauthored two one-act plays, *Rita's Haircut* and *Litany of the Clothes*. Her fiction and personal essays have appeared in *Sun Dog, There and Back*, and *Buffalo*, the Sunday magazine of the *Buffalo News*.

Carla Kaplan is Associate Professor of English at Yale University, where she also teaches in Women's Studies, African-American Studies, and American Studies. The recent recipient of a fellowship at the Schomburg Center for Research in Black Culture for her work on modernism, race, and identity, she is the author of *The Erotics of Talk: Women's Writing and Feminist Paradigms* (1996).

Gramley Library
Salem College
Winston-Salem, NC 27108